REACHING COMMON GROUND

REACHING COMMON GROUND

A COMPREHENSIVE GUIDE *to* CONFLICT RESOLUTION

FREDERICK T. GOLDER

LUMINARE PRESS
WWW.LUMINAREPRESS.COM

Luminare Press
442 Charnelton St.
Eugene, OR 97401
www.luminarepress.com

LCCN: 2020907625
ISBN: 978-1-64388-328-1

To my wife, Caron;
Our Children, Rachel, David, and Naomi;
Their Spouses, Michael, Shera, and Joseph;
Our Grandchildren, Jared and Noah,
Pauline and Alexandra,
Hannah and Emma

CONTENTS

Part One
SOURCES OF CONFLICTS

Part Two
TYPES OF CONFLICTS

Introduction

OUR SOCIETY HAS BECOME OVERWHELMINGLY ADVERSARIAL and confrontational, with consequences not only in our ability to solve problems but also in our personal relationships. Many of today's most contentious issues are framed as us-versus-them identity-based conflicts: men against women, blacks against whites, citizens against immigrants, and liberals against conservatives. Political correctness is drowning out diverse opinions. People are verbally and sometimes physically attacked for expressing opposing viewpoints. Labeling and name-calling are used to stifle any dissenting opinions. The inability to communicate effectively with people from different cultures and backgrounds is a major problem.

As an attorney, professor, and mediator, I have learned the most effective methods for resolving conflicts using collaborative communication skills. My book *Reaching Common Ground* is a guide to understanding the nature of conflict in all its facets. It provides effective methods for resolving conflicts despite differences in personality, core values, gender, race, religion, culture, national origin, age, sexual orientation, economic status, and power imbalances.

The better you understand the many challenges, the better you will be able to effectively resolve your conflicts while maintaining positive relationships with others. Learn how to turn confrontation into dialogue, dialogue into understanding, understanding into effective resolution of conflicts. We need these skills now more than ever.

My book is divided into three parts. Part One explains the sources of conflicts. Part Two describes the most frequent types of conflicts. Part Three provides the tools you need to resolve your conflicts successfully. The Appendix of Questionnaires provides insights into the differences that can impair our ability to resolve conflicts successfully.

Conflict is inevitable in human interactions. Before language, humans had two ways of dealing with conflicts: (1) fight; or (2) flight. Language provided another alternative. Now people could engage in rational conversations and work together to find better ways of resolving conflicts—COOPERATION.

Despite the evolutionary gift of language, people continued to resolve many conflicts violently through war and other forms of intentional killing. History records at least 300 million people killed in wars, 150 million from genocide, and 160 million for political reasons.

There was a time when violence may have been necessary for human survival. Violence is no longer necessary and poses an existential threat to life on Earth. People act to satisfy their own needs. Hidden biases prevent us from fully understanding those needs. It is even more difficult to understand the needs of others. When needs are not met, emotional and psychological problems result. Some people may resort to violence when their needs are not met, not realizing that their needs can be met by nonviolent means. *Reaching Common Ground* explains that by understanding and satisfying the needs of the parties, we can resolve our conflicts constructively, reduce violence, and create a more cooperative world.

Humans are the only life form that has evolved on this planet that has the ability to alter the environment significantly. Prior to the emergence of modern humans (*Homo sapiens*), life on our planet adapted to the environment or became extinct. Natural selection ensured that organisms best adapted to their environment were more likely to survive and reproduce. This was true of humans until they learned how to change their environment. When this happened, humans replaced nature as the planet-altering force. Unless we learn to resolve conflicts constructively, we run the risk of destroying our planet. This is the great challenge we now face.

Conflicts can be destructive, neutral, or constructive depending on how they are resolved. Confrontation and war are not inevitable.

Neither is cooperation or peace. Failed negotiations between nations can result in war, death, and destruction. Successful negotiations result in peace treaties, compatible relationships, and cooperative ventures.

Professor Steven Pinker opines that: "Most people agree that life is better than death. Health is better than sickness. Sustenance is better than hunger. Abundance is better than poverty. Peace is better than war. Safety is better than danger. Freedom is better than tyranny. Equal rights are better than bigotry and discrimination. Literacy is better than illiteracy. Knowledge is better than ignorance. Intelligence is better than dull-wittedness. Happiness is better than misery. Opportunities to enjoy family, friends, culture, and nature are better than drudgery and monotony."[1] I would add that cooperation is better than confrontation. While things have improved, there is no guarantee that they will continue to improve. Only by actively engaging with each other in a positive and constructive way can we ensure a better future.

Although people are social animals, they are also egocentric. It takes a special effort to see the world from any perspective other than our own. Egocentrism can cause us to make incorrect assumptions about what other people are thinking or feeling. We have a natural tendency to think that our beliefs are true because we believe them. We may feel superior to others believing that only we possess THE TRUTH. We may forget information that does not support our thinking, to remember information that does. We do not accept facts that contradict our core values or beliefs.

Each of us has core values and deeply held beliefs. Some values and beliefs are shared, but many will differ. Beliefs affect our attitudes. Attitudes and beliefs influence our behavior. These values, beliefs, and attitudes can be based on facts, perceptions, superstition, faith, biases, or prejudices. Believing something is true does not make it so. A person is likely to disregard anything that opposes his or her view and embrace anything that supports it. Many people believe that the way they see things is the way everyone sees them or should see them.

We may use heuristics when making decisions. While heuristics are useful in solving many problems and making judgments quickly and efficiently, sometimes these rule-of-thumb strategies can lead to making erroneous decisions. Some common heuristics include the availability heuristic, the representativeness heuristic, and the affect heuristic.

The availability heuristic involves making decisions based upon how easy it is to bring something to mind. When you are trying to make a decision, you might quickly remember a number of relevant examples. Since these are more readily available in your memory, you may judge these outcomes as being more common or frequently occurring. For example, if you are thinking of flying and suddenly think of a number of recent airline accidents, you might decide air travel is too dangerous and travel by car instead. Air disasters come to mind, and the availability heuristic makes you think plane crashes are more common than they actually are.

The representativeness heuristic involves making a decision by comparing the present situation to the most representative mental prototype. When you are trying to decide if someone is trustworthy, you might compare aspects of the individual to other mental examples you hold. An older woman might remind you of your grandmother, so you might assume that she is kind and trustworthy.

The affect heuristic involves making choices that are strongly influenced by the emotions that an individual experiences at that moment. People are more likely to see decisions as having higher benefits and lower risks when they are in a positive mood. Negative emotions, on the other hand, lead people to focus on the potential downsides of a decision rather than the possible benefits.

While heuristics can speed up our problem and decision-making process, they can lead to poor decisions. Because something has worked in the past, this does not mean that it will work again. Relying on an existing heuristic can make it difficult to see alternative solutions or come up with more effective options. Using mental shortcuts to classify and categorize people can lead to prejudice and stereotyping.

Dr. Robert B. Cialdini[2] identifies six psychological principles that influences human behavior: (1) Commitment and Consistency—This causes us to repeat things that we have done in the past without considering that present circumstances may dictate a different approach; (2) Reciprocity—This may cause us to give up something without thinking because the other person has given us something. When this is used as an exploitation tactic, you can avoid this by refusing to give up anything; (3) Social Proof—This may cause us to do something that may not be prudent because everyone else is doing it. When someone is trying to exploit you, you can avoid this by making sure the data is accurate; (4) Authority—This may cause us to trust people who wear a uniform or have impressive credentials. When this occurs, you ask yourself these questions: "Is this person truly an expert?" "How truthful can we expect the expert to be?" "Does the expert have something to gain by convincing us?" (5) Scarcity—The perceived scarcity of some object may cause us to take an action we would not have taken if we thought about it. When this happens, you can avoid buying the object if you decide that you are buying it because of its limited availability rather than because it is something you need; (6) Affinity—There are a number of factors, such as physical attractiveness, similarity, compliments, familiarity, and association that unconsciously affect our feelings for a person that may affect our decision-making process and cause us to act contrary to our best interests. When this occurs, you can avoid making a bad decision by asking yourself if you would make the same decision if you did not like the person.

Consciousness refers to your individual awareness of your unique thoughts, memories, feelings, sensations, and environment. It is that part of your mind that is responsible for logic and reasoning. The conscious mind also controls all the actions you do, like walking or talking. This awareness is subjective and unique to you. Your conscious experiences are constantly shifting and changing. For example, one moment you may be focused on reading this book. Your consciousness may then shift to the memory of a conversation you had earlier with a co-worker. Next, you might notice how uncomfortable your chair is, or maybe you are mentally planning dinner. This ever-shifting stream of thoughts can change dramatically from one moment to the next. You receive information through your five senses.

All of this information is stored in your preconscious or subconscious mind. The subconscious mind is a like a big memory bank that stores your beliefs, memories, and life experiences. The information stored in your subconscious mind always affects your behavior and actions in different situations. For example, if you lack self-confidence because of certain beliefs that you have about yourself (stored in your subconscious mind), you might start to feel anxious around people. In that case, you felt anxious because your subconscious mind had false information that made you believe that you were in danger when in fact you were not. The subconscious mind not only affects your behavior, it also affects your perception. If you saw two people smiling while looking at you, you might believe that they were making fun of you. Your subconscious mind follows a rule called "you get what you focus on." Because you had a false belief about yourself, you found proof for it even though it was not accurate.

The subconscious mind makes everything you say and do fit a pattern consistent with your self-concept. You can actually reprogram your thought patterns by inserting positive and success-oriented sound bites. By focusing your thoughts on uplifting ideas, your subconscious will begin to implement a positive pattern in your thinking and in your outlook on life. The subconscious mind does not think or reason independently. It obeys the commands it receives from the conscious mind. The subconscious mind is an unquestioning servant that works constantly to make your behavior fit a pattern consistent with your *emotionalized* thoughts, hopes, and desires. The conscious mind *commands* and the subconscious mind *obeys*. The subconscious is that part of you that is outside of your conscious awareness, which creates automatic programs, such as beliefs, behaviors, and attitudes. The key to changing these automatic behaviors and beliefs is to effectively communicate with your subconscious. You can do this by using Affirmations or Mindful Awareness.

Affirmations are statements of positive intent as if they are already occurring. Affirmations are an attempt to counteract the negative self-talk with the positive. Focus on the behavior you want rather than what you do not want. For example, "I don't want to smoke" should be "I am a nonsmoker." Focus on the present rather than the future. For example, "I don't want to eat chocolate" should be "I only eat healthy food." Affirmations can program yourself into a more empowering set of automatic behaviors. Subliminal messages are a form of affirmations given at a subconscious level, which avoids negative feelings and allows change without much conscious effort.

Mindful Awareness is the ability to make yourself consciously aware of the types of thoughts you are having. When you observe a negative thought you can immediately counter it by thinking "Cancel that, what I mean is..." and insert a positive affirmation. The skill of Mindful Awareness allows you to become aware of and program your subconscious mind rather than allowing the subconscious to make the decision for you.

Dr. Viktor E. Frankl, a concentration camp survivor during World War II, wrote in his best-selling memoir, *Man's Search for Meaning*, "Everything can be taken from a man but one thing: the last of human freedoms—to choose one's attitude in any given set of circumstances, to choose one's own way."[3] Dr. Frankl developed a theory of psychotherapy he called logotherapy. In logotherapy, the patient is confronted with and reoriented toward the meaning of his life. A person's search for meaning is the primary motivation in life. This meaning is unique and must and can be fulfilled by that individual alone. What a person needs is the striving and struggling for a worthwhile goal—the call of a potential meaning waiting to be fulfilled by the person. The meaning of life differs from person to person, from day to day, and from hour to hour. What matters is not the meaning of life in general but rather the specific meaning of life at a given moment. To put the question in general terms is comparable to the question posed to a chess champion: "Tell me, Master, what is the best move in the world?" There is no best move or even a good move apart from a particular situation in a game and the particular personality of one's opponent. The same holds for human existence. One should not search for an abstract meaning of life. Everyone has his or her own specific mission in life to carry out. The logotherapist's role consists of widening and broadening the patient's field so that the whole spectrum of potential meaning becomes conscious and visible. "Every human being has the freedom to change at any instant... the individual personality remains essentially unpredictable. The basis for any prediction would be represented by biological, psychological, or sociological conditions. One of the main features of human existence is the capacity to rise above such conditions, to grow beyond them. Man is capable of changing the world for the better if possible, and of changing himself for the better if necessary."[4]

The conscious mind communicates to the outside world and the inner self through speech, pictures, writing, physical movement, and thought. The subconscious mind is in charge of our recent memories, and is in continuous contact with the resources of the unconscious mind. The subconscious mind has a much stronger sense of awareness of your surroundings than your conscious mind (your "sixth sense") and is always active, even when asleep. It obeys orders from your conscious mind. If you focus your conscious thoughts on negative things, then your subconscious will obediently deliver the feelings, emotions, and memories that you have associated with that type of thinking. Those feelings will become your reality. You can then be caught up in a continuous loop of negativity, fear, and anxiety, constantly looking for the bad in every situation. If you focus on positive things, your reality will become positive.

Negative thoughts can create anxiety, anger, resentment, jealousy (an array of emotions), which can lead to depression and self-destructive behavior, such as addictions, which derail us from what we want most in life. Negative thinking saps our energy, erodes our self-confidence, and can put us in a bad mood. Awareness and an attitude of self-compassion can redirect our negative thoughts to more positive ones.

Our thoughts can be our own worst enemy. You may be "feeding" your negative thoughts by allowing them to rule your mind. When you have a negative thought, ask yourself, "What is this thought doing for me?" The answer is they are disempowering you. You can immediately feel more empowered by focusing on something positive in your life. We can create greater peace, confidence, and a more positive outlook by learning how to manage our thoughts.

The unconscious mind is the storehouse of all memories and past experiences, which have been repressed through trauma or consciously forgotten and no longer important to us. The unconscious constantly communicates with the conscious mind via our subconscious and provides us with the meaning to all our interactions with the world, filtered through our belief system. Subconscious and unconscious biases affect our perceptions, making it more difficult to resolve our differences constructively.

The confirmation bias causes a person to search for, interpret, and remember information in a way that confirms one's preconceptions. People may react to disconfirming evidence by strengthening their belief rather than by questioning it. If you believe you are better informed, it may be difficult to see problems from another perspective. There may be a tendency to underestimate the influence or strength of feelings, in either oneself or others. People may draw different conclusions from the same information, depending on how and who presents it. Actor-observer bias overemphasizes the influence of their personality and underemphasizes the influence of their situation. The false consensus effect creates a tendency for people to overestimate the degree to which others agree with them. The halo/demonizing effect creates a tendency for a person's positive or negative traits to "spill over" from one personality area to another in others' perceptions of them. The superiority bias causes some to overestimate desirable qualities and underestimate undesirable qualities, relative to other people. The projection bias may create a tendency to unconsciously assume that others share one's current emotional states, thoughts, and values. The in-group bias causes others to give preferential treatment to people in their group. The self-serving bias creates a tendency to claim more responsibility for successes than failures. It may also manifest itself as a tendency to evaluate ambiguous information in a way that is beneficial to their interests. The illusion of truth effect may cause people to identify statements as true when they have previously heard them, even though not true. Thus, a person is more likely to believe a familiar statement than an unfamiliar one. The group attribution error causes some to believe that the characteristics of an individual are reflective of the group or assume that group decision outcomes reflect the preferences of group members, even when information is available that clearly suggests otherwise.

We are not likely to be consciously aware of these biases. All of these subconscious or unconscious biases affect our ability to communicate effectively, to find common ground, and to resolve conflicts in a peaceful and constructive manner. By understanding these biases and using the methods described in my book, you will be better able to successfully resolve your conflicts.

For purposes of this book, a "conflict" will be defined as a "difference of opinion between two or more persons each seeking a particular outcome." If the parties genuinely want to resolve their conflict, it is essential that they have a full understanding of each other's perspective regarding the conflict.

Conflicts arise on a daily basis in many different situations. Successful resolutions of these conflicts can lead to harmonious relationships, satisfying work experiences, and a more productive life. After reading this book, you will understand the nature of conflict and will have the tools you need to resolve conflicts constructively and peacefully.

PART ONE

SOURCES OF CONFLICTS

The difference between what we do and what we are capable of doing would suffice to solve most of the world's problems."

—MOHANDAS KARAMCHAND GANDHI

Chapter 1

GENETIC DIFFERENCES

M any differences shape how we see the world. Some differences are inherited (nature) and some come from our environment (nurture). Although we are strongly influenced by our genes and memes,[5] we have a conscious mind that can alter those influences. This self-reflective consciousness allows us to write our own programs for action.[6] Each of us can be the producer and director of our own life, but only by exerting a concerted, conscious effort.

The billions of humans alive today belong to one species: *Homo sapiens*. Our roots extend back 300,000 years to the emergence of the first modern humans in Africa. This amazing story of adaptation and survival is written in the language of our genes. In all species, there is variation among individual members, such as gender, size, shape, weight, skin tone, hair, and eye color. Despite these differences, the DNA (or deoxyribonucleic acid) of all human beings living today is *99.9%* alike. DNA is the molecule that carries the genetic information in all cellular life forms, including some viruses.

A gene is the basic physical and functional unit of heredity. Genes are made up of DNA. Some genes contain instructions to make molecules called proteins. Many genes do not code for proteins. In humans, genes vary in size from a few hundred DNA bases to more than 2 million bases. Humans have between 20,000 and 25,000 genes. A genome is an organism's complete set of DNA, including all of its genes. Each genome contains all of the information needed to build and maintain that organism. In humans, a copy of the entire genome—more than 3 billion DNA base pairs—is contained in all cells that have a nucleus.

Every person has two copies of each gene, one inherited from each parent. Most genes are the same in all people, but a small number of genes (less than 1 percent of the total) are slightly different between people. Alleles are forms of the same gene with small differences in their sequence of DNA bases. These small differences contribute to each person's unique features.

Some genes have a variety of different forms, which are located at the same position, or genetic locus, on a chromosome. Humans are called diploid organisms because they have two alleles at each genetic locus, with one allele inherited from each parent. Each pair of alleles represents the genotype of a specific gene. Genotypes are described as homozygous if there are two identical alleles at a particular locus and as heterozygous if the two alleles differ. Alleles contribute to the organism's phenotype, which is the outward appearance of the organism. Alleles are dominant or recessive. When an organism is heterozygous at a specific locus and carries one dominant and one recessive allele, the organism will express the dominant phenotype. Alleles can also refer to minor DNA sequence variations between alleles that do not necessarily influence the gene's phenotype.

Certain traits are inherited from our parents. Heritability estimates range from zero to one. Heritability close to zero indicates that almost all of the variability in a trait among people is due to environmental factors, with very little influence from genetic differences. Characteristics such as religion, language, and political preference have a heritability of zero because they are not under genetic control. Heritability close to one indicates that almost all of the variability in a trait comes from genetic differences, with very little contribution from environmental factors.

It is essential that we understand these differences, because genetic differences impact on our ability to solve our problems and resolve our conflicts successfully.

GENDER DIFFERENCES

There are significant differences in how men and women communicate. This does not mean that one form of communication is better than another one. It just means that men and women communicate differently. By understanding these differences, you will be better able to resolve conflicts that will inevitably arise. While many men and women share these characteristics, not everyone does, and there are many variations.

Some common differences between men and women:

Attitude towards tasks vs. relationships: Women tend to be more relationship oriented and accomplish tasks by building relationships first. They then know whom to ask and are comfortable asking others to get things done. Men tend to be more task oriented and go straight to the task. They build their relationships when they are in the task or project.

Processing Information: When women have to make a decision they will often process and express options out loud while men tend to process internally until they come up with a solution. Women often think that the man is being unresponsive to suggestions because of their silence, and men often think that women are looking for approval when they process out loud or do not know what they are doing. Some men may think that a woman's way of processing is a sign of weakness. It is not.

Leadership Style: Women are more relationship oriented, and they tend to lead by consensus. Men tend to be more hierarchical and will include only the people closest to them at their level when they think it is necessary.

Communication Styles: In non-verbal behavior, women will nod their head to show that they are listening. Men leave the conversation thinking that a head nod means agreement and will be surprised to find out that the woman did not agree. When a woman is speaking to a man and he does not say anything and stays in neutral body language to show that he is listening, a woman will interpret that as the man being bored or not understanding what she is saying. This posture can lead the woman to become very uncomfortable and repeat what she is saying or ask the man each time if he understands what she is saying. The man may then interpret the comments as a sign of insecurity, or talking too much. These thoughts can lead him to think she is not assertive or confident to be a leader. Women will use more direct eye contact in conversation to create relationships and connections, which men may take as a challenge to their power or position. Women will approach a man from the front while men often approach from the side at an angle, which is how each of them tends to stand or sit when talking to others. Men interpret the face to face as too personal, or aggressive, and women will interpret the talking side to side as though not being upfront or evasive.

Talk time: Men take up more time and space at meetings, while women try to aim for more equality in the room. Despite stereotypes to the contrary, studies have shown that men talk more than women. Men interrupt women and talk over them much more than women interrupt men. All of this can lead to the type of miscommunication based on assumptions of why members of the other sex are using certain verbal and non-verbal behaviors.

Women often try to get their point across by asking many types of questions: defiant, informational, and rhetorical. The questions may be designed to present an opposition or gather data. Men's contributions to arguments are often simple and direct. Men are so straightforward in contrast to women's questions that men might not realize there is a conflict. When both parties realize they are in disagreement, their communication styles may be impacted. Men are concerned with being right and less concerned about anyone else's feelings. This perceived lack of compassion upsets women. Men dislike questions, interpreting them as censure, and they may react by closing down emotionally.

This pattern leads women to become increasingly suspicious and wary.

From an early age, females learn to give compliments. Compliments are a way of reaching out to one another, an offer of affirmation and inclusion. Men are more likely to volunteer evaluations instead of giving compliments. Similarly, they will not seek out compliments because they want to avoid being critiqued themselves. These differing approaches complicate communication. If a woman asks a question with the hope of being praised or flattered, a man may see it as a way to offer advice, thereby affecting their relative power. The advice-giver is automatically shifted to a higher position, with the woman having lower status.

Women use apologies to try to create or maintain connections. Men, on the other hand, are concerned with what an apology might do. It might lower them to a subordinate position. After a male-female quarrel, gender differences can prolong negative feelings. While a man fears losing power and avoids apologizing, a woman might consider this insensitive behavior, and become offended and annoyed.

Men and women have very different ways of trying to get what they want, which can make it difficult to come to a resolution of any conflict. Women are typically in conversation mode; they are more likely to ask questions to get others to acquiesce through agreement. Men often interpret this approach as manipulation. They will make statements rather than suggestions. Their objective is to get their way directly and quickly. If that does not work, they will exit the discussion; they may either be angry or simply less passionate about the subject. These conversations may result in misunderstandings. Men may be resentful, believing women are trying to trick them. If men do not participate in back and forth negotiations, women may feel slighted. Men tend to focus on facts and seek immediate resolutions; action is the conversational goal. Women desire more extensive talk about problems, sharing feelings, and finding common experiences.

Different styles can lead to misunderstandings, which can impede conflict resolution. Do not use this information to stereotype all men or all women, as not everyone fits these generalizations. These are typical, and a large majority of men and women display some of these characteristics. Both men and women need to be aware of each other's styles of communication both verbal and non-verbal in order to avoid miscommunication in resolving their differences. There may also be subconscious or unconscious stereotyping and biases that prevent resolution of conflicts.

There is enormous diversity in communication style and practices within each gender group. Most women and many men have at their disposal a variety of conversational and speech skills, which they may draw upon, depending on the situation, the purposes, the context, and the roles they are playing.

Who Talks the Most?
In mixed-gender groups, at public gatherings, and in many informal conversations, men spend more time talking than do women. In one experiment, the men with expertise talked longer than the women with expertise. Men initiate more interaction than do women.

Who Interrupts?
Men are more likely than women to interrupt people speaking. A study of faculty meetings revealed that women are more likely than men to be interrupted. Some interruptions that women experience come from other women. Women, who do interrupt, are more likely to interrupt other women than men. Women are more likely than men to allow an interruption of their talk to be successful. They do not resist the interruption as much as men do.

What About Gender Patterns in Formal Group Meetings?
In meetings, men gain the "floor" more often, and keep the floor for longer periods of time, regardless of their status in the organization. In professional conferences, women take a less active part in responding to papers. When women do ask a question, they take less time in asking it than do men. Women are less likely to ask multiple questions and are more likely to phrase their question in personal terms.

What are the Gender Patterns in Informal Group Meetings?

When the meeting is an informal, collaborative venture, women display a fuller range of language ability. In this setting, women excel, people jointly build an idea, operate on the same wavelengths, and have deep conversational overlaps.

Is There a "Women's Language" Connoting Uncertainty and Deference?

The use of tag questions ("It's really cold in here, isn't it?"), disclaimers ("I may be wrong, but..."), and question statements ("Won't you close the door?") all decrease the perceived assertiveness of speech. However, research has not confirmed that women and men differ in the frequency of their use of these forms. Raters perceive those who use a deferential language style (super polite language, hedges, and hesitations) as having less power but more personal warmth.

Does it Matter who Talks More?

People who talk more are more likely to be perceived as dominant and controlling. Those who talk the most in decision-making groups also tend to become the leaders. "Task leadership behaviors," such as asking questions, setting up structures and procedures for the groups, giving information and opinions, and identifying and solving problems are important. Interrupters are perceived as more successful and driving, but less socially acceptable, reliable, and companionable than the interrupted speaker. In a study of trial witnesses, undergraduate student observers saw both female and male witnesses who use powerful language as being more competent, intelligent, and trustworthy than those who use powerless language.

What are Some Ways Women are Affected by These Patterns?

When someone is interrupted often or her comments are ignored, she may believe that what she has to say is not important. Women are less likely than men to have confidence in their ability to make persuasive arguments. Many women feel inhibited in formal, mixed-gender groups. Some women create their own passive participation—by allowing interruptions, by not taking advantage of natural pauses in the conversation, or by asking questions without explaining the context out of which the question emerged. Some women, when they do gain the "floor," talk too fast as though they know they are about to be interrupted.

Are Gender Differences in Communication Patterns Related to Power?

When people are strangers, they expect less competence from women than from men. If women are known to have prior experience or expertise related to the task, are assigned leadership roles, then women show greatly increased verbal behaviors in mixed-sex groups. A study of court witnesses found that educated professionals who have high social status were less likely to use "powerless language," regardless of gender. Differences in communication patterns may be linked to power, and are context-specific. Differences are socially created and therefore may be socially altered. Other studies have found that talking time is related to gender, i.e., men spend more time talking than women. In many organizations, the more powerful, usually men, spend more time talking than the less powerful.

Is Assertiveness in Women Viewed Negatively by Others?

In several controlled studies using undergraduate students, assertive behavior exhibited by females was evaluated as positively as the same behavior exhibited by males. The least-valued behavior is the self-effacing assertive. Subordinates prefer a supervisor to balance a task-orientated style with a relationship-oriented style. Research further suggests that the adoption of task behaviors, i.e., a focus on getting things done, enhances a woman's adaptability in the organization. The healthiest and best-liked individuals, male or female, were assertive, decisive, and intellectual, rather than nurturing, responsive, and emotional. Therefore, women may want to focus on task and impression-management goals in their interactions.

Strategies for Women to Communicate more Effectively with Men

Learn to state exactly what you want and face the risk of being criticized. This may not be a "safe" position, but it is an honest one. Focus on stating your own position rather than how the other person is reacting to you. State your own needs and do not back down even if the immediate response is not acceptance. Stop self-limiting behaviors, such as allowing interruptions or laughing after making a serious statement. Practice taking risks and overcoming fear. Learn to focus on a task and regard it as at least as important as the relationship among the people doing the task. Stop turning anger and blame inward. Make positive statements about yourself. Do not be a victim. Support other women.

Women and men often miscommunicate because of their different perspectives. Some of these differences appear below:

MEN:	WOMEN:
Live in a world of status	Live in a world of connections
Conversations are negotiations for power	Conversations are negotiations for closeness
Want to preserve independence	Want to preserve intimacy
Seek to win, avoid failure	Seek closeness, avoid isolation
Avoid taking orders, since it demonstrates low status and loss of independence	Accept taking orders, if perceived as forming a connection
Seek control	Seek understanding
Prefer inequality and asymmetry	Prefer equality and symmetry
Are adversarial with conflicting goals	Are synergistic with common goals
Value differences	Value similarities
Goal of conversation: transmit information	Goal of conversation: maintain interaction
Offer advice	Seek connection and understanding

Nonverbal Communication

Examples of nonverbal communication are fingers tapping; eyes squinting; legs crossing; hands fluttering; heads nodding. Nonverbal communication involves varying levels of body expression, with women usually functioning at high intensity. Faces are animated and hands are in motion, often touching others. Men are more conservative in facial movement and body contact; however, they do tend to be unreserved in sitting styles, such as, sprawling, stretching, and spreading out. The intensity level for women drops when seated, as they tend to draw in by keeping arms and legs close to their bodies.

How does nonverbal communication impact male and female communication? Women's actions focus on maintaining the relationship: providing attention and encouraging participation. The goal for men depends on the task. If they want to appear in charge, they use their bodies to control the discussion space. If they want to preserve calm and prevent emotional escalation, they are likely to be impassive.

One specific aspect of nonverbal communication is body orientation. If a man will not make eye contact or face his female conversational partner, she, who perceives conversation as integral to relationships, may interpret this as a lack of interest. He may become annoyed that she is rejecting his efforts. His relaxed body position is actually helping him concentrate. The differences in physical alignment can make it difficult for talkers to reconcile the two styles.

Imagine, a happy hour after work. On one side of the room, there is a group of women, deep in conversation. Their chairs are all turned toward each other, and they continually make eye contact. On the other side of the room, there is a group of men. Men sit at angles to each other. During much of their discussion, their eyes roam around the room, glancing at each other infrequently. Each cluster is engaged in their preferred style of talk. When group members are engaged with the other gender, these preferences may cause problems.

SKIN COLOR DIFFERENCES

From a scientific perspective, there is only one race, the human race. All people, regardless of the color of their skin share 99.99+% of the same genetic materials. Therefore, the division of people into "races" is arbitrary and artificial. The consensus of current scientific evidence shows that the physical and behavioral traits shared by all people originated from apelike ancestors and evolved over a period of approximately six million years. Humans first evolved in Africa, and much of human evolution occurred on that continent. We all started out with dark skin.

Therefore, "race" is a recent human invention. It is about culture, not biology. However, the concept of "race" and "racism" are embedded in our institutions and in everyday life. Skin color, one of our most visible physical features, has long been used to divide people into artificial "racial" categories. Variations in human skin are adaptive traits that correlate closely to geography and the sun's ultraviolet radiation, not "racial" differences. A certain amount of ultraviolet radiation (UVR) from the sun helps the human body use vitamin D to absorb the calcium necessary for strong bones. However, too much UVR can strip away folate (folic acid), an essential nutrient to the development of healthy fetuses. Skin pigmentation developed as the body's way of balancing its need for vitamin D and folate. Those closer to the equator had darker skin to prevent folate deficiency. As some groups moved into regions farther from the equator where UVR levels are lower, natural selection favored lighter skin, which allowed enough vitamin D-forming UVR to penetrate their skin.

While some people talk about "racial" differences, the real differences are caused by social, cultural, or other "non-racial" differences. The news media and our institutions constantly talk about people in "black" and "white" giving us the false impression that skin color is somehow related to other qualities or traits. It is not. Words that have negative connotations, like "blackball," "blacklist," "black mark," or "black sheep," adds to the stereotypical notion that "black" is bad and "white" is good. Thus, talking in terms of "black" and "white," skin color differences may impact on perceptions that need to be addressed if people with different skin colors seek to resolve their conflicts.[7] Low expectations for dark skinned people are likely to induce behavior that will cause the expectations to be fulfilled. If a person with dark skin is considered incapable of holding responsible positions, he will not be hired for those positions; he will have no opportunity to gain relevant experience in those positions; and lacking any such experience, he is likely to be incapable of performing in a responsible position.

When one is treated as inferior, he will act inferior. When he is perceived as inferior, he will begin to feel inferior. Treating "blacks" as inferiors to "whites" in America has a long, shameful history. It took a civil war to free "blacks" from slavery. Although the use of slaves was inconsistent with the Declaration of Independence, America, like other countries, had slaves. Ironically, the first man to fall in the 1770 Boston massacre demonstration for freedom from England was Crispus Attucks, a black slave.

Following the Civil War (1861-1865), slavery was finally abolished in America *de jure*. The Thirteenth Amendment passed in 1865 declared that, "Neither slavery nor involuntary servitude, except as a punishment for crime whereof the party shall have been duly convicted, shall exist within the United States, or any place subject to their jurisdiction." The Fourteenth Amendment passed in 1868 declared that, "All persons born or naturalized in the United States, and subject to the jurisdiction thereof, are citizens of the United States and of the state wherein they reside. No state shall make or enforce any law which shall abridge the privileges or immunities of citizens of the United States; nor shall any state deprive any person of life, liberty, or property, without due process of law; nor deny to any person within its jurisdiction the equal protection of the laws." The Fifteenth Amendment declared that, "The right of citizens of the United States to vote shall not be denied or abridged by the United States or by any state on account of race, color, or previous condition of servitude."

Although the passage of the 13th, 14th, and 15th Amendments to the Constitution granted blacks the same legal protections as whites, former slaves and others of African descent were treated unequally through the "Jim Crow" laws. After 1877, and the election of Republican Rutherford B. Hayes, southern and border states began restricting the liberties of blacks. Unfortunately, the Supreme Court helped undermine the Constitutional protections of blacks with the infamous *Plessy v. Ferguson* (1896) case, which legitimized Jim Crow laws and the Jim Crow way of life.

Jim Crow was the name of the racial caste system that operated primarily, but not exclusively in southern and border states, between 1877 and the mid-1960s. Jim Crow was more than a series of rigid anti-black laws. It was a way of life. Under Jim Crow, dark-skinned Americans were relegated to the status of second-class citizens. Jim Crow represented the legitimization of anti-black racism. Many Christian ministers and theologians taught that whites were the Chosen people, blacks were cursed to be servants, and God supported racial segregation. Craniologists, eugenicists, phrenologists, and Social Darwinists, at every educational level, buttressed the belief that blacks were innately, intellectually, and culturally inferior to whites. Pro-segregation politicians gave eloquent speeches on the great danger of integration: the mongrelization of the white race. Newspaper and magazine writers routinely referred to blacks as "niggers," "coons," and "darkies;" and worse, their articles reinforced anti-black stereotypes. All major societal institutions reflected and supported the oppression of blacks.

In 1890, Louisiana passed the "Separate Car Law," which purported to aid passenger comfort by creating "equal but separate" cars for blacks and whites. No public accommodations, including railway travel, provided blacks with equal facilities. The Louisiana law made it illegal for blacks to sit in coach seats reserved for whites, and whites could not sit in seats reserved for blacks. In 1891, a group of blacks decided to test the Jim Crow law. Homer A. Plessy, who was seven-eighths white and one-eighth black (therefore, black), sat in the white-only railroad coach. He was arrested. Plessy's lawyer argued that Louisiana did not have the right to label one citizen as white and another black for the purposes of restricting their rights and privileges. In *Plessy*, the Supreme Court stated that so long as state governments provided legal process and legal freedoms for blacks equal to those of whites, they could maintain separate institutions to facilitate those rights. The Court, by a 7-2 vote, upheld the Louisiana law, declaring that racial separation did not necessarily mean an abrogation of equality. In practice, this represented the legitimization of two societies: one white, and advantaged; the other, black, disadvantaged, and despised.

The Jim Crow system was undergirded by the following beliefs or rationalizations: whites were superior to blacks in all important ways, including but not limited to intelligence, morality, and civilized behavior; sexual relations between blacks and whites would produce a mongrel race, which would destroy America; treating blacks as equals would encourage interracial sexual unions; any activity which suggested social equality encouraged interracial sexual relations; if necessary, violence must be used to keep blacks at the bottom of the racial hierarchy. Blacks were denied the right to vote by grandfather clauses (laws that restricted the right to vote to people whose ancestors had voted before the Civil War), poll taxes (fees charged to poor blacks), white primaries (only Democrats could vote, only whites could be Democrats), and literacy tests ("Name all the Vice Presidents and Supreme Court Justices throughout America's history").

Jim Crow states passed statutes severely regulating social interactions between the races. Jim Crow signs were placed above water fountains, door entrances and exits, and in front of public facilities. There were separate hospitals for blacks and whites, separate prisons, separate public and private schools, separate churches, separate cemeteries, separate public restrooms, and separate public accommodations. In most instances, the black facilities were grossly inferior—generally, older, less well kept. In other cases, there were no black facilities—no Colored public restroom, no public beach, no place to sit or eat.

Jim Crow laws touched every aspect of everyday life. The Jim Crow laws and system of etiquette were supported by violence, real and threatened. Blacks who violated Jim Crow norms, for example, drinking from the white water fountain or trying to vote, risked their homes, their jobs, even their lives. Whites could physically beat blacks with impunity. Blacks had little legal recourse against these assaults because the Jim Crow criminal justice system was all white: police, prosecutors, judges, juries, and prison officials. Violence was instrumental for Jim Crow. It was a method of social control. The most extreme forms of Jim Crow violence were lynchings. The great majority of lynchings occurred in southern and border states, where the resentment against blacks ran deepest. Many whites claimed that, although lynchings were distasteful, they were necessary supplements to the criminal justice system because blacks were prone to violent crimes, especially the rapes of white women.

With this as a backdrop, it is understandable that there will be difficulties resolving conflicts between black and white people, not because of their "race," but because of this historical context.

In trying to find common ground in resolving conflicts between or among people of different colors, establish ground rules:

1. Listen respectfully, without interrupting.

2. Respect one another's views.

3. Criticize ideas, not individuals.

4. Commit to learning, not debating.

5. Avoid blame and speculation.

6. Avoid inflammatory language.

7. Focus the discussion on issues.

8. Prepare a list of questions to guide the discussion.

9. Listen to one another and exchanging viewpoints.

10. Increase insight and lessen defensiveness.

11. Use active listening and working on the ability to tolerate opposition.

12. Respect diversity of opinions and the varying knowledge.

13. Acknowledge tension between key underlying values.

14. Recognize strong feelings and perspectives that may be unpredictable.

Even within a well-planned and thoughtful discussion, statements can be made, and tones of voice used, that will cause emotional responses of anger, confusion, hurt, fear, surprise, or embarrassment. Such moments are called "triggers." Responses to triggers may include:

Avoidance: Avoiding future encounters and withdrawing emotionally from people or situations that trigger us.

Silence: Not responding to the situation, although it is upsetting, not saying or doing anything.

Misinterpreting: Feeling on guard and expecting to be triggered, we misinterpret something said and are triggered by our misinterpretation, not the words.

Attacking: Responding with the intent to lash back or hurt whoever has triggered us.

Laughing: Being overcome by awkwardness or tension and bursting out in laughter, which can be misinterpreted.

Launching asides or side conversations: Being unable to suppress commentary.

Internalizing: Accepting the trigger, believing it to be true.

Being confused: Feeling angry, hurt, or offended, while unsure why we feel that way or what to do about it.

Naming: Identifying what is upsetting us to the triggering person or organization.

Confronting: Naming what is upsetting us to the triggering person or organization and demanding that the behavior or policy be changed.

Startling with surprise: Responding to the trigger in an unexpected way, such as reacting with constructive humor that names the trigger and makes people laugh.

Using discretion: Deciding not to address the trigger at the time, fearing physical retribution.

SEXUAL ORIENTATION DIFFERENCES

Sexual orientation refers to an enduring pattern of emotional, romantic, and/or sexual attractions to men, women, or both sexes. Sexual orientation also refers to a person's sense of identity based on those attractions, related behaviors, and membership in a community of others who share those attractions. Research over several decades has demonstrated that sexual orientation ranges along a continuum, from exclusive attraction to the other sex to exclusive attraction to the same sex. Studies also indicate that less than 10% of the population identify as being lesbian, gay, bisexual, or transgender. Sexual orientation is usually discussed in terms of three categories: heterosexual (having emotional, romantic, or sexual attractions to members of the other sex), gay/lesbian (having emotional, romantic, or sexual attractions to members of one's own sex), and bisexual (having emotional, romantic, or sexual attractions to both men and women). This range of behaviors and attractions has been described in various cultures and nations throughout the world. Many cultures use identity labels to describe people who express these attractions. In the United States, the most frequent labels are *lesbians* (women attracted to women), *gay men* (men attracted to men), and *bisexual people* (men or women attracted to both sexes). However, some people may use different labels or none at all.

Sexual orientation is distinct from other components of sex and gender, including biological sex (the anatomical, physiological, and genetic characteristics associated with being male or female), gender identity (the psychological sense of being male or female), and social gender role (the cultural norms that define feminine and masculine behavior).

Sexual orientation is commonly discussed as if it were solely a characteristic of an individual, like biological sex, gender identity, or age. This perspective is incomplete because sexual orientation is defined in terms of relationships with others. People express their sexual orientation through behaviors with others, including such simple actions as holding hands or kissing. Thus, sexual orientation is closely tied to the intimate personal relationships that meet deeply felt needs for love, attachment, and intimacy. In addition to sexual behaviors, these bonds include nonsexual physical affection between partners, shared goals and values, mutual support, and ongoing commitment. Therefore, sexual orientation is not merely a personal characteristic within an individual. Rather, one's sexual orientation defines the group of people in which one is likely to find the satisfying and fulfilling romantic relationships that are an essential component of personal identity for many people.

There is no consensus among scientists about the exact reasons that an individual develops a heterosexual, bisexual, gay, or lesbian orientation. Although much research has examined the possible genetic, hormonal, developmental, social, and cultural influences on sexual orientation, no findings have emerged that permit scientists to conclude that sexual orientation is determined by any particular factor or factors. Many think that nature and nurture both play complex roles. Most people experience little or no sense of choice about their sexual orientation.

Lesbian, gay, and bisexual people in the United States have encountered extensive prejudice, discrimination, and violence because of their sexual orientation. Intense prejudice against lesbians, gay men, and bisexual people was widespread throughout much of the 20th century.

Public opinion studies over the 1970s, 1980s, and 1990s routinely showed that, among large segments of the public, lesbian, gay, and bisexual people were the target of strongly held negative attitudes. More recently, public opinion has increasingly opposed sexual orientation discrimination, but expressions of hostility toward lesbians, gay men, and bisexuals still exist. Bisexual individuals may face discrimination from some lesbian and gay men as well as from heterosexual people.

Sexual orientation discrimination takes many forms. Some surveys indicate that verbal harassment and abuse are nearly universal experiences among lesbian, gay, and bisexual people. The HIV/AIDS pandemic is another area in which prejudice and discrimination against lesbian, gay, and bisexual people have had negative effects. Early in the pandemic, the assumption that HIV/AIDS was a "gay disease" contributed to the delay in addressing the massive social upheaval that AIDS would generate. This disease has disproportionately affected gay and bisexual men. The association of HIV/AIDS with gay and bisexual men and the inaccurate belief that some people held that all gay and bisexual men were infected served to further stigmatize lesbian, gay, and bisexual people.

Prejudice and discrimination have social and personal impact. On the social level, prejudice and discrimination against lesbian, gay, and bisexual people are reflected in the everyday stereotypes of members of these groups. These stereotypes persist even though they are not supported by evidence, and they are often used to excuse unequal treatment of lesbian, gay, and bisexual people. For example, limitations on job opportunities, parenting, and relationship recognition are often justified by stereotypical assumptions about lesbian, gay, and bisexual people.

On an individual level, such prejudice and discrimination may also have negative consequences, especially if lesbian, gay, and bisexual people attempt to conceal or deny their sexual orientation. Although many lesbians and gay men learn to cope with the social stigma against homosexuality, this pattern of prejudice can have serious negative effects on health and well-being. Individuals and groups may have the impact of stigma reduced or worsened by other characteristics, such as race, ethnicity, religion, or disability. Some lesbian, gay, and bisexual people may face less of a stigma. For others, skin color, national origin, religion, disability, or other characteristics may exacerbate the negative impact of prejudice and discrimination.

Sexual prejudice, sexual orientation discrimination, and antigay violence can be sources of stress for lesbian, gay, and bisexual people. Although social support is crucial in coping with stress, antigay attitudes and discrimination may make it difficult for lesbian, gay, and bisexual people to find such support.

One of the most powerful influences on heterosexuals' acceptance of gay people is having personal contact with an openly gay person. Antigay attitudes are far less common among members of the population who have a close friend who is gay. Most scientists today agree that sexual orientation (including homosexuality and bisexuality) is the result of a combination of environmental, emotional, hormonal, and biological factors. In other words, there are many factors that contribute to a person's sexual orientation, and the factors may be different for different people.

However, homosexuality and bisexuality are not caused by the way a child was reared by his or her parents, or by having a sexual experience with someone of the same sex when the person was young. Also, being homosexual or bisexual does not mean the person is mentally ill or abnormal in some way, although there may be social problems that result from prejudicial attitudes or misinformation.

A person's sexual orientation may affect the way he or she looks at conflict and ways to resolve them. Looking at a person's sexual orientation in a judgmental way will likely create an impediment to resolving the conflict. If you refer to a person's sexual orientation as a sexual preference, you are likely to antagonize that person and make it more difficult to resolve any conflicts. Keep in mind that people of all walks of life may have sexual orientations toward the same sex, but they see things from their own perspective that may have nothing to do with their sexual orientation. Sexual orientation has nothing to do with a person's intelligence, morality, or qualities as a person.

AGE DIFFERENCES

The age of the persons seeking to resolve their differences can significantly impact on how conflicts get resolved. We look at conflicts differently at age 20, 30, 40, 50, or 60. Be aware of these differences.

Maslow and Kohlberg describe six stages of human growth and development.[8] All ages are considered psychological, not chronological age, as developmental lag (not acting your age) is a universal phenomenon. Following is a synopsis of what happens at each of six stages of development:

LEVEL ONE (PRE-ADULT)
Dependency: *How do I survive?*

There are not many adults living at level one. A level one adult cannot take care of himself well. Cannot keep a job. Does not have much social skill. People at level one are most concerned with where their next meal is coming from and what is happening today. They do not plan for the future. They are not proactive. The key word that applies to them is extreme dependency.

LEVEL TWO (AGE 20-30)
Personal Power: *How do I establish myself in the world?*

Most adults start out at level two. The challenges of life are how to get by and become a viable person. Primary concerns are establishing oneself in the world, which means getting ahead, getting an education, making money, making connections, competing for a place in society.

Because of their needs for certainty and viability, level two people are concerned with power, self and other control, right and wrong, and winning/losing. This is a high anxiety time in life and the challenges are great. Most personal empowerment books and seminars are designed, consciously or unconsciously, to address level two needs.

LEVEL THREE (AGE 30-35)
Belonging: *Where do I fit in?*

Once the need for viability in the world is met, we tend to relax a little and focus on more social needs, like belonging. We tend to reach out and get involved in the community. We may be raising a family at this point, so we want to be more involved. Kids may lead us to greater involvement in church, schools, and other families. Or, since we are less concerned with money, competition and the dog eat dog world (having won many battles and satisfied much of the need), we want to reach out to others and find out where we belong. Level three is a time for being socially concerned. We may tend to seek others' approval or catering to social expectations. We find our place in the world through the back and forth process of reaching out to others and receiving feedback.

LEVEL FOUR (AGES 35-45)
Deep Self-Awareness: *What is really important to me?*

Once we are viable in the world and know where we belong, we are ready to explore our identity at a deeper level. We are free to begin to question what is really important in life. This leads us to discover our values. Our values may be different than our parents' values, or they may be the same. We may find we value things that our friends do not value. This is often a period of introspection. We have worked hard. We have joined in and played the game. Now, we want to know what really is important to us. We have lived half of our lives. For what? What really matters?

Discovering what is really important sets us apart from the crowd. At level four, we become less concerned about what other people think. Our identity finally becomes clear. We know what we value, even if it does not comply with social expectations. As a result, as we progress, we often become more selective in how we socialize.

LEVEL FIVE (AGE 45-65)
Life Mission: *What is my purpose?*

After a longer period of mature introspection and values clarification, we are prepared to fully comprehend and embrace the purpose of our life. At this point, we are viable, comfortable with where we belong, and we know what is most important in life. This is an ideal situation in which to identify and expand our mission. From here on, the level of focus on what matters most is extraordinarily high. We are filled with the kind of purpose that can only come from years of paying our dues.

LEVEL SIX (AGE 65+)
Self-Acceptance: *How did I do?*

Having successfully met so many critical developmental milestones over the course of a lifetime, we now enter into a rare, self-actualized state of being in which we basically are at peace with ourselves. We feel at home in our bodies, comfortable in our own skin. We are beyond internal strife and conflict, beyond any need for social approval and content with our lot in life. We enjoy who we have become and are able to express ourselves genuinely and honestly. In spite of our acceptance and enjoyment of life, we understand and accept our ultimate passing.

In seeking to find common ground in resolving conflicts, be mindful of age differences.

Chapter 2

ENVIRONMENTAL
DIFFERENCES

G enetic differences, unlike environmental ones, are fixed.[9] Although there is little you can do about your environmental differences, understanding these differences can help you deal with conflict in a more constructive way.

Intelligence, like most aspects of human behavior and cognition, is a complex trait influenced by both genetic and environmental factors. Most definitions of intelligence include the ability to learn from experiences and adapt to changing environments. Where we are born and raised have a significant impact on how we see the world. Just as we have no control over our genetic differences, we have no control over where we are born or how we are nurtured. To solve our problems and resolve our conflicts successfully, we need to understand these environmental differences.

CULTURAL DIFFERENCES

Culture influences our behavior. Culture is a learned behavior, which can be defined as all the accepted and patterned ways of behavior that a group of people follow. Often we assume that our way of doing things is the right way, the best way, or the only way. When you have people from different cultures, you can have serious conflicts. What is important in one culture may not be important in a different culture. Cultures have different sets of values that may make resolving conflicts more difficult. Communicating across cultures is challenging.

Each culture has set rules that its members take for granted. Few of us are aware of our own cultural biases because cultural imprinting begins at a very early age. While some of a culture's knowledge, rules, beliefs, values, phobias, and anxieties are taught explicitly, most of the information is absorbed subconsciously.

One's own culture provides the "lens" through which we view the world; the "logic" by which we order it; and the "grammar" by which it makes sense. Culture is central to what we see, how we make sense of what we see, and how we express ourselves.

When people from different cultural backgrounds work together, cultural values sometimes conflict. We can misunderstand each other, and react in ways that can hinder relationships. We may not be aware of the affect that our culture has on us. We may not even be aware that our cultural values or assumptions are different from other people.

A method of communication, which is proper and correct in one culture, may be ineffective or even offensive in another. In reality, no culture is right or wrong, better or worse—just different. There is no single best approach to communicating with one another. The key to cross-cultural success is to develop an understanding of, and a deep respect for, the differences.

Even two people belonging to the same culture may not respond in exactly the same way. Generalizations are valid to the extent that they provide clues on what you will most likely encounter when dealing with members of a particular culture.

High-Context vs. Low-Context

International communication is influenced by cultural differences. The choice of communication medium can have cultural overtones. The determining factor may not be the degree of industrialization, but rather whether the particular country falls into a *high-context* or *low-context culture*. High-context cultures (Mediterranean, Slav, Central European, Latin American, African, Arab, Asian, American-Indian) leave much of the message unspecified, to be understood through context, nonverbal cues, and between-the-lines interpretation of what is actually said. By contrast, low-context cultures (most Germanic and English-speaking countries) expect messages to be explicit and specific.

Sequential vs. Synchronic

Some cultures think of time sequentially, as a linear commodity to "spend," "save," or "waste." Other cultures view time synchronically, as a constant flow to be experienced in the moment, and as a force that cannot be contained or controlled. In *sequential cultures* (like North American, English, German, Swedish, and Dutch), businesspeople give full attention to one agenda item after another. In *synchronic cultures* (including South America, southern Europe, and Asia) the flow of time is viewed as a sort of circle, with the past, present, and future all interrelated. This viewpoint influences how an organization in those cultures acts concerning deadlines, strategic thinking, investments, developing talent from within, and "long-term" planning.

Orientation to the past, present, and future is another aspect of time in which cultures differ. Americans believe that the individual can influence the future by personal effort, but since there are too many variables in the distant future, they favor a short-term view. Synchronistic cultures' context is to understand the present and prepare for the future. Any important relationship is a durable bond that goes back and forward in time, making it disloyal not to favor friends and relatives in business dealings.

Affective vs. Neutral

In international business practices, both reason and emotion play a role. Which one plays the dominant role depends on whether we are *affective* (readily showing emotions) or emotionally *neutral* in our approach. Members of neutral cultures do not telegraph their feelings, but keep them carefully controlled and subdued. In cultures with high affect, people show their feelings openly by laughing, smiling, scowling, crying, shouting, or walking out of the room. This does not mean that people in neutral cultures are cold or unfeeling, but in the course of normal business activities, neutral cultures are more careful to monitor the amount of emotion they display. Emotional reactions were found to be least acceptable in Japan, Indonesia, the United Kingdom, Norway, and the Netherlands, and most accepted in Italy, France, the United States, and Singapore.

The six fundamental patterns of cultural differences—which vary from one another, are described below. The descriptions highlight some of the recurring causes of cross-cultural communication difficulties. As you enter into multicultural dialogue or collaboration, keep these generalized differences in mind. Next time you find yourself in a confusing situation, and you suspect that cross-cultural differences are at play, review this list. Ask yourself how culture may shape your own reactions. Try to see the world from someone else's point of view.

Different Communication Styles

Communication styles vary widely between and within cultures. The use of language is one aspect of communication style. Across cultures, some words and phrases are used differently. Even in countries that share the English language, the meaning of "yes" varies from "maybe," "I'll consider it" to "definitely so," with many shades in between.

Another major aspect of communication style is the relative importance of non-verbal communication. Non-verbal communication includes not only facial expressions and gestures, but also seating arrangements, personal distance, and sense of time. Different norms regarding the appropriate degree of assertiveness in communicating can add to cultural misunderstandings. For example, some white Americans consider raised voices to be a sign that a fight has begun, while some black, Jewish, and Italian Americans often feel that a raised voice is a sign of an exciting conversation among friends. As a result, some white Americans may react with greater alarm to a loud discussion than would members of some American ethnic or non-white racial groups.

Different Attitudes Toward Conflict

Some cultures view conflict as a positive thing, while others view it as something to be avoided. In the United States, conflict is not usually desirable; but people often are encouraged to deal directly with conflicts that do arise. Face-to-face meetings customarily are recommended as the way to work through whatever problems exist. In contrast, in many Eastern countries, open conflict is experienced as embarrassing or demeaning, differences best worked out quietly. A written exchange might be the favored means to address the conflict.

Different Approaches to Completing Tasks

From culture to culture, there are different ways that people move toward completing tasks. Some reasons include different access to resources, different judgments of the rewards associated with task completion, different notions of time, and varied ideas about how relationship-building and task-oriented work should go together.

When working together effectively on a task, cultures differ with respect to the importance placed on establishing relationships early on in the collaboration. A case in point, Asian and Hispanic cultures tend to attach more value to developing relationships at the beginning of a shared project and more emphasis on task completion toward the end. Europeans and Americans tend to focus immediately on the task at hand, and let relationships develop as they work on the task. This does not mean that people from any one of these cultural backgrounds are more or less committed to accomplishing the task, or value relationships more or less; it means they may pursue them differently.

Different Decision-Making Styles

The roles individuals play in decision-making vary widely from culture to culture. For example, in the United States, decisions are frequently delegated—that is, an official assigns responsibility for a particular matter to a subordinate. In many Southern European and Latin American countries, there is a strong value placed on holding decision-making responsibilities oneself. When decisions are made by groups of people, majority rule is a common approach in the United States; while in Japan consensus is the preferred mode. Be aware that individuals' expectations about their own roles in shaping a decision may be influenced by their cultural frame of reference.

Different Attitudes Toward Disclosure

In some cultures, it is not appropriate to be frank about emotions, about the reasons behind a conflict or a misunderstanding, or about personal information. Keep this in mind when you are in a dialogue or when you are working with others. When you are dealing with a conflict, be mindful that people may differ in what they feel comfortable revealing. Questions that may seem natural to you—What was the conflict about? What was your role in the conflict? What was the sequence of events? The variation among cultures in attitudes toward disclosure is also something to consider before you conclude that you have an accurate reading of the views, experiences, and goals of the people with whom you are working.

Different Approaches to Knowing

Notable differences occur among cultural groups when it comes to epistemologies—that is, the ways people come to know things. European cultures tend to consider information acquired through cognitive means, such as counting and measuring, more valid than other ways of coming to know things. Compare that to African cultures' preference for affective ways of knowing, including symbolic imagery and rhythm. Asian cultures' epistemologies emphasize the validity of knowledge gained through striving toward transcendence.

These different approaches to knowing could affect ways of analyzing a community problem or finding ways to resolve it. Some members of your group may prefer library research to better understand a shared problem and identify possible solutions. Others may prefer to visit places and people who have experienced similar challenges to get a feel for what has worked elsewhere.

Respecting Our Differences and Working Together

In addition to helping us to understand our own cultural frames of reference, knowledge of these six patterns of cultural difference can help us to understand the people who are different from us. An appreciation of patterns of cultural difference can assist us in processing differences in ways that are respectful of others, not faultfinding or damaging.

Anthropologists Avruch and Black have noted that, when faced by an interaction that we do not understand, people tend to interpret the others involved as "abnormal," "weird," or "wrong." This tendency can lead to prejudice. If this propensity is either consciously or unconsciously integrated into organizational structures, then prejudice takes root in our institutions—in the structures, laws, policies, and procedures that shape our lives. Consequently, it is vital that we learn to control the human tendency to translate "different from me" into "less than me." We can learn to do this.

We can learn to collaborate across cultural lines as individuals and as a society. Awareness of cultural differences does not have to divide us. It does not have to paralyze us either for fear of not saying the "right thing." In fact, becoming more aware of our cultural differences, as well as exploring our similarities, can help us communicate with each other more effectively. Recognizing where cultural differences are at work is the first step toward understanding and respecting each other.

Learning about different ways that people communicate can enrich our lives. People's different communication styles reflect deeper philosophies and worldviews that are the foundation of their culture. Understanding these deeper philosophies gives us a broader picture of what the world has to offer us.

H. Ned Seelye, in *Teaching Culture, Strategies for Intercultural Communication*, identifies six skills that nurture and support intercultural communication: (1) Cultivating curiosity about another culture (or another segment or subculture of one's own culture) ; (2) Recognizing that role expectations and other social variables such as age, sex, social class, religion, ethnicity, and place of residence affect the way people speak and behave; (3) Realizing that effective communication requires discovering the culturally conditioned images that are invoked in the minds of people when they think, act, and react to the world around them; (4) Recognizing that situational variables and convention shape behavior in important ways; (5) Understanding that people generally act the way they do because they are using options their society allows for satisfying basic physical and psychological needs, and that cultural patterns are interrelated and tend to support need satisfaction mutually; (6) Developing the ability to evaluate the strength of a generalization about the target culture (from the evidence substantiating the statements), and to locate and organize information about the target culture from the library, the mass media, people, and personal observation.[10]

Learning about people's cultures has the potential to give us a mirror image of our own. We have the opportunity to challenge our assumptions about the "right" way of doing things, and consider a variety of approaches. We have a chance to learn new ways to solve problems that before seemed intractable.

Prejudice and stereotypes separate us from groups of people who could be friends and partners in working for change. Talking with people different from ourselves can energize us to take on the challenge of improving our communities and our world.

NATIONAL ORIGIN DIFFERENCES

People born in different countries have different national origins. Your national origin also refers to belonging to a group with the same culture, traditions, history, language, and other general similarities. Citizenship is not the same as national origin. Citizenship is the status of a person recognized under the custom or law of a state that bestows on that person the rights and the duties of citizenship. For example, a person born in the United States is automatically a citizen of the United States. A person born in another country can become a citizen of the United States by applying for citizenship through a legal process.

Different national origins may have different ways of looking at conflict and methods of resolution. Therefore, one needs to be aware of one's national origin. One's national origin may or may not be an impediment to conflict resolution.

While everyone has a national origin, the origin of all modern humans is most likely Africa. Although there are three models to explain the origin of modern humans, the current dominant theory, known as the Recent African Origin or Out of Africa model, is that many of us emigrated out of Africa about 60,000 years ago. When modern humans began to leave Africa, they largely or entirely replaced other archaic human species outside the continent.[11]

A second theory, the Multiregional Model, holds that there were parallel lines of evolution in each inhabited region of Africa, Europe, Asia and Australasia, glued together by interbreeding across the human range. Under this model, there was no real 'origin' for the modern form of *Homo sapiens*. A feature like a chin might have evolved in a region such as Africa and spread through interbreeding followed by selection if it was an advantageous characteristic. Another feature, like our high forehead, might have evolved elsewhere and then spread through interbreeding.

A third theory, the Assimilation Model, holds that modern humans evolved out of Africa, but more gradually. Under this theory, Neanderthals and archaic people like them were assimilated through widespread interbreeding. Thus, the establishment of modern human features occurred via a blending of populations rather than a rapid replacement.

The United States Department of State currently recognizes 195 independent countries, thereby providing 195 potential national origins. There are roughly 6,500 spoken languages in the world today. However, about 2,000 of those languages have fewer than 1,000 speakers. The most common languages are Mandarin (over 900 million); Spanish (over 400 million); English (over 350 million); Hindi/Urdu (over 320 million); Arabic (over 300 million); Portuguese (over 215 million); Bengali (over 205 million); Russian (over

155 million); Japanese (over 125 million); Punjabi (over 102 million). The Spanish language, spoken by more than four hundred million people, is the official language in twenty-one countries: Argentina, Bolivia, Chile, Colombia, Costa Rica, Cuba, Dominican Republic, Ecuador, Equatorial Guinea, El Salvador, Guatemala, Honduras, México, Nicaragua, Panamá, Paraguay, Peru, Puerto Rico, Spain, Uruguay, and Venezuela. In 2014, there were 58 sovereign states and 21 non-sovereign entities where English was an official language. The Arabic language is spoken in 22 countries in the Middle East and North Africa: Algeria, Bahrain, the Comoros Islands, Djibouti, Egypt, Iraq, Jordan, Kuwait, Lebanon, Libya, Morocco, Mauritania, Oman, Palestine, Qatar, Saudi Arabia, Somalia, Sudan, Syria, Tunisia, the United Arab Emirates, and Yemen.

Each individual is impacted differently by national origin. It may make little difference or it may be significant. For example, Israel and most of the Middle East countries have been in conflict for many years. It is likely that resolving a conflict between an Israeli and an Arab might be more difficult in comparison to resolving a conflict between a Canadian and an Australian.

Chapter 3

PERSONALITY TYPES

ifferent personality types affect the way we view and resolve conflicts. Personality is made up of patterns of thoughts, feelings, and behaviors that make a person unique. Personality is not determined by a single factor, but by an accumulation of many factors. Some of those factors are psychological, while others are physical, biological, and hereditable. Most personality psychologists consider three factors in personality development: (1) Heredity; (2) Culture; and (3) Family Influences.

Heredity is an important factor in determining personality, as most determinants, such as physical characteristics, gender, psychology, and more, are passed down through genes. The biological factors include genetic, physical appearance, physique, and rate of maturation. Aggressiveness, nervousness, timidity, and sociability are strongly influenced by genes.

Individual differences in abilities, aptitudes, and skills have a significant impact on personality. There are two basic types of abilities: cognitive and physical. Psychologists have identified many types of cognitive abilities. Jum C. Nunnally grouped them under *general intelligence* identifying and describing them into eight categories:[12]

Verbal ability: understand and use written and spoken language.

Numerical ability: solve arithmetic problems and deal with numbers.

Reasoning ability: solve problems and understand principles by which different problems can be solved.

Deductive ability: reach appropriate conclusions from an array of observations or evaluate the implications of a series of facts.

Ability to see relationships: see how things are related to each other and then apply this knowledge to other relationships and solutions.

Ability to remember: recall things ranging from simple associations to complex groups of statements or sentences.

Spatial ability: determine the location or arrangement of objects in relation to one's own position and to imagine how an object would appear if its position in space were altered.

Perceptual: uncover visual patterns and see relationships within and across patterns.

Physical abilities can be divided into two categories:

1. **Motor skill:** manipulate objects in an environment.

2. **Physical skill:** a person's fitness and strength.

These abilities vary with each individual and are measurable. A person may have a high verbal ability but low spatial abilities. Even if you have a high verbal ability relative to others (genetic), the extent to which that ability is used and developed depends on your environment (nurture).

Howard Gardner's theory of intelligence divides "intelligence" into eight different categories:[13]

1. Visual-Spatial Intelligence

Strengths: Visual and spatial judgment.
People who are strong in visual-spatial intelligence are good at visualizing things. These individuals are good with directions as well as maps, charts, videos, and pictures.

Characteristics:
Enjoys reading and writing
Good at putting puzzles together
Good at interpreting pictures, graphs, and charts
Enjoys drawing, painting, and the visual arts
Recognizes patterns easily

2. Linguistic-Verbal Intelligence

Strengths: Words, language, and writing.
People who are strong in linguistic-verbal intelligence are able to use words well, both when writing and speaking. These individuals are good at writing stories, memorizing information, and reading.

Characteristics:
Good at remembering written and spoken information
Enjoys reading and writing
Good at debating or giving persuasive speeches
Able to explain things well
Often uses humor when telling stories

3. Logical-Mathematical Intelligence

Strengths: Analyzing problems and mathematical operations.
People who are strong in logical-mathematical intelligence are good at reasoning, recognizing patterns, and logically analyzing problems. These individuals think conceptually about numbers, relationships, and patterns.

Characteristics:

Excellent problem-solving skills

Enjoys thinking about abstract ideas

Likes conducting scientific experiments

Good at solving complex computations

4. Bodily-Kinesthetic Intelligence

Strengths: Physical movement, motor control.

Those who have high bodily-kinesthetic intelligence are good at body movement, performing actions, and physical control. People who are strong in this area tend to have excellent hand-eye coordination and dexterity.

Characteristics:

Good at dancing and sports

Enjoys creating things with his or her hands

Excellent physical coordination

Tends to remember by doing, rather than hearing or seeing

5. Musical Intelligence

Strengths: Rhythm and music.

People who have strong musical intelligence are good at thinking in patterns, rhythms, and sounds. They have a strong appreciation for music and are good at musical composition and performance.

Characteristics:

Enjoys singing and playing musical instruments

Recognizes musical patterns and tones easily

Good at remembering songs and melodies

Rich understanding of musical structure, rhythm, and notes

6. Interpersonal Intelligence

Strengths: Understanding and relating to other people.

Those who have strong interpersonal intelligence are good at understanding and interacting with other people. These individuals are skilled at assessing the emotions, motivations, desires, and intentions of those around them.

Characteristics:

Good at communicating verbally
Skilled at nonverbal communication
Sees situations from different perspectives
Creates positive relationships with others
Good at resolving conflict in groups

7. Intrapersonal Intelligence

Strengths: Introspection and self-reflection.

Individuals who are strong in intrapersonal intelligence are good at being aware of their own emotional states, feelings, and motivations. They enjoy self-reflection and analysis, including daydreaming, exploring relationships with others, and assessing their personal strengths.

Characteristics:

Good at analyzing his or her strengths and weaknesses
Enjoys analyzing theories and ideas
Excellent self-awareness
Clearly understands the basis for his or her own motivations and feelings

8. Naturalistic Intelligence

Strengths: Finding patterns and relationships to nature.

Naturalistic is the most recent addition to Gardner's theory and has been met with more resistance than his original seven intelligences. According to Gardner, individuals who are high in this type of intelligence are more in tune with nature and are interested in nurturing, exploring the environment, and learning about other species. These individuals are aware of even subtle changes to their environments.

Characteristics:
Interested in subjects such as botany, biology, and zoology
Good at categorizing and cataloging information easily
May enjoy camping, gardening, hiking, and exploring the outdoors
Doesn't enjoy learning unfamiliar topics that have no connection to nature

Gardner's theory has come under criticism from both psychologists and educators opining that Gardner's definition of intelligence is too broad and that his eight different "intelligences" simply represent talents, personality traits, and abilities. Despite those criticisms, the theory of multiple intelligences enjoys considerable popularity with educators, who utilize multiple intelligences in their teaching philosophies and work to integrate Gardner's theory into the classroom. Learning more about the multiple intelligences can help you better understand your own strengths and weaknesses and those of others.

All human beings live in a society, an interacting group of people with a distinctive culture, a body of stored knowledge, a characteristic way of thinking, feelings, attitudes, goals, ideals, and value systems. Culture regulates our lives and influences the development of personality by prescribing and limiting what will be required for the development of personality. Each culture expects and trains its members to behave in the ways that are acceptable to the group. Each culture has its own concepts, needs, and specific techniques of child rearing, as well as a set of expectations regarding patterns of approved behavior. There are cultural variations in the methods of achieving such goals as to perpetuating the group and maintaining solidarity, or for satisfying basic needs of its members. There are cultural pre-scriptions for different types of child rearing according to the various groups. Children from different socio-economic backgrounds differ in personality structure, behavior, and attitudes. They differ with respect to achievement motivation—the basic need leading to success in life. Middle-class parents, in general, stress achievement strongly, but lower-class parents do not. Sociological analysis suggests that the lower-class child develops little capacity to "delay gratification," because for that child, the future is uncertain. The variation in social class leads to the setting of a variety of aim, modes, and methods in developing social behavior and causes individuals to vary in the development of personality.

The child's first social learning occurs at home. His earliest experiences with his family, particularly his mother, are critical in determining his attitude and expectations toward other individuals. The mother remains most important to him because she gratifies his primary needs for food, for alleviation of his pain and source of pleasure, and for warmth. The infant soon learns to search for and approach his mother whenever he is hungry, in pain, or uncomfort-able. If the mother is nurturing and gratifies his needs promptly and effectively, she rewards the child's "approach" responses, and these are likely to be repeated. Positive approach responses gradually generalize to other people, and the child develops a positive social attitude. The earliest interactions between mother and child lay the groundwork for the child's development of trust and mistrust. The parental attitude (in child-rearing process) toward the child's growing independence and reactions to exploration strongly influence the development of important motives, like, curiosity, and the drives for autonomy, inde-pendence, mastery, competence, and achievement.

Permissive and easygoing parents will allow their child to explore and investigate freely, encouraging and rewarding curiosity and inde-pendent behavior. As a result, their children will actively manipulate their environment, thereby developing self-confidence, spontaneity, and the desire for mastery over their surroundings. Parents who severely restrict their children in exploring and manipulating their environment and inhibit the development of motivation for autonomy will ultimately lead to the child's dependent behavior. Over-protected children tend to become submissive, compliant, and passive. Children from democratic homes, characterized by general permissiveness, frequent conversing with children, emphasis on the child's decision-making, problem solving, and helping them to rationalize behavior, lead to strengthening their (children's) ego-strength and strong self-concept in the future. By contrast, children brought up in authoritative (controlled, restricted) homes, homes with clear-cut rules, prohibitions, and restrictions tend to be quiet, well-behaved, shy, and socially unassertive. Those from the highly "indulgent" homes show almost the same behavior as shown by those of the restricted and overprotected children.

One study on human behavior published in Science Advances revealed that 90% of the population can be classified into four basic personality types: Optimistic, Pessimistic, Trusting, and Envious. Envious is the most common type with 30% compared to 20% for each of the other groups.

A study conducted by Northwestern University in 2018 involving more than 1.5 million questionnaire respondents found at least four distinct *clusters* of personality types: average, reserved, self-centered, and role model. They were based on the five widely accepted basic personality traits: neuroticism, extraversion, openness, agreeableness, and conscientiousness.[14]

Average: Average people are high in neuroticism and extraversion, while low in openness. Females are more likely than males to fall into the Average type.

Reserved: The Reserved type is emotionally stable, but not open or neurotic. They are not particularly extraverted but are somewhat agreeable and conscientious.

Role Models: Role Models score low in neuroticism and high in all the other traits. The likelihood of being a role model increases dramatically with age. These are people who are dependable and open to new ideas. More women than men are likely to be role models.

Self-Centered: Self-Centered people score very high in extraversion and below average in openness, agreeableness, and conscientiousness. There is a very dramatic decrease in the number of self-centered types as people age, both with women and men.

There are a number of personality tests that have been developed and used over the years to determine personality types. Some of these personality tests are listed below:

The Eysenck Personality Inventory (EPI) measures two pervasive, independent dimensions of personality, Extraversion-Introversion and Neuroticism-Stability, which account for most of the variance in the personality domain.

2

The Herrmann Brain Dominance Instrument (HBDI) is a system to measure and describe thinking preferences in people. The HBDI identifies four different modes of thinking:

    A. Analytical thinking—Key words: Auditive, logical, factual, critical, technical, and quantitative; Preferred activities: collecting data, analysis, understanding how things work, judging ideas based on facts, criteria, and logical reasoning;

    B. Sequential thinking—Key words: safekeeping, structured, organized, complexity or detailed, planned; Preferred activities: following directions, detail oriented work, step-by-step problem solving, organization, and implementation;

C. Interpersonal thinking—Key words: Kinesthetic, emotional, spiritual, sensory, feeling; Preferred activities: listening to and expressing ideas, looking for personal meaning, sensory input, and group interaction;

D. Imaginative thinking—Key words: Visual, holistic, intuitive, innovative, and conceptual; Preferred activities: Looking at the big picture, taking initiative, challenging assumptions, visuals, metaphoric thinking, creative problem solving, long term thinking.

The Taylor-Johnson Temperament Analysis is an instrument for assessing the influence of an individual's personal characteristics in relationships. The test is used in counseling for couples or individuals, premarital sessions, and marriage enrichment. T-JTA aids professionals in identifying individual improvement and providing the client with self-awareness with factors affecting relationships.

4

The Temperament and Character Inventory (TCI) is a set of tests designed to identify the intensity of and relationships between the seven basic personality dimensions of Temperament and Character, which interact to create the unique personality of an individual. *Temperament* refers to the automatic emotional responses to experience and is moderately heritable (i.e., genetic, biological) and relatively stable throughout life. The four measured temperament dimensions are: A. Novelty Seeking (NS); B. Harm Avoidance (HA); C. Reward Dependence (RD); D. Persistence (PS). *Character* refers to self-concepts and individual differences in goals and values, which influence voluntary choices, intentions, and the meaning and salience of what is experienced in life. Differences in character are moderately heritable and moderately influenced by socio-cultural learning. Character traits mature in progressive steps throughout life. The three measured character dimensions are: A. Self-Directedness (SD); B. Cooperativeness (CO); C. Self-Transcendence (ST).

The DISC Profile, published by Wiley, is a non-judgmental tool used for discussion of people's behavioral differences. There are four dimensions to DISC:

> **A.** Dominance—Person places emphasis on accomplishing results, the bottom line, confidence; Behavior—sees the big picture; can be blunt; accepts challenges; gets straight to the point;
>
> **B.** Influence—Person places emphasis on influencing or persuading others, openness, relationships; Behaviors— shows enthusiasm; is optimistic; likes to collaborate; dislikes being ignored;
>
> **C.** Steadiness—Person places emphasis on cooperation, sincerity, dependability; Behaviors—does not like to be rushed; calm manner; calm approach; supportive actions;
>
> **D.** Conscientiousness—Person places emphasis on quality and accuracy, expertise, competency; Behaviors— enjoys independence; objective reasoning; wants the details; fears being wrong.

The Forté Primary Profile identifies an individual's natural interpersonal communication style preferences. The profile is measured through four dimensions:

A. Patience/Impatience—The Pace Strength (Represented graphically as Patient to Impatient or Paced to Urgent). The Patient or paced individual is relaxed, easygoing, steady, amiable, warm, dependent, sincere, likable, and a good listener. The paced person likes peace and harmony, likes to be cooperative, likes to save time, and likes time to adjust to changes. The Impatient or urgent person is action-oriented and does not tolerate delays for extended periods of time. This person often has to do things twice for lack of adequate planning. Impatient people have a strong sense of urgency, both for themselves and for those around them. It is important for these individuals to keep busy and have others respond quickly to them. They learn quickly and prefer variety as opposed to a single area of concentration. Their sense of urgency often drives them to seek out new, exciting situations, which offer them a change of pace.

B. Conformity/Non-Conformity—The Systems Strength (Represented graphically as Conformist to Non-Conformist or Systematic to Independent). The Conformist or systematic person, depending upon environment and experience, will be careful, accurate, precise, thorough, skillful, dependable, meticulous, conservative, prudent, anxiety-prone, worrisome, sensitive to criticism, and a perfectionist. This person prefers to work systematically, wants outcomes to be "right," and wants to be fair. The Non-Conformist or independent person is characterized by a generalist orientation to life. This person exhibits an independent attitude, with a tendency to avoid detail work. These individuals usually are uninhibited, candid, and relate well to activities that take them out of ordinary or prescribed situations. These individuals want freedom and minimal controls, both in work and personal relationships. They can be resistant to controls and will tend to rationalize.

C. Dominance/Non-Dominance—The Decision Style Strength (Represented graphically as Dominant to Non-Dominant or Controlling to Cooperative). The Dominant or controlling person is results-oriented and primarily concerned with getting things done. Dominant people are hard-driving, to the point, and dislike indecisiveness. They appear outwardly secure, and are innovative, venturesome, ingenious, big-picture oriented, and sometimes abrasive. They are trouble-shooters, decisive, and risk-takers. The Non-Dominant or cooperative person is characterized by a non-threatening way of working with others. This person is not forcefully demanding. A Non-Dominant person will seldom impose upon others, is mild-mannered, composed, and often modest. They prefer direction.

D. Extroversion/Introversion—The People Strength (Represented graphically as Extroverted to Introverted or Outgoing to Reserved). The Extrovert or outgoing person is people-oriented. Extroverts are friendly, pleasant, persuasive, emphatic, enthusiastic, talkative, stimulating, motivating, and optimistic. They are good mixers and good coordinators. The Extrovert likes to be with and influence people. Introverted or reserved people are selective in whom they place their trust; they take greater care in protecting their private life and prefer not to speak without weighing the potential consequences. They are creative, have an individualistic side that can manifest itself in a vivid imagination, and the ability to think things through to a conclusion. They tend to be contemplative, enjoy quiet, and do not need others around for self-fulfilling activities.

7

The HEXACO Personality Inventory-Revised is an instrument that assesses the six major dimensions of personality: A. Honesty-Humility; B. Emotionality; C. eXtraversion; D. Agreeableness (versus Anger); E. Conscientiousness; F. Openness to Experience.

8

The Newcastle Personality Assessor is a brief tool for assessing the Big Five described as follows:

Openness: Characterized by imagination and insight. Those high in this trait also tend to have a broad range of interests. People who are high in this trait tend to be more adventurous and creative. People low in this trait are often much more traditional and may struggle with abstract thinking. People who are high on the openness continuum are typically: very creative; open to trying new things; focused on tackling new challenges; happy to think about abstract concepts. Those who are low on this trait: dislike change; do not enjoy new things; resist new ideas; not very imaginative; dislike abstract or theoretical concepts.

Conscientiousness: Characterized by high levels of thoughtfulness, good impulse control, and goal-directed behaviors. Those high in conscientiousness tend to be organized and mindful of details. Those who are high on the conscientiousness continuum also tend to: spend time preparing; finish important tasks right away; pay attention to details; enjoy having a set schedule. People who are low in this trait tend to: dislike structure and schedules; make messes and not take care of things; fail to return things or put them back where they belong; procrastinate important tasks; fail to complete the things they are supposed to do.

Extraversion: Characterized by excitability, sociability, talkativeness, assertiveness, and high amounts of emotional expressiveness. People who are high in extraversion are outgoing and tend to gain energy in social situations. People who are low in extraversion (or introverted) tend to be more reserved and have to expend energy in social settings. People who rate high on extraversion tend to: enjoy being the center of attention; like to start conversations; enjoy meeting new people; have a wide social circle of friends and acquaintances; find it easy to make new friends; feel energized when they are around other people; say things before they think about them. People who rate low on extraversion tend to: prefer solitude; feel exhausted when they have to socialize a lot; find it difficult to start conversations; dislike making small talk; carefully think things through before they speak; dislike being the center of attention.

Neuroticism: Characterized by sadness, moodiness, and emotional instability. Individuals who are high in this trait tend to experience mood swings, anxiety, irritability, and sadness. Those low in this trait tend to be more stable and emotionally resilient. Individuals who are high in neuroticism tend to: experience a lot of stress; worry about many different things; get upset easily; experience dramatic shifts in mood; feel anxious. Those who are low in this trait are typically: emotionally stable; deal well with stress; rarely feel sad or depressed; do not worry much; very relaxed.

Agreeableness: Characterized by trust, altruism, kindness, affection, and other prosocial behaviors. People who are high in agreeableness tend to be more cooperative while those low in this trait tend to be more competitive and even manipulative. People who are high in the trait of agreeableness tend to: have a great deal of interest in other people; care about others; feel empathy and concern for other people; enjoy helping and contributing to the happiness of other people. Those who are low in this trait tend to: take little interest in others; do not care about how other people feel; have little interest in other people's problems; insult and belittle others.

9

The Myers-Briggs Test of personality is based on Carl Jung's theory of psychological types. The Myers-Briggs Type Indicator (MBTI) is an assessment of personality based on preferences in four dimensions. Each dimension has two opposite personality preferences: extraversion or introversion; sensing or intuition; thinking or feeling; judging or perceiving. Each of the eight preferences is represented by a capital letter. People will have some traits of all eight preferences; however, they will be more inclined towards one preference in each pair. The four paired dimensions are described below:

Extraversion (E) or Introversion (I): How we gain energy. Do you prefer to focus on the outer world or on your own inner world? Extroverts direct energy outwardly and are energized by the outside world. Introverts direct energy inwardly and are energized by reflecting on their inner world.

Sensing (S) or INtuition (N): How we receive information. Do you prefer to focus on the basic information or do you prefer to interpret and add meaning? Sensors learn through their five senses, through facts. Intuitives learn through patterns, impressions, and possibilities.

Thinking (T) or Feeling (F): How we make decisions. When making decisions, do you prefer to first look at logic and consistency or first look at the people and special circumstances? Thinkers make decisions based on facts. Feelers make decisions based on values.

Judging (J) or Perceiving (P): Our lifestyle preference. Do you prefer to have things decided or do you prefer to stay open to new information and options? Judgers prefer their world to be structured and planned. Perceivers prefer their world to be open-ended.

Each MBTI personality type consists of 4 letters. The first letter is E or I (how you get your energy), the second letter is S or N (how you learn), the third letter is T or F (how you make decisions), and the fourth letter is J or P (how you organize your life). The combinations of the four letters make up sixteen personality types:

1. Giver: Extraverted Intuitive Feeling Judging; Extraverted Feeling with Introverted Intuition (ENFJ) - focuses on others; caring and concerned; good public speaker.

2. Inspirer: Extraverted Intuitive Feeling Perceiving; Extraverted Intuition with Introverted Feeling (ENFP) - prefers variety and challenge; lively and creative; good sense of humor.

3. Executive: Extraverted Intuitive Thinking Judging; Extraverted Thinking with Introverted Intuition (ENTJ) - likes to be in charge; energetic and confident; enjoys a good debate.

4. Visionary: Extraverted Intuitive Thinking Perceiving; Extraverted Intuition with Introverted Thinking (ENTP) - seeks variety and change; clever and creative; good problem-solver.

5. Caregiver: Extraverted Sensing Feeling Judging; Extraverted Feeling with Introverted Sensing (ESF) - likes to be needed; outgoing and warmhearted; good team player.

6. Performer: Extraverted Sensing Feeling Perceiving; Extraverted Sensing with Introverted Feeling (ESFP) - prefers to talk; friendly and upbeat; generous with friends and family.

7. Guardian: Extraverted Sensing Thinking Judging; Extraverted Thinking with Introverted Sensing (ESTJ) - seeks being in charge; meets problems head-on; gets things done.

8. Doer: Extraverted Sensing Thinking Perceiving; Extraverted Sensing with Introverted Thinking (ESTP) - prefers to always be on the go; confident and charming; strong sense of fun.

9. Protector: Introverted Intuition with Extraverted Feeling; Introverted Intuitive Feeling Judging (INFJ) - likes to work toward a vision; sensitive to others; keenly aware of emotions.

10. Idealist: Introverted Intuitive Feeling Perceiving; Introverted Feeling with Extraverted Intuition (INFP) - likes pursuing own interests; dislikes rules and deadlines; strong inner values.

11. Scientist: Introverted Intuitive Thinking Judging; Introverted Intuition with Extraverted Thinking (INTJ) - prefers to come up with fresh ideas; original thinker; highly independent.

12. Thinker: Introverted Intuitive Thinking Perceiving; Introverted Thinking with Extraverted Intuition (INTP) - seeks to be precise and logical; quiet and self-reliant; deep thinker.

13. Nurturer: Introverted Sensing Feeling Judging; Introverted Sensing with Extraverted Feeling (ISFJ) - likes to be helpful; loyal and dependable; pays attention to details.

14. Artist: Introverted Sensing Feeling Perceiving; Introverted Feeling with Extraverted Sensing (ISFP) - seeks to live and let live; easygoing and likable; enjoys simple pleasures.

15. Duty Fulfiller: Introverted Sensing Thinking Judging; Introverted Sensing with Extraverted Thinking (ISTJ) - wants things to be orderly; reliable and responsible; good with facts and figures.

16. Mechanic: Introverted Sensing Thinking Perceiving; Introverted Thinking with Extraverted Sensing (ISTP) - prefers to stand back and observe; quiet and curious; highly independent.

10

The Enneagram Personality Test identifies nine core personality types. While the nine personality types are distinct, they are also interlinked. Each of us has a dominant personality type that drives how we think, behave, learn, see the world, and evolve. The nine types are described below:

1. Reformer: Rational, idealistic, principled, purposeful, self-controlled, and perfectionistic.

2. Helper: Caring, interpersonal; generous, demonstrative, people-pleasing, and possessive.

3. Achiever: Success-oriented, pragmatic, adaptable, excelling, driven, and image-conscious.

4. Individualist: Sensitive, introspective, expressive, dramatic, self-absorbed, and temperamental.

5. Investigator: Intense, cerebral, perceptive, innovative, secretive, and isolated.

6. Loyalist: Committed, security-oriented, engaging, responsible, anxious, and suspicious.

7. Enthusiast: Busy, variety-seeking, spontaneous, versatile, acquisitive, and scattered.

8. Challenger: Powerful, dominating, self-confident, decisive, willful, and confrontational.

9. Peacemaker: Easygoing, self-effacing, receptive, reassuring agreeable, and complacent.

Chapter 4

BIAS, STEREOTYPING, AND PREJUDICE

B iases, stereotyping, and prejudices can impede the ability of people to find common ground in resolving conflicts and disputes. Bias may be defined as preference in favor of or against one thing, person, or group compared with another. It is a tendency to believe that some people, ideas, customs, religions, cultures, or other traits are better than others resulting in treating some people unfairly. People will embrace any evidence or experience that reinforce their biases, but disregard any evidence or experience that contradicts them.

Bias is perpetuated by conformity with in-group attitudes and socialization by their culture. Bias is an inclination to hold a partial perspective, often accompanied by a refusal to consider the possible merits of alternative points of view. Biases are learned implicitly within cultural contexts. People may develop biases toward or against an individual, an ethnic group, a nation, a religion, a social class, or political party. Biased means one-sided, lacking a neutral viewpoint, or not having an open mind. Bias can come in many forms and is often synonymous with prejudice or bigotry.

A stereotype is an exaggerated belief, image, or distorted truth about a person or group—a generalization that allows for little or no individual differences or social variation. Stereotypes are based on images in mass media or reputations passed on by parents, peers, and other members of society. Stereotypes can be positive or negative. Mass media routinely utilizes stereotypes as a shorthand method to paint a mood, scene, or character. The elderly, for example, are routinely portrayed as being frail and forgetful, while younger people are often shown as vibrant and able. Stereotypes can also be conveyed by omission in popular, as when TV shows present an all-white world. Once learned, stereotypes and prejudices resist change, even when evidence fails to support them or points to the contrary.

The word "prejudice" can literally be broken down into "pre" and "judgment." Prejudice comes from our pre-judging other people's habits, customs, culture, religion, clothes, ways of speaking, and values. We often do this with no basis for the judgment other than the fact that their culture, customs, values, religious beliefs are different from our own. What we call Truth is very often a social construction that differs across cultures. When we are confined to a single culture, it is incredibly difficult to see that one's viewpoints are not the only viewpoints. Simply put, prejudice is a preconceived opinion that is not based on facts, reason, or actual experience. Stereotypes can lead to faulty beliefs and can also result in both prejudice and discrimination.

Conformity to social norms may be a cause of prejudice in some cases. People who tend to be more conformist would also likely be more prejudiced. The higher levels of prejudice against people of color in the southern United States compared to the north is a result of the greater social acceptability of this kind of prejudice in the south.

Influences that cause individuals to be "racist" or "sexist," may come from peers, parents, and group membership. Conforming to social norms means people adopt the "normal" set of behaviors associated with a particular group or society.

Behavior considered appropriate within a social group can influence prejudice and discrimination. People may have prejudiced beliefs and feelings and act in a prejudiced way because they are conforming to what is regarded as normal in the social groups to which they belong.

For example, with respect to miners, below ground, where the social norm was friendly behavior towards work colleagues, 80% of the white miners were friendly towards the black miners. Above ground, where the social norm was prejudiced behavior by whites to blacks, this dropped to 20%. The white miners were conforming to different norms above and below ground. Whether or not prejudice is shown depends on the social context within which behavior takes place.

Hidden bias tests measure unconscious or automatic biases. Your willingness to examine your own possible biases is an important step in understanding the causes of stereotypes and prejudice. The ability to distinguish friend from foe helped early humans survive, and the ability to quickly and automatically categorize people is a fundamental quality of the human mind. Categories give order to life. We group other people into categories based on social and other characteristics.

We use heuristics when making quick decisions. While heuristics are useful in solving many problems and making judgments quickly, they can lead to erroneous decisions. Some of the more common heuristics include the availability heuristic, the representativeness heuristic, and the affect heuristic.

The availability heuristic involves making decisions based upon how easy it is to bring something to mind. When you are trying to make a decision, you might quickly remember a number of relevant examples. Since these are more readily available in your memory, you may judge these outcomes as being more common or frequently occurring. For example, if you are thinking of moving to another city and remember reading about rising crime rates there, you might decide not to move there even though the crime rate is less than where you live. The availability heuristic leads you to think that the crime rate is higher there than it actually is.

The representativeness heuristic involves making a decision by comparing the present situation to the most representative mental prototype. When you are trying to decide if someone is honest, you might compare aspects of the individual to other mental examples you hold. The person reminds you of your mother, so you might immediately assume that she is trustworthy.

The affect heuristic involves making choices that are strongly influenced by the emotions that an individual is experiencing at that moment. People are more likely to see decisions as having higher benefits and lower risks when they are in a positive mood. Negative emotions, on the other hand, lead people to focus on the potential downsides of a decision rather than the possible benefits.

While heuristics can speed up our problem and decision-making process, they can lead to errors. Because something has worked in the past does not mean that it will work again. Relying on an existing heuristic can make it difficult to see alternative solutions. Using mental shortcuts to classify and categorize people can lead to bias, stereotyping, and prejudice.

Hidden biases may be related to discriminatory behavior in a wide range of human interactions, from employment to choices of housing and schools. There is growing evidence that hidden biases may affect split-second, life-or-death decisions, such as the shootings of black men incorrectly thought to be holding guns. Unconscious prejudices and stereotypes may also affect court jury deliberations and other daily tasks requiring judgments of human character. People who argue that prejudice is not a big problem today are, ironically, demonstrating the problem of unconscious prejudice. Because these prejudices are outside our awareness, they can be denied.

Hidden bias has emerged as an important clue to the disparity between public opinion, as expressed by America's creed and social goals, and the amount of discrimination that still exists.

A cognitive bias is a mistake in reasoning, evaluating, remembering, or other cognitive process, often occurring as a result of holding onto one's preferences and beliefs regardless of contrary information. People create their own subjective social reality from their own perceptions; their view of the world may dictate their behavior. Cognitive biases may lead to perceptual distortion, inaccurate judgment, illogical interpretation, or what is broadly called irrationality. Some cognitive biases are taken to be adaptive and may lead to success in the appropriate situation. Cognitive biases may allow speedier choices when speed is more valuable than precision. Other cognitive biases are a "by-product" of human processing limitations due to an absence of appropriate mental mechanisms, or just from human limitations in information processing.

Some of the more common cognitive biases may be grouped in the following ways:

Social Cognition Biases:

Correspondence Bias: The tendency to infer that people's behavior corresponds to their disposition (personality).

Actor/Observer Difference: The tendency to see other people's behavior as dispositionally caused but focusing more on the role of situational factors when explaining one's own behavior.

Self-Serving Attributions: Explanations for one's successes that credit internal, dispositional factors and explanations for one's failures that blame external, situational factors may be distorted by the need to maintain and enhance self-esteem.

Belief in a Just World: The assumption that bad things happen to bad people and good things happen to good people.

Reciprocity Bias: When people feel a sense of obligation after they receive something.

Own-Race Bias: People are better at recognizing faces of their own race than those of other races.

Ultimate Attribution Error: The tendency to make dispositional attributions about an entire group of people.

In-group bias: The tendency to reserve positive feelings and special treatment to people we have defined as being part of our in-group (the group with which a person identifies and of which he or she feels a member), and negative feelings and unfair treatment to people we have defined as being part of our out-group (groups which an individual does not identify with).

Out-group homogeneity bias: The perception that those in the out-group are more similar (homogenous) to each other than they really are, as well as more similar than the members of the in-group are (i.e., the belief that "they are all alike").

Illusory Correlation: The tendency to see relationships, or correlations, between events that are actually unrelated; this is one-way stereotypes form and endure.

False Consensus Effect: The tendency for people to overestimate the extent to which others agree with them.

Bandwagon Effect: The tendency to follow the actions or beliefs of others because individuals prefer to conform, or because individuals derive information from others.

Reasoning Biases:

Anchoring: The common human tendency to rely too heavily on the first piece of information offered (the "anchor") when making decisions.

Representativeness Heuristic: The tendency for people to use similarity or representativeness as a proxy for probabilistic thinking; this can lead to base-rate neglect, the tendency for people to insufficiently take into account the overall frequency (base rate) of an event in a population.

Commitment and Consistency Bias: A pattern of behavior in which an individual or group will continue to rationalize their decisions, actions, and investments when faced with increasingly negative outcomes rather than alter their course of behavior.

Hindsight Bias: The tendency for people to exaggerate how much they could have predicted an outcome after knowing that it occurred.

Projection Bias: The tendency for people to exaggerate the degree to which their future tastes will resemble their current tastes.

Impact Bias: The tendency to overestimate the intensity and duration of our emotional reactions to future negative events.

Bias Blind Spot: Recognizing the impact of biases on the judgment of others, while failing to see the impact of biases on one's own judgment.

Conjunction Fallacy: The tendency to assume that specific conditions are more probable than general ones.

Gambler's Fallacy: The false belief that in a sequence of independent draws from a distribution, an outcome that has not occurred for a while is more likely to come up on the next draw.

Hot-Hand Fallacy: The false or exaggerated belief that a person's performance varies systematically over the short run.

Availability Heuristic: The tendency for people to assess the frequency of a class or the probability of an event by the ease with which instances or occurrences can be brought to mind.

Anchoring and Adjustment Heuristic: The tendency for people to answer a question by starting at some first-pass guess based on memory or the environment, and adjust that guess until they are satisfied with the answer.

Curse of Knowledge: If you know something, you cannot appreciate what it is like not to know it.

Confirmation Bias: Tendency to search for or interpret information in a way that confirms one's preconceptions, causing people to actively seek out and assign more weight to evidence that confirms their beliefs, and ignore or under weigh evidence that could disconfirm their beliefs. A form of Confirmation Bias where the impression is positive is called the Halo Effect. If the impression is negative, it may be referred to as a Demonizing Effect. An observer's overall impression of a person, company, brand, or product influences the observer's feelings and thoughts about that entity's character or properties.

Memory Biases:

Primacy Effect: Tendency to weigh initial events more than subsequent events. People tend to recall items that were at the beginning of a list rather than items that were in the middle of a list.

Recency Effect: Tendency to weigh recent events more than earlier events. People tend to recall items that were at the end of a list rather than items that were in the middle of a list.

To resolve conflicts peacefully, you need to be aware of these biases and prejudices. If people are aware of their hidden biases, they can monitor and attempt to ameliorate hidden attitudes before they are expressed through behavior. This can include attention to language, body language, and to the stigmatization felt by target groups. A change in behavior can modify beliefs and attitudes. A conscious decision to be egalitarian might lead one to widen one's circle of friends and knowledge of other groups. Such efforts may, over time, reduce the strength of unconscious biases.

Chapter 5

ECONOMIC DISPARITY AND POWER IMBALANCES

 conomic disparity and power imbalances can be a challenge to resolving conflicts peacefully and effectively.

ECONOMIC DISPARITY

Economic disparities in the distribution of economic assets and income can lead to conflicts. Horizontal inequalities can occur between different ethnic, religious, or regional groups. Economic inequalities include access to and ownership of financial, human, natural resource-based, and social assets. They also include inequalities in income levels and employment opportunities.

A country may have a highly equal distribution of income overall, but it may be divided very unevenly between particular cultural groups. Focusing on inequalities between different groups draws attention to discriminatory relationships between groups in a society. Conflicts are more likely to occur where there are large inequalities between different groups. One of the major reasons there is economic inequality within modern market economies is because wages are determined by a market, and are influenced by supply and demand A job where there are many willing workers (high supply) but only a small number of positions (low demand) will result in a low wage for that job. This is because competition between workers drives down the wage. An example of this would be low-skill jobs such as dish-washing or customer service. These jobs require very little skill, which results in a high supply of willing workers. Competition amongst workers would tend to drive down the wage, since if any one worker demands a higher wage, the employer can simply hire another employee at an equally low wage. A job where there are few willing workers (low supply), but a high demand for the skills these workers have will result in high wages for that job. This is because competition between employers will drive up the wage. An example of this would be high-skill jobs such as data scientists or capable CEOs. Competition amongst employers tend to drive up wages, since if any one employer demands a low wage, the worker can simply quit and easily find a new job at a higher wage.

While the above examples tend to identify skill with high demand and wages, this is not necessarily the case. For example, highly skilled computer programmers in western countries have seen their wages suppressed by competition from computer programmers in India who are willing to accept a lower wage. The final results amongst these supply and demand interactions is a gradation of different wages representing income inequality within society. There are many reasons for economic differences between people and countries. Richard Lynn and Tatu Vanhanen, in their book, *IQ and the Wealth of Nations*, opine that the most significant factor is IQ.[15]

One important factor in the creation of inequality is the variable ability of individuals to get an education. Education, especially education in an area where there is a high demand for workers, creates high wages for those with this education. Those who are unable to afford an education generally receive much lower wages. Many economists believe that a major reason the world has experienced increasing levels of inequality since the 1980s is because of an increase in the demand for highly skilled workers in high-tech industries. This has resulted in an increase in wages for those with an education, but has not increased the wages of those without an education, leading to greater inequality.

The existence of different genders, cultures, and religions within a society can contribute to economic differences. The idea of the gender gap explains the reasons there are different levels of income for different genders. Culture and religion can play a role in creating inequality by either encouraging or discouraging wealth-acquiring behavior and providing a basis for discrimination. Individuals belonging to certain racial and ethnic minorities are found more often among the poor than others.

Wealth condensation is a process by which, in certain conditions, newly-created wealth tends to become concentrated in the possession of already-wealthy individuals or entities. According to this theory, those who already hold wealth have the means to invest in new sources of creating wealth or to otherwise leverage the accumulation of wealth and are the beneficiaries of the new wealth. Over time, wealth condensation can significantly contribute to the persistence of inequality within society. As an example of wealth condensation, truck drivers who own their own trucks consistently make more money than those who do not since the owner of a truck can escape the rent charged to drivers by owners (Even taking into account maintenance and other costs). Hence, a truck driver who has wealth to begin with can afford to buy his own truck in order to make more money. A truck driver who does not own his own truck makes a lesser wage and is therefore unable to buy his own truck to increase his income.

Related to wealth condensation are the effects of inter-generational inequality. The rich tend to provide their offspring with a better education, increasing their chances of achieving a high amount of income. Furthermore, the wealthy often leave their offspring with a hefty inheritance, jump starting the process of wealth condensation for the next generation.

There are many factors that tend to constrain the amount of economic inequality within society. Progressive taxation, where the rich are taxed more than poor, is effective at reducing the amount of income inequality in society. The Nationalization or subsidization of essential goods and services, such as food, healthcare, education, and housing can reduce the amount of inequality in society by providing goods and services that everyone needs cheaply or free. Governments can thereby effectively increase the disposable income of the poorer members of society.

There is a correlation between income inequality and social cohesion. In more equal societies, people are much more likely to trust each other, engage in greater community activities, and have lower crime rates. There is also a correlation between socioeconomic status and health. It is not only the poor who tend to be sick when everyone else is healthy, but there is a continual gradient, from the top to the bottom of the socio-economic ladder, relating status to health. This is referred to as the "SES (socio-economic status) Gradient."[16] The SES Gradient is a composite measure of an individual's economic and sociological standing. It is a complex assessment measured in a variety of ways that account for a person's work experience and economic and social position in relation to others, based on income, education, and occupation. Socioeconomic status has been a powerful determinant of health.

Some of the metrics of socioeconomic status include: (1) highest level of education attained; (2) education of parents; (3) current occupation; (4) net income; (5) household income; (6) wealth (assets, capital). People are usually separated into groups based on these metrics, from least advantaged to most advantaged, or low, medium, or high SES. There are many complex factors in the relationship between socioeconomic status and health. People with relatively few resources may not have very good access to healthcare services, or even transportation to get medical care. They may not have the time to focus on their health, or have sufficient education to realize the impact that certain elements have on their health. Priorities can also vary; one person might be trying to maintain good health, while another person is a single mother trying to maintain a family with a minimum wage job. The stress related to a person's socioeconomic status alone may impact his or her health. Regardless of the mechanism, there is a strong association between SES and health. As a general rule, wealthy people tend to be in better health than people of poorer status.

There appears to be a significant impact of socioeconomic status on a multitude of diseases, including: (1) Cardiovascular disease; (2) respiratory disease; (3) mental health-related disorders. Lower socioeconomic status has been linked to chronic stress, heart disease, ulcers, type 2 diabetes, rheumatoid arthritis, certain types of cancer, and premature aging. Economic inequality is bad for everyone's health.

Economic disparity reduces distributive efficiency within a society. Inequality reduces the sum total of personal utility because of the decreasing marginal utility of wealth. For example, a house may provide less utility to a single billionaire as a summer home than it would to a homeless family of five. The marginal utility of wealth is lowest among the richest. An additional dollar spent by a poor person will go to things providing a great deal of utility to that person, such as basic necessities like food, water, and healthcare. An additional dollar spent by a much richer person will most likely go to things providing relatively less utility to that person, such as luxury items. From this standpoint, for any given amount of wealth in society, a society with more equality will have higher aggregate utility. In societies where inequality is lower, population wide satisfaction and happiness tend to be higher.

There are various schools of thought regarding economic inequality. Marxism favors an eventual communist society where distribution is based on an individual's needs rather than his ability to produce, social class, inheritance, or other factors. In such a system inequality would be low or non-existent assuming everyone had the same "needs." Classical liberals and libertarians generally do not take a stance on wealth inequality, but believe in equality under the law regardless of whether it leads to unequal wealth distribution. In most western democracies, the desire to eliminate or reduce economic inequality is generally associated with the political left. The main practical argument in favor of reduction is the idea that economic inequality reduces social cohesion and increases social unrest, thereby weakening the society.

The main disagreement between the western democratic left and right, is basically a disagreement on the importance of each effect, and where the proper balance point should be. Both sides generally agree that the causes of economic inequality based on non-economic differences (race, gender, etc.) should be minimized. There is strong disagreement on how this minimization should be achieved. The acceptance of economic inequality is generally associated with the political right.

One argument in favor of the acceptance of economic inequality is that, as long as the cause is mainly due to differences in behavior, the inequality provides incentives that push the society towards economically healthy and efficient behavior, and is therefore beneficial. In addition, capitalists see orderly competition and individual initiative as crucial to economic prosperity and accordingly believe that economic freedom is more important than economic equality.

Another argument is that more inequality does not necessarily mean more poverty, and that although poverty is bad, inequality is not bad in itself. A policy can be considered good if it makes some wealthy people wealthier without making anyone poorer, although it increases the total amount of inequality.

A third argument is that capitalism, especially free market capitalism, results in voluntary transactions among parties. Since the transactions are voluntary, each party at least believes that they are better off after the transaction. According to the subjective theory of value, both parties will indeed be better off after the transaction (assuming there is no fraud or extortion involved).

Economic inequality has existed in a wide range of societies and historical periods; its nature, cause and importance are open to broad debate. A country's economic structure or system (such as capitalism, socialism, and everything in between), ongoing or past wars, and individuals' different abilities to create wealth are all involved in the creation of economic inequality. Economic inequality among different individuals or social groups is best measured within a single country. This is due to the fact that country-specific factors tend to obscure inter-country comparisons of individuals' incomes. A single nation will have more or less inequality depending on the social and economic structure of that country.

POWER IMBALANCES

Power is a person's ability to exert influence and control. Power dynamics describes how power affects a relationship between two or more people. There are seven main types of power:

Coercive power: The ability to offer punishments to deter certain actions. For example, a police officer can arrest a person thought to be committing a crime.

Reward power: The ability to give out rewards for desired behavior. For example, a parent may reward their child with a cookie in exchange for doing chores.

Formal power: Also called legitimate or titular power. This power comes from having an official position. For example, CEOs of companies can fire workers below them.

Connection power: The ability to offer access to certain people or resources. For example, an agent can introduce an actor to a film producer.

Referent power: Influence that comes from being liked by others. For example, a popular, charismatic student may create a new fashion trend at school.

Informational power: Influence that comes from knowledge and information. For example, a spy may know the location of an enemy base.

Expert power: Influence that comes from having exceptional skills. For example, a talented doctor may have a lot of power where medical treatment is needed.

These types of power may overlap in some situations. It is common for an individual to have multiple types of power. Power dynamics are present in nearly every human social interaction—between workers and managers, parents and children, romantic partners, and friends. Power affects all aspects of social life, from the workplace to the home. Power is not inherently negative. For example, the ability of a parent to influence his toddler's actions can help keep him out of harm's way. But if a person abuses his power, it has the capacity to do great harm. In most conflict situations, one party may have more power than the other party. When the power differential is substantial, this usually has a significant effect on both the substance and process of the dispute. If one side is far more powerful than the other one, they are likely to simply impose their solution on the other side, who will be forced to accept it, because they have no other choice.

Alternatively, the high power parties may simply refuse to enter into a negotiation, because they have no need to. They can get what they want without compromising, or in any way giving in to the other side. They pursue their alternative to negotiation, which usually involves persuasion and/or force.

Another possibility is that the low-power parties will refuse to negotiate, because they fear they will be co-opted or otherwise forced to make compromises they do not want to make. Low power parties often engage in advocacy and violent or nonviolent direct action in an effort to build their power before they are willing to enter into a negotiation process.

Power relationships do not only, however, derive from our formal powers. Members of particular groups, which have consistently experienced disempowerment within the society in which they are based, may feel distrustful and disempowered in all relationships with people outside those groups, regardless of the "official" power balance; conversely, individual members of such groups may have developed considerable personal strength and confidence through challenging such disempowerment. Individuals also vary considerably in their personal confidence and sense of power; an aggressive, or even particularly self-confident and charismatic, individual may wield great power over a less assertive individual in an apparently more powerful position.

Many of us will try to avoid conflict situations or try to placate the people concerned, but this does not always work. Strategies for dealing with this type of situation can be useful. All of us have experienced difficult situations at some times in our lives. In any difficult situation, there is often a power imbalance. In any relationship, there is power involved. By this we mean who holds the power in a relationship and in communication. If two people are involved in a conversation and they both hold equal power, then there is no imbalance, but this is rare. Power may be influenced by a number of factors:

Gender: can influence the power in a relationship. A male arguing with a female may have more power in some situations. In other situations, the female may have more power.

Intelligence: in some situations, one person in an argument may have a higher level of intelligence than the other person, so may use that intelligence to intimidate the other person.

Size: a large man towering above a shorter man can be intimidating for the shorter man and thereby empower the larger man.

Age: being older can give power. An older man talking about his experiences to a younger person and sharing his knowledge can give greater power to the older person. But in other situations, a younger person may have more power. For example, a younger person coming into an industry may have more up to date knowledge and more useful skills than an older person, so there can be a power imbalance.

Experience: our experience of the world, in a job, or in a particular area of life can give us power over another.

Qualifications: a person's qualifications can sometimes give him more power.

Knowledge: of a particular topic can create power, as one person may know more than another.

Although gross power imbalances are a problem for conflict resolution, so too is equality of power. It is has been argued that wars or other deep-rooted international or ethnic conflicts cannot be resolved until they become "ripe." A variety of factors contribute to "ripeness," but one of the most commonly agreed-upon factors is that a conflict has reached a hurting stalemate when it becomes clear to both sides that neither side can ever win, and the costs of continuing the struggle are far higher than the costs of ending it. While it takes equality of power to reach this point, the losses entailed in so doing are extremely severe. Thus, both power equality and power inequality pose challenges and problems for dispute resolution.

Power struggles frequently make their way into our personal interactions and cause conflict. Trying to one-up someone or put them down is never constructive, just as allowing someone to devalue you or overpower you is never constructive. These destructive behaviors can lead to downward spirals both in our relationships and our ability to resolve conflicts. Instead of engaging in a power struggle, try to balance power relationships, so that each person comes out with his or her values and self-respect intact.

We all operate, for much of the time, within relationships in which the power balance is uneven. Such power imbalances can affect communication in a variety of ways. If we feel ourselves to have relatively less power, we may be fearful of saying what we really think, of asking for explanations, or of asking for what we need. We may be inclined to be uncritical of what we are told, or, conversely, angry and distrustful, depending on the quality of the relationship. If we have the greater power within a relationship, we may be more likely to set the agenda, make assumptions, and be unaware of other people's opinions or feelings. Conversely, we may worry that what we are hearing is what the other person thinks we want to hear.

Power imbalances can interfere significantly with communication, by setting the terms of debate and closing down some avenues of discussion. They also can arouse strong emotions, and these in themselves can interfere with open and accurate communication. Power imbalances can also be conveyed through communication, through the words we use, our tone of voice, and very strongly through body language.

Conversation is the key in any sort of power balancing situation. Be clear about what you want and what the other person wants. Stick to facts and avoid insinuating or stating that the other person is wrong or that they are causing a problem. Always focus on the matter, desired behavior, or outcome, and not on personal traits. Stated another way, focus on the conflict that needs to be resolved, not on the parties.

Try to talk face to face and not through text messages, emails, or phone conversations. Facial and body language are an important source of clarification and humanizes the interaction, while technology tends to distance us. It is far easier to forget how we can harm others with a barb or insult through the interface of the computer, whereas seeing someone's reaction in front of us clarifies this instantly.

Avoid getting defensive or speaking in negative tones. As soon as you sound whining, victimized, or angry, the emotions start to get the better of the conversation.

Be sure to listen carefully and to get clarification when necessary. Do not be afraid to ask questions. They are a great way to get more insight into the other person and their thoughts. You can never learn anything while you are talking. You can only learn when you listen.

Bear in mind that both of you might have a valid perspective of a conflict regardless of the power imbalance. This can be confronting for both of you, but it is also empowering, as potentially you have a range of solutions available provided you can accept that both sides have valid perspectives. It would be unusual if there were only one right way to achieve most things.

Define the conflict as a mutual matter, a problem you must solve together. Focus on shared interests. From the outset, the person holding the position of more power may be inclined to state the problem as being one caused by the person with less power. This needs to be challenged immediately by defining the problem as a mutual issue.

If you are the person holding the high power position, you can limit your own power rather than using it to gain an upper hand. Refrain from continued destructive patterns, either by speech or action. Be aware of your own behavior and regulate yourself. Look for opportunities to find options that will benefit both sides.

If you find yourself in the low power position, emphasize the interdependence that you and the other person have between each other. High power individuals will likely avoid this and minimize any recognition of interdependence. Point out emotional, behavioral, economic, or other dependence on each other. This is especially important in close or intimate relationships. Focus should not be put on the amount of power or influence that each person has over the other, but on achieving the balance between the parties and drawing each other into mutual understanding.

Significant change in power relations rarely comes from radical or aggressive confrontation. Careful and thoughtful understanding and planning will likely lead to small but important changes. Work toward an issue in common, even if it is on a very basic issue in the conflict. The more things you can find in common the more likely you are to reach a resolution of the conflict.

Stay actively engaged. Remember that no power position is a permanent condition. Be sure to speak your mind but also stick to providing the "big picture" and balanced ideas. Stay connected to your values and the outcome that you perceive as worthy throughout times of intensity or difficulty in your dialog with the other person.

A conflict should only be avoided or ignored where it is trivial or unimportant. Otherwise, it needs to be dealt with, whatever your power relationship. An ignored minor conflict can quickly escalate into a major problem. Seek third party intervention when you have reached an impasse. Seeking outside help to resolve a conflict is not a sign of weakness. Any fool can make war. It requires great strength to make peace. A power imbalance becomes a problem when it affects self-determination. There are many forms of imbalance. An example of informational imbalance would be when a spouse does not disclose a hidden asset in divorce mediation. Self-determination is in jeopardy because your choice of outcomes is not real. The imbalance could be emotional where one party is overpowering or taking advantage of a meeker or less confident participant. Or a party might have better self-control in difficult situations. The imbalance could be intellectual, verbal, or an imbalance of experience. The imbalance could be simply between the numbers of parties at the table. For example, it is not unusual for a Special Education mediation case to have many people on the side representing the school system, and only one or two on the parent's side of the table.

Power imbalance can also manifest itself via information. One party may have more information or experience than the other. For example, one person in a marriage manages all of the finances for the home. If they are in divorce mediation, then an ability to make financial decisions may be out of balance. A way to balance self-determining power could be appealing to the use of outside resources.

The important question is not how much power does a party have, but rather does the party have enough power for self-determination. There may be circumstances where power imbalance is inevitable, even preferable. Even so, empowering a self-determination process could be of immense value in many relationships, organizations, and teams.

Power dynamics can and often do affect interpersonal relationships. In relationships that are strong and healthy, power is generally equal or close to equal. Partners may not have equivalent kinds of power: one partner may have more financial resources while the other has more social connections. However, influence is often reciprocal. Healthy partners often work together respectfully and each have a hand in decision-making.

A balanced relationship, one in which power is, for the most part, held equally, might be represented by some of the following elements: (1) both partners know their value; (2) partners listen to each other and make changes based on the feelings and interests of the other; (3) partners respect each other, even in times of disagreement; partners talk to each other, especially when issues develop or miscommunications occur.

Problems can develop when there is a power imbalance in the relationship. For example, if a person makes more money than his partner, she may begin to feel entitled to make all decisions about how the money is spent, rather than seeking her partner's opinion. In cases of abuse, an individual may try to limit his partner's power through isolation and threats so that he can have complete control. Meanwhile, the partner without power may grow resentful or feel taken for granted. She may withdraw from the relationship to protect her own self-esteem. For example, someone who considers herself the less attractive partner in a relationship may feel insecure and avoid intimacy.

Common power-related issues that come up in a professional environment include:

Salary and wage negotiation: Bargaining power comes into play when discussing salary at time of hire or during a review. In some cases, the employee has more bargaining power and may be able to negotiate a higher salary. This could happen if the employee has a unique skillset, has increased company revenue, or is needed by the company for a specific reason. In other cases, the company may have more bargaining power. This could happen in fields where there is a lot of competition for jobs.

Promotion and job assignments: An employee who has skills that are in demand in the marketplace can demand promotions or favorable job assignments. The bargaining power of the parties are always dependent on the supply and demand of the skillset of the employee.

Bullying or harassment: In workplace settings, bullying often goes unpunished because of imbalanced power dynamics. If a person with more power bullies another person in the company, the person being bullied may avoid telling anyone due to fear of retaliation. It is not always easy to find a new position, and a person who needs steady income may decide putting up with bullying is preferable to unemployment. People can also misuse power in the workplace by forcing others to complete menial tasks unrelated to their job (such as getting coffee) or to put up with harassment.

PART TWO

TYPES OF CONFLICTS

*"People fail to get along because they fear each other;
they fear each other because they don't know each
other; they don't know each other because they
have not communicated with each other."*

—MARTIN LUTHER KING, JR.

Chapter 6

FAMILY, NEIGHBOR, AND SCHOOL CONFLICTS

C onflicts in families, with neighbors, and in schools occur frequently. Unresolved intrapersonal conflicts with family members, neighbors, and schools can give rise to anxiety, depression, and a multitude of self-defeating behaviors. School conflicts can have a devastating effect on a child's future welfare. If you avoid dealing with these conflicts constructively, serious problems can occur. Do not put your effort and energy into avoiding what you do not want. Put your energy into what you do want, an effective resolution.

FAMILY CONFLICTS

A family is made up of many unique individuals, each with a range of thoughts, viewpoints, and opinions on almost every subject and situation. When you add extended family members with their countless beliefs and personal opinions, conflicts are inevitable. Conflict is simply the natural and healthy progression of any relationship. In an integrated family, each person's goals matter to each other. How you deal with these conflicts determines whether you will maintain positive and constructive relationships.

There are many different types of family conflicts and many different causes for these conflicts, including: learning to live as a new couple; money issues; birth of a baby; birth of other children; child going to school; child becoming a young person; young person becoming an adult; separation or divorce; child rearing; child custody; moving to a new house or country; traveling long distances to work; commuting interstate for work; change in financial circumstances; staying too long; calling on the phone too often or too little; meddling in your business; telling you how to live your life.

The opinions, values, and needs of parents can change and find they are no longer compatible. It is normal to disagree with each other from time to time. Occasional conflict is part of family life, however, ongoing conflict can be stressful and damaging to relationships. Some people find it difficult to manage their feelings and become intentionally hurtful, aggressive, or even violent. Communicating in a positive way can help reduce conflict, and when conflicts do arise, they can be resolved in a more peaceful way.

Your first impulse may be, "you are right," and you will try to win the argument at any cost. Finding a peaceful resolution can be difficult, if not impossible, when both parties think they are right. A better approach is listening to each other, considering it as a joint problem, and finding a solution together.

As in most successful negotiations, separate the problem from the person. Cool off first if you feel too angry to talk calmly. The goal is to resolve the conflict, not to win the argument. Do not expect the other party to always agree with your point of view. Respect the other person's point of view by paying attention and listening. Create options. Use objective criteria. Work to find common ground. When the parties to the conflict are invested in the resolution, it is more likely to be successful. Let the person tell the story from his or her perspective. Stay calm. Do not get emotional. Do not interrupt the other person while he or she is speaking. Listen to what they are saying to understand what they mean. Check that you understand them by asking questions. Communicate your side of the story clearly and honestly. Resist the urge to bring up other unresolved but unrelated issues. Avoid being judgmental.

Come up with as many possible solutions as you can. Try to find solutions that will satisfy the needs of both parties. Make sure everyone clearly understands the chosen resolution. Be hard on the problem, not the people. Using blame, shame, or guilt to get someone to do something will not help your relationship. Instead, address the problem rather than laying blame on another. When two people who are stakeholders in a relationship are at odds, they sometimes may say and do irrational things, project, deny, and shift blame. All this drama has nothing to do with solving your problem. The goal is to work with your spouse, rather than being adversarial. Remember that your problem is mutual. You need your spouse in order to solve this problem and reach a resolution. It takes two to have an argument. Reframe your problem as a mutual problem and use "we" language. "We need to decide what to do with the credit card debt" gets a different reception then "You need to deal with your credit card debt." Think about the situation from your spouse's point of view, even if you think he is wrong. Acknowledge your spouse's feelings without being patronizing. When your spouse knows he is safe from automatically being blamed for a situation, he will be able to think strategically rather than defensively. You will be able to work cooperatively and collaboratively. Part Three provides other methods for resolving conflicts, but the five steps listed below are very effective in resolving family disputes.

Five Steps for Resolving Family Conflicts

Step 1: Learn to Listen

You can only learn when listening, not when talking. When a person speaks to you, you know only the words spoken and the person's impact on you. You do not know the person's intentions. Do not make assumptions about intentions.

A. Blend visibly and audibly.

B. Give feedback to show you are listening.

C. Clarify by asking open-ended questions (what, who, where, when, how).

    1. Classification questions can help gather more accurate information, shows that you care about what is said, and better understand hidden agendas.

D. Summarize what you heard.

    1. When you summarize, if you missed something, they will tell you.

    2. You show that you are making a serious effort to understand.

E. Confirm that you understand. Good listening requires an open and honest curiosity about the other person. Listening is only effective if it is authentic, i.e., because you care. Three skills that good listeners employ: (1) Inquiry; (2) Paraphrasing; (3) Acknowledgement.

Step 2: Keep an Open Mind

Our assumptions about their intentions may be wrong. We often assume the worst in other people (Demonizing affect). We treat ourselves more charitably (Halo affect). Our conclusions are often based on the impact of their behavior on you. Assumptions about bad intentions affects behavior and how we behave can affect how we are treated and can then be self-fulfilling. Good intentions do not sanitize bad impact. Disentangle impact and intent. Listen for feelings and reflect on your intentions. What did the other person actually say or do? What was the impact on you? Based on this impact, what assumption are you making about what the other person intended?

Step 3: Use empathy

Try to see things through the other person's eyes. Look at things in a neutral, nonjudgmental way. Acknowledge emotional issues. The goal is to find a solution to the problem not to blame. Focusing on blame inhibits our ability to learn what is causing the problem and to find anything meaningful to correct it. Blame is about judging; contribution is about understanding. The problem is created in the past; the solution is found in the future.

Step 4: Speak to be Understood
State your positive intent. Tell your truth. Express your feelings without judging, attributing, or blaming.

Step 5: Work Together
Rarely can you change someone else's mind or force someone to change his or her behavior. Seldom can you change someone's opinion because of facts and arguments. Keep the conversation constructive. Work for mutual understanding not necessarily mutual agreement. Learn their story. Express your views and feelings. Focus on the interests and needs of the parties. Brainstorm creative ways to satisfy the needs of both sides. Begin from the third story. The goal is to understand his perspective better, share yours, and talk about how to go forward together. Reframe toward a learning conversation and away from blame. The conversation is not likely to move in a positive direction until the other person feels heard and understood.

In every explicit message, there is an implicit message.

Explicit Statement	Implicit Message	Third Story
If you contest Dad's will, it's going to tear the family apart.	You're selfish, ungrateful, and don't care about the family. Care about the family.	I wanted to talk about Dad's will. You and I have different understandings of what Dad intended, and what's fair to each of us. I want to understand why you see things the way you do, and to share with you my perspective and feelings. I have strong feelings and fears about what a court fight would mean for the family.
I was upset by what you said in front of our supervisor.	At worst, you betrayed me—at best, you were stupid.	I wanted to talk to you about what happened in the meeting this morning. I was upset by something you said. I wanted to explain what was bothering me, and also hear your perspective on the situation.
Your son Nathan can be difficult in class—disruptive and argumentative. You've said in the past that things at home are fine, but something must be troubling him.	Your son is a troublemaker, probably because you're a bad parent who's created a lousy home environment. What are you hiding?	I wanted to share with you my concerns about Nathan's behavior in class, and hear more about what you think may be contributing to it. Maybe together we can determine what's motivating Nathan and how to handle it.

Problem solving consists of gathering information, testing your perceptions, creating options that meet both parties' primary concerns, or at least finding fair ways to resolve the differences. Ask their advice.

Ask what would persuade them. Tell them what would persuade you.

Dealing with children is a great source of conflict. There are methods that will help resolve many of these conflicts. Learn to acknowledge their feelings. This will also go a long way in preventing conflicts and problems.

When your child comes to you with a problem: (1) listen carefully; (2) acknowledge their problem; (3) give their problem a name; (4) let them find a solution to their problem. Children need to have their feelings accepted and respected. While feelings can be accepted, certain actions must be limited.

How can you get your child to cooperate? The methods that do not work include: (1) blaming and accusing; (2) name-calling; (3) threats; (4) commands; (5) lecturing and moralizing; (6) warnings; (7) martyrdom statements; (8) comparisons; (9) sarcasm; (10) prophecy.

The methods used to resolve conflicts in other situations can be used to resolve conflicts with your children. Step 1: Talk about your child's feelings and needs; Step 2: Talk about your feelings and needs; Step 3: Brainstorm together to find a mutually agreeable solution: Step 4: Write down all ideas without evaluating or judging; Step 5: Decide which solution works best for both of you.

When your child has done something you disapprove of, instead of punishing your child, try a problem-solving approach: (1) express your feelings strongly without attacking your child's character; (2) state your expectations; (3) show the child how to make amends; (4) give the child a choice; (5) take action; (6) create options that will satisfy your needs and your child's needs.

Encourage your child to be independent: (1) let them make choices; (2) show respect for their efforts; (3) let them answer their questions; (4) encourage them to use outside sources; (5) encourage their choices. Instead of evaluating what your child has done, describe what you see and how you feel, and use a word to describe your child's praiseworthy behavior.

Look for opportunities to show the child in a new light. Put children in situations where they can see themselves in a new light.

Let children overhear you say something positive about them. Model the behavior you would like to see.

Separation, Divorce, or Child Custody

Cases involving separation, divorce, or child custody require special attention. In these cases, there could be problems regarding domestic violence or child abuse that may impose a serious threat to one of the parties. The terms "domestic violence" or "domestic abuse" means a pattern of behavior characterized by the use of various tactics, both criminal and non-criminal, to control and coerce an intimate partner by fear and intimidation, which may or may not be apparent to outside observers. The threat of physical or sexual violence is the ultimate coercive tactic, although this threat may only be carried out infrequently. Besides acts and threats of physical and sexual violence, abusers use money, children, isolation, and emotional and psychological abuse to control their spouses or partners. Other tactics include: belittling their partners; threatening self-harm if the partner leaves; interfering with their partners' work or educational opportunities; stalking; and harming pets or property. Some abusers harshly enforce strict household rules, or closely monitor their partners, restricting their access to transportation or means of communication. Each abuser has a unique pattern of coercion, which is best known to the abused partner.

Some abused individuals will readily talk about the violence that they are experiencing or have experienced if they feel safe and supported. Others, when asked, may not identify their experiences as "domestic violence," or they may disclose this incrementally, as trust in the person asking the question develops.

Some abused individuals may not disclose abuse in their relationships out of shame, fear of retaliation, or fear of negative consequences resulting from such disclosures. Abused individuals may be reluctant to disclose abuse due to past negative responses to disclosures of abuse.

The ability and willingness to disclose abuse may be enhanced when abused individuals think that the inquiring professional will believe their allegations, that it is safe to share, and that sensitive information will be handled responsibly by the system. Inquiries about specific behavior (rather than inquiries about "domestic violence") may yield important information in cases where the abused individual has not identified the perpetrator's conduct as abusive. If abuse is disclosed or identified, it is common for abused individuals to minimize it, or to accept some responsibility for it. Minimizing and accepting responsibility is sometimes a coping mechanism, which makes the abuse less frightening to abused individuals by framing it as something within their control.

Where domestic violence exists, mediation is unlikely to be appropriate for resolving the dispute. This presumption can be overcome, but only if the abused party desires to participate in mediation and the circumstances of the individual case indicate that mediation will be a safe, effective tool for all concerned. The decision to order, initiate, or continue mediation despite a presumption against mediation should be made on a case-by-case basis. The most important factor to consider in deciding whether to proceed with mediation is whether the abused party wants to mediate. Mediation should not proceed if the abused party does not wish to participate. Other factors to consider are: (1) ability to negotiate for oneself; (2) physical safety for all concerned; (3) ability to reach a voluntary, uncoerced agreement; (4) ability of the mediator to manage a case involving domestic violence; and (5) likelihood that the abuser will use mediation to discover information that can later be used against the abused party, or to otherwise manipulate court processes.

Parties should be informed that continuing the mediation is a voluntary process and that they may withdraw for any reason. Skilled mediators are well aware of the potential for violence in domestic cases and will not mediate a case without going through a comprehensive process to determine the suitability of mediation to resolve the dispute. Mediators use a number of domestic violence screening tools. One such screening tool is set forth below developed by a court mediation program:

Screening Questionnaire

Section 1: General Questions

a) Is there anything you would like to ask me or tell me before we continue?

b) Please tell me about your situation.

c) Could you tell me about how the decision to divorce or separate was reached?

d) Do you want to mediate? If so, why? If not, why not?

Section 2: Control, Coercion, Intimidation, Fear

a) When you look back over time, how were decisions made in your marriage/relationship? Please provide examples. How did you feel about the way decisions were made? Possible follow-up questions as appropriate: How did you make major decisions, for instance, where your children went to school? In making major purchases?

b) What happens when you speak your mind and express your point of view to [insert name]? (Possible follow up questions as appropriate: What happens specifically? Can you give me some examples? What does it look like? And then what happens…, and then what happens…, and then what happens…., etc.)

c) Has [insert name] ever interfered with your relationships with family or friends, or with your children? (Follow up questions as appropriate: Can you tell me more about it? Can you give me some examples?)

d) Has [insert name] ever made it difficult for you to have money you need for things for yourself or the family?

(Follow up questions as appropriate: Tell me more about it. Can you give me some examples?)

e) When you and [insert name] disagree, fight and/or are angry with each other, what happens?

1. Would you feel more comfortable if your attorney was present with you during the mediation sessions?

Yes_____No_____

2. Would you feel more comfortable if you and [insert name] were in separate rooms during the mediation sessions?

Yes_____No_____

3. Would you feel more comfortable if you and [insert name] arrived and departed at separate times or weren't in the building at the same time?

Yes_____No_____

4. (If the mediator and parties are comfortable with available technology) Would you feel more comfortable if the mediation took place over the telephone, Internet, or by videoconference?

Yes_____No_____

Section 3: Violence/Fear of Violence

Caution: If there is a "yes" answer to questions 3a-3p, advise the party that mediation may NOT be appropriate. If the abused party still wants to mediate, continue through the screening process.

a) Have there ever been any physical confrontations between you and [insert name]?

Yes_____No_____

(Follow up questions as appropriate to determine whether mediation can safely occur: Can you tell me what happened? Have there been any other physical confrontations?)

b) Do you ever feel afraid of [insert name]? What are you afraid of? Tell me about the time you felt most afraid. Do you think that [insert name] has ever felt afraid of you? What do you think he/she may be afraid of?

Yes_____No_____

c) Do you ever feel afraid for yourself, your children, or others based on a look from [insert name] or actions of [insert name]? If so, tell me about it.

Yes_____No_____

d) Has [insert name] ever caused you to feel threatened or harassed by following you, interfering with your work or education, making repeated phone calls to you, using social media or sending you unwanted letters, emails, text messages, faxes, or gifts? Can you tell me more about it?

Yes_____No_____

e) Have either of you ever been arrested? If so, what happened?

Yes_____No_____

f) Have either of you been convicted of a crime? If so, what happened?

Yes_____No_____

g) Is there currently or has there ever been an order limiting contact between the two of you, for example, a Personal Protection Order or a No Contact Order? Can you tell me more about this?

Yes_____No_____

h) Has there ever been a violation of the order, whether or not the violation was ever reported? Can you tell me about it?

Yes_____No_____

i) Have you or [insert name] ever applied for an order to limit contact between the two of you (for example, a PPO that was denied?

Yes_____No_____

j) Are either of you currently restrained from contacting any other person by a PPO or other court order?

Yes_____No_____

Can you say more about that?

k) Has [insert name] ever pushed, shoved, hit, kicked, spit on, choked, strangled, restrained, or pulled your hair? If so, what happened?

Yes_____No_____

l) Has [insert name] ever damaged or destroyed your property or harmed or threatened to harm your pets? Your children's property or pets? If so, what happened?

Yes_____No_____

m) Are there any guns or other weapons in your home/either of your homes? If so, do you have any concerns about them?

Yes_____No_____

n) Does [insert name] carry a gun outside of the home? If so, does this cause you any concern?

Yes_____No_____

o) Has [insert name] ever used a weapon in a way that felt threatening to you, or threatened your children? Can you tell me more about it?

Yes_____No_____

p) Have you ever been afraid that [insert name] would kill or injure you or anyone else close to you? Has [insert name] ever threatened to hurt or kill him/herself? Can you tell me more about it?

Yes_____No_____

NOTE: If there is a "YES" answer to the following question, discontinue the screening process. If the parties are together in a mediation session, safely terminate the process and explore safety options.

q) Do you feel you are in danger right now?

Yes_____No_____

Section 4: Children (if applicable)

a) How are the children doing?

b) Do you have any concerns about the safety of the children? If so, please describe.

Yes_____No_____

c) Has [insert name] ever talked about taking the children away from you? Has [insert name] ever interfered with or prevented you from seeing them? Please describe.

Yes_____No_____

d) Is there an open abuse or neglect case involving your children? Tell me about it.

Yes_____No_____

Section 5: Attorney Awareness of Violence

(If attorney is not present) Have you ever told your attorney what you've told me? It is generally important for your attorney to know about things we've talked about. Is there a concern you have about telling your attorney?

Yes_____No_____

Section 6: Other Considerations Regarding Ability to Negotiate

Note: In addition to domestic violence, the following are other factors that may affect a parties' ability to mediate. This is not an exhaustive list of screening questions that impact a parties' ability to negotiate. The issues may or may not be present in cases involving domestic violence.

a) Do you believe alcohol or drug use have ever caused difficulties for either of you? (If so, how recent? What is the current status of treatment? If yes, how do you think this may impact mediation?

Yes_____No_____

b) Do you believe mental health issues or emotional problems have ever caused difficulties for either of you? (If yes, how recently? What is the current status of treatment? If yes, how do you think this may impact mediation?

Yes_____No_____

Section 7: Conclusion

Is there anything I haven't asked you about that you'd like to tell me?
      Now that we have had a chance to discuss your situation and mediation, how do you feel about going forward with mediation? Do you feel any pressure to mediate?

The mediator should always be mindful of any factor that would make mediation physically or emotionally unsafe for any participant, or that would impede a voluntary and safe resolution of the issues. Some examples of those impediments would include: domestic abuse, neglect or abuse of a child, mental illness or impairment, inability to understand or communicate in the language in which the mediation is conducted.

NEIGHBOR CONFLICTS

There are a number of conflicts that can occur between neighbors. According to a recent study, the top five neighbor conflicts involve: (1) Noise (48% of all conflicts). It may be from late-night parties, loud music, noise sensitivity, or different sleep schedules that result in one neighbor waking up the other; (2) Pets and animals (29%). The problem usually stems from the owner's failure to properly handle or train the animal; (3) Children's behavior (21%). Much like pets, children running onto your property, being loud, or defacing your property can often be the result of their parents—i.e., your adult neighbors—not properly monitoring their children; (4) A visual nuisance, the property's appearance, trash, etc. (18%). Many eyesores, such as unkempt lawns, offensive signs, or overflowing trash cans can lead to ill will between neighbors; (5) Property boundaries (17%).

Resolving these types of conflict can sometimes be difficult and may lead to legal actions and other forms of retaliation. Great care and caution must be used if the conflict is to be resolved successfully. Unless you are planning to move or your neighbor is planning to move, you will be living with that neighbor. There are nonprofit organizations in many communities dedicated to helping resolve neighbor conflicts. If the conflict is particularly difficult, that may be your first resort for dealing with the particular conflict. Look at the conflict as a problem that needs to be solved, not an opportunity to attack your neighbor.

Do not make it personal. Identify the problem that needs to be solved. Explore options that would solve the problem. Select a mutually agreeable solution.

SCHOOL CONFLICTS

There are a number of different conflicts that can occur at school: (1) teacher to teacher; (2) teacher to administrator; (3) teacher to student; (4) student to student; (5) parent to teacher; (6) parent to administrator; (7) parent to student.

There are many different reasons for these conflicts. People come from different backgrounds and may have different values. Conflicts may be caused by personality clashes, poor communication, personal problems, religious differences, cultural differences, among other reasons. To resolve these conflicts, it is essential that you understand the root cause or causes of the conflict. Often, the underlying cause is not apparent.

The same strategies that are used to resolve conflicts in other settings should be employed in the school setting. However, more patience and discretion may be needed.

The administrators need to encourage respect for different viewpoints. Teachers are part of a team. The administrators should focus on team building and creating an atmosphere where effective learning can take place. When conflict does occur, which is inevitable, use it as a learning opportunity.

Students may have conflicts over grades, power struggles, discipline, personality clashes, culture, religion, skin color, economic differences, and many other issues that may not be school related but are brought into the classroom from the outside.

Some useful strategies in resolving these types of conflicts may include parent-student-teacher conferences to discuss any problems or conflicts, building relationships with parents that instill trust with one another, having open communication, working with students to build classroom rules, and having an open door policy. Treat the conflict as a learning experience. Finding ways of handling different personalities is an important life lesson. Train students to engage in peer mediation to encourage students to solve their problems themselves. Methods for resolving these disputes can be found in Part Three.

Chapter 7

CULTURAL AND RELIGIOUS CONFLICTS

~~~~~~~~~~~~

C ulture consists of the behaviors, rules, values, beliefs, symbols, systems of language and communication, and practices people share, which are passed along by communication and imitation from one generation to the next. Culture also includes the collective practices people participate in, such as religious ceremonies. Religion is a shared collection of transcendental beliefs that are passed on from believers to converts. Adherents hold these beliefs to be sacred and based on (1) formally documented doctrine (*organized religion*), or (2) established cultural practices (*folk religion*). Culture and religion form a central part of many individuals' identity. Culture and religion are formed by our environment (nurture). We generally adopt the culture and religion of the place and time where and by whom we were raised. Richard Dawkins, a British evolutionary biologist, first used the term *meme* in his book, *The Selfish Gene*.[17] He defined meme as a unit of cultural imitation parallel to biological genes and considered them, in a manner similar to "selfish" genes, as being in control of their own reproduction and thus serving their own ends. Understood in those terms, memes carry information, are replicated, and are transmitted from one person to another. Memes have the ability to evolve, mutating at random and undergoing natural selection, with or without impacts on human fitness (reproduction and survival).

Within a culture, memes take a variety of forms, such as an idea, a skill, a behavior, a belief, a phrase, or a particular fashion. The replication and transmission of a meme occurs when one person copies a unit of cultural information comprising a meme from another person. The process of transmission is carried out primarily by means of verbal, visual, or electronic communication ranging from books and conversation to television, email, or the Internet. Those memes most successfully copied and transmitted become the most prevalent within a culture. Memes may be considered inherently harmful, since, according to some scholars, memes are parasites or viruses of the mind; once assimilated into the human mind, their chief purpose becomes their own replication, with humans having little or no control over them. Some memes, which are benign or beneficial, can become dangerous after they are seeded in the human mind. They lend themselves to being misused or abused. Memes associated with religious or political ideas may benefit the people who carry them; however, those same memes, when imposed on people whose religious or political memes are different, may cause harm, such as the brutal conflicts between Sunni and Shia Muslims. Memes associated with religious or political ideas may be abused, as in the case of religious cults or extremist groups.

Since cultural and religious conflicts can be very difficult to resolve where people have different core values and beliefs, exercise care when dealing with these issues.

CULTURAL CONFLICTS

Cultural conflicts arise because of the differences in values and norms of people from different cultures and are characterized by different behaviors, memes, and communication styles. A person acts according to the values and norms of his or her culture. One holding a different worldview might interpret his or her behavior from an opposite standpoint. This situation creates misunderstandings that can lead to conflicts. People of mainstream America, the Anglo culture, perceive their behavior and beliefs as an ultimate norm, forgetting that Anglo culture is just one of the multiple cultures existing in the United States. As a result, when negotiating across cultures, we bring different perspectives to the bargaining table, which in turn may result in potential misunderstandings and a lower likelihood of exploring and discovering integrative, or value-creating, solutions.

Cultural misunderstandings occur for two main reasons: First, we tend to rely on stereotypes, which are often pejorative and can lead to distorted expectations about your counterpart's behavior and costly misinterpretations. Instead of relying on stereotypes, focus on prototypes, i.e., cultural averages on dimensions of behavior or values. For example, Japanese negotiators tend to have more silent periods during their talks than, say, Brazilians. There can be a great deal of variability within each culture, meaning that some Brazilians speak less than some Japanese do. It would be a mistake to expect a Japanese negotiator you have never met to be reserved; however if the negotiator is especially quiet, you might better understand the behavior in light of the prototype. Awareness of your own cultural prototypes can help you anticipate how your counterpart might interpret your bargaining behavior.

Second, we tend to interpret others' behaviors, values, and beliefs through the lens of our own culture. To prevent incorrect assumptions, we need to learn about the other party's culture. This means not only researching the customs and behaviors of different cultures, but also understanding why people follow these customs and exhibit these behaviors. Before any negotiation, take time to study the person on the other side of the bargaining table, including the various cultures to which he or she belongs, whether the culture of a country, the culture of a profession, or the particular company's corporate culture.

In one case, a group of women wrote an excellent and detailed proposal, but did badly during the interview part of the evaluation. It happened because those women were from a culture where establishing personal relationships preceded business relationships. These women felt uncomfortable when government officials did not allow time for casual conversation and immediately moved toward firing questions at them.

The following case exemplifies how one cultural group unintentionally hurt the feelings of the other. The city of Kenai, Alaska was planning a celebration commemorating when the first Russian fur traders came to the region. A Native tribe, which lived in Alaska for a thousand years, was offended by the implication that before the Russians came to the region, no civilization existed there. By recognizing the Native Alaskan culture, a serious conflict was avoided, and the Kenai Bicentennial Visitors and Cultural Center was completed. Accommodating the different cultural interests helped the region to recognize its historical past.

Identifying cultural conflicts

Cultural conflict has three dimensions. To the two dimensions that every conflict has (content and relational), cultural conflict adds the third one, "a clash of cultural values." This third dimension constitutes the foundation of the conflict, since it determines personal identity.

The following signs can identify cultural conflict: (1) it usually has complicated dynamics. Cultural differences mentioned above tend to create complex combinations of expectations about one's own and others' behavior; (2) if addressing content and relational issues does not resolve the conflict, it can be rooted in cultural differences; (3) conflict reoccurs or arises strong emotions even though the issue of disagreement is insignificant.

Resolving cultural conflicts

The resolution of cross-cultural conflict begins with determining whether cultural issues are involved. There are three ways of dealing with cross-cultural conflict resolution:

1. Probing for the cultural dimension: The resolution process should start with the parties' acknowledgment that their conflict has a cultural dimension. Next, there should be willingness on all sides to deal with all conflict dimensions, including the cultural one. Third, systematic phased work on the conflict is needed. There are four phases in dealing with cultural conflicts: (1) parties describe the offensive behavior in each other; (2) get an understanding of the other party's cultural perceptions; (3) learn how the problem would be handled in the other's culture; (4) develop conflict solutions. Resolution of the conflict is particularly complicated if the conflict arose, not just out of misunderstanding of the other's behavior, but also because of incompatible values.

2. Learning about other cultures: People can prevent cross-cultural conflicts by learning about cultures of those whom that they come in contact with. This knowledge can be obtained through training programs, general reading, talking to people from different cultures, and past experiences. Important aspects of cultural education are understanding your own culture and developing cultural awareness by understanding the values and beliefs of other cultures. Avoid cultural stereotypes.

3. Altering organizational practices and procedures: Often the organizational structure reflects the norms of just one culture. In such cases, structural change is necessary to make the system more sensitive to cultural norms of other people. Conflict, depending on the outcome, can be a positive or negative experience. With changing demographics, cultural differences can become an acute issue. Many groups resist assimilation by preserving their cultural distinctiveness. As a result, cultural conflict education is an essential tool for maintaining healthy relations in organizations and society in general.

Guidelines for Multicultural Collaboration

Learn from generalizations about other cultures, but do not use those generalizations to stereotype or oversimplify your ideas about another person. The best use of a generalization is to add it to your storehouse of knowledge so that you better understand and appreciate other interesting, multi-faceted human beings.

Do not assume that there is one right way (yours!) to communicate. Question your assumptions about the "right way" to communicate. Think about your body language; postures that indicate receptivity in one culture might indicate aggressiveness in another.

Do not assume that breakdowns in communication occur because other people are on the wrong track. Search for ways to make the communication work, rather than searching for who to blame for the breakdown.

Listen actively and empathetically. Try to put yourself in the other person's shoes, especially when that person's perceptions or ideas are very different from your own. You might need to operate at the edge of your own comfort zone.

Respect others' choices about whether to engage in communication with you. Honor their opinions about what is going on.

Stop, suspend judgment, and try to look at the situation as an outsider.

Be prepared for a discussion of the past. Use this as an opportunity to develop an understanding from "the other's" point of view, rather than getting defensive or impatient. Acknowledge historical events that have taken place. Be open to learning more about them. Honest acknowledgment of the mistreatment and oppression that have taken place on the basis of cultural differences is vital for effective communication.

Awareness of current power imbalances and an openness to hearing each other's perceptions of those imbalances is necessary for understanding each other and working together.

Cultural norms may not apply to the behavior of any particular individual. We are all shaped by many factors—genes, cultural background, family, education, and personalities. Check your interpretations if you are uncertain what is meant.

RELIGIOUS CONFLICTS

Religion is at the core of much of the strife around the world. When eternal salvation is at stake, compromise can be difficult or even sinful. Religion is also important because, as a central part of many individuals' identity, any threat to one's beliefs is a threat to one's very being.

Keep in mind that more people than ever before are identifying as atheist, agnostic, or otherwise nonreligious. Religiously unaffiliated people—sometimes called the "nones"—account for 16% of the world's population, and they make up the largest "religious group" in seven countries and territories. They are the *second-largest* group in roughly half (48%) of the world's nations. While either Christians or Muslims make up the largest religious group in nine out of ten nations around the globe, "nones" rank second in size in most of the Americas and Europe, as well as in many countries in sub-Saharan Africa.

The Richard Dawkins Foundation promotes scientific literacy and a secular worldview by: (1) teaching the value of science, and (2) advancing secularism.[18] The Foundation sees religious extremism as a threat to the advancement of science, personal freedoms, and human dignity. Making secular views welcome in politics and policy-making will advance human safety, security, health, achievement, prosperity, and most of all, science. Religion should not influence scientific inquiry or public policy.

The Center for Inquiry (CFI) strives to foster a society free of the dogmatic influence of religion and pseudoscience.[19] CFI's vision is a world in which evidence, science, and compassion—rather than superstition, pseudoscience, or prejudice guide public policy. Old superstitions, prejudices, and magical thinking need to be discarded and replaced with facts, evidence, and critical thinking.

The relationship between religion and conflict is complex. All religions have their accepted dogma, or articles of belief, that followers must accept without question. This can lead to inflexibility and intolerance in the face of other beliefs. After all, if it is the word of

God, how can one compromise it? At the same time, scripture and dogma are often vague and open to interpretation. Conflict can arise over whose interpretation is the correct one. This conflict cannot be solved because there is no decision maker. The winner generally is the interpretation that attracts the most followers, and those followers must also be motivated to action. While the majority of any faith generally hold moderate views and are amenable to compromise, the extremists are motivated to bring their interpretation of God's will to fruition.

Religious extremists can contribute to conflict escalation. They see radical measures as necessary to fulfilling God's will. If the world is a struggle between good and evil, it is hard to justify compromising with the devil. Any sign of moderation can be seen as abandoning God's will. In circumstances where moderate ways are not perceived to have produced results, whether social, political, or economic, the populace may turn to extreme interpretations for solutions. Without legitimate mechanisms for religious groups to express their views, they may be more likely to resort to violence. Those who call for violence see themselves as divinely directed.

Many religions also have significant strains of evangelism, which can create conflict. Believers are called upon to spread the word of God and increase the numbers of the flock. For example, the effort to impose Christianity on subject peoples was an important part of the conflict surrounding European colonization. Similarly, a group may seek to deny other religions the opportunity to practice their faith. This derives from a lack of respect for other faiths.

Religious fundamentalists are primarily driven by displeasure with modernity. Motivated by the marginalization of religion in modern society, they act to restore faith to a central place. There is a need for purification of the religion in the eyes of fundamentalists. The spread of Western materialism is often blamed for increases in gambling, alcoholism, and loose morals in general. Al-Qaeda, for example, claims it is motivated by this neo-imperialism as well as the presence of foreign military forces in the Muslim holy lands. The

liberal underpinning of Western culture is also threatening to tradition in prioritizing the individual over the group, and by questioning
the appropriate role for women in society. The growth of the New
Christian Right in the United States indicates that Westerners also
feel that modern society is missing something. Conflict over abortion
and the teaching of evolution in schools are examples of issues that
some feel religious tradition has been abandoned.

Religious nationalists can produce extremist sentiments because
they tend to view their religious traditions as so closely tied to their
nation or their land that any threat to one of these is a threat to one's
existence. Therefore, religious nationalists respond to threats to their
religion by seeking a political entity in which their faith is privileged
at the expense of others. It is likely that religious symbols will come
to be used to forward ethnic or nationalist causes. This has been the
case for Catholics in Northern Ireland, the Serbian Orthodox church
in Milosevic's Yugoslavia, and Hindu nationalists in India.

The global media has paid significant attention to religion and
conflict, but not the ways in which religion has played a powerful
peacemaking role. This excessive emphasis on the negative side of
religion and the actions of religious extremists generates interfaith
fear and hostility. Media portrayals of religious conflict can confuse
rather than inform. It does so by misunderstanding goals and alliances
between groups, thereby exacerbating polarization. The tendency to
carelessly throw around the terms 'fundamentalist' and 'extremist'
masks significant differences in beliefs, goals, and tactics.

In virtually every heterogeneous society, religious difference
serves as a source of potential conflict. Ignorance of other faiths can
cause potential tension, but it does not necessarily mean conflict will
result. Religion is not necessarily conflictual but, as with ethnicity or
race, religion serves, as a way to distinguish one's self and one's group
from the other. Often, the group with less power, be it political or
economic, is more aware of the tension than the privileged. When
the privileged group is a minority, such as the Jews historically were
in Europe, they are often well aware of the latent conflict. There are

steps that can be taken to head off conflict. Interfaith dialogue can increase understanding.

When religion is a potential source of conflict, a triggering event can cause the conflict to emerge. At this stage in a conflict, grievances, goals, and methods often change to make the conflict more difficult to resolve. In a crisis, group members may see extremists as those who can produce what appear to be gains, at least in the short-term. In such situations, group identities are even more firmly shaped than the other group, thereby reinforcing the message of extremists that one's religion is threatened by another faith that is diametrically opposed. Often, historic grievances are recast as being the responsibility of the current enemy. At that stage, tactics often come detached from goals and radical interpretations are increasingly favored. Once martyrs have been sacrificed, it becomes increasingly difficult to compromise because their lives will seem to have been lost in vain.

Religious conflicts can often be resolved by promoting an awareness of the positive peace building and reconciliatory role religion has played in many conflict situations. Interfaith dialogue would be beneficial at all levels of religious hierarchies and across all segments of religious communities. When silence and misunderstanding are all too common, learning about other religions would be a powerful step forward. Being educated about other religions does not mean conversion but can facilitate understanding and respect for other faiths.

Religion and Violence

Since the beginning of religion, wars have been fought in the name of different gods and goddesses. Even today, most violent conflicts contain religious elements linked up with ethno-national, inter-state, economic, territorial, and cultural issues. Conflicts based on religion tend to become dogged, tenacious, and brutal. When conflicts are couched in religious terms, they become transformed into value conflicts. Unlike issues, such as resource conflicts that can be resolved by pragmatic and distributive means, value conflicts have a tendency to become mutually conclusive or zero-sum issues. They entail strong judgments of what is right and wrong, and parties believe that there cannot be a common ground to resolve their differences. In a world where many governments and international organizations are suffering from a legitimacy deficit, one can expect a growing impact of religious discourses on international politics. Religion is a major source of soft power. It can be used or misused by religions and governmental organizations to pursue their own interests. It is therefore important to develop a more profound understanding of the basic assumption underlying the different religions and the ways in which people adhering to them see their interests. It is useful to identify elements of communality between the major religions.

Some religious organizations support structural violence by endorsing a centralized and authoritarian decision-making structure and by repressing egalitarian forces. The causes of religious wars and other religion related violence have not disappeared. Without a change in the environments of public discourses within and between religious organizations, demagogy and rhetorical intolerance will prevail.

With respect to war and peace, the religious approaches could be divided into two main categories: pacifism and just war doctrine. Many varieties of pacifism can be distinguished: optimistic, mainstream, and pessimistic. For some, it means an unconditional rejection of participation in armed struggle; for others, it refers to an active engagement in peace-making. The Quakers traditionally have devoted themselves to the dismantling of enemy-images and reconciliation. Religious organizations can and should make efforts to overcome religious-intolerance, sectarianism, or nationalism and develop an ecumenical climate. As a start, Christians, Jews, and Muslims can develop a systematic analysis of their divergences and convergences, and their potential for conflict and find ways to cooperate. Any peace process should be seen as a learning experience for all the people concerned. A sustainable peace demands not only a mutually satisfying resolution of a specific conflict, but also a reconciliation of the past and a constructive engagement towards the future.

Religions and religious organizations have an under-utilized potential for constructive conflict management:

First, more than two thirds of the world population belong to a religion. In 2019, these were the religious constituency: Christian-32.8%; Muslim-22.5%; Hindu-13.8%; Buddhist-7.2%; .2% Jewish; other-11.8%, which includes folk and traditional religions. About 11.8% of the world's population has no religious affiliation. Religious organizations have a huge infrastructure with a far-reaching global network reaching to all corners of the world.

Second, religious organizations can mobilize people and cultivate attitudes of forgiveness and conciliation. They can do a great deal to prevent dehumanization. They have the capacity to motivate and mobilize people for a more peaceful world. Religious and humanitarian organizations encourage voluntarism in all countries. They are problem-solvers. They do not seek conflict. They respond to needs.

Third, religious organizations can rely on a set of soft power sources to influence the peace process. To mediate, religious organizations can rely on several sources of power. There could be the referent power that stems from the mediation position of a large and influential religious family. Closely related could be legitimate power or the claim to moral rectitude, the right to assert its views about the appropriateness and acceptability of behavior. Religious leaders could refer to their 'spiritual power' and speak in the name of God.

Fourth, religious organizations could use hard sources of power. Some have reward power, not only in terms of promising economic aid, but also by granting personal audiences. Coercive power can be used by mobilizing people to protest certain policies.

Fifth, non-governmental peace services can fulfill tasks for which the traditional diplomacy is not well equipped. They could provide information not readily available to traditional diplomats; they could create an environment where parties could meet without measuring their bargaining positions, without attracting charges of appeasement, without committing themselves, and without appearing to seek peaceful solutions at the expense of other important interests. They could monitor the conflict dynamics, involve the people at all levels, and assess the legitimacy of peace proposals and agreements.

Sixth, most can make use of their transnational organization to provide peace services.

Finally, religious organizations are in the field and could fulfill several of the above peace services.

Several weaknesses limit the impact of religious organizations in building a world free from conflict. Several religious organizations are still perpetrators of different kinds of violence. In many of today's conflicts, they remain primary or secondary actors or behave as passive bystanders. Religious organizations tend to be reactive players. They respond better to humanitarian relief efforts after a conflict has escalated rather than preventing violence. Most peace making or peace-building efforts are uncoordinated and lack effective cooperation. More professional expertise in conflict analysis and management is critical.

Although more people are becoming secular and scientifically oriented to finding solutions to the world's problems, religion still can and should play a role in helping people of different religious backgrounds to find common ground.

Chapter 8

POLITICAL CONFLICTS

P olitical conflicts are inevitable, since people have different ideas of how to deal with social problems as they arise. A political conflict may be defined as a positional difference regarding values relevant to a society—the conflict items—between at least two decisive, directly involved actors, which is implemented using observable and interrelated conflict means that lie beyond established regulatory procedures and threaten a core state function or the order of international law, or hold out the prospect to do so. The substance of a political conflict is a discrepancy, depicted by the concept of positional difference. A positional difference is a perceived incompatibility of content, thought, or concept.

Social conflicts involve the following elements: First, there have to be at least two persons capable of intellectual and imaginative power and of communicating it; Second, there has to be reciprocal and correlated action and communication between these persons, in order to be aware of the incompatibility of their content, thought, and concept; Third, communication has reference to a certain topic and action to a certain object. Political conflicts are a subtype of social conflicts. The "political" about political conflicts accrues from its relevance for society as a whole, from the fact that there are no accepted mechanisms for settlement and from the involvement of significant groups of the society.

Political philosophy begins with the question: what ought to be a person's relationship to society? The subject seeks the application of ethical concepts to the social sphere and deals with the variety of forms of government and social existence that people could live in. It also provides a standard by which to analyze and judge existing institutions and relationships.

Although linked by a range of philosophical issues and methods, political philosophy can be distinguished from political science. Political science predominantly deals with existing states of affairs, and tends to be amoral in its descriptions. It seeks a positive analysis of social affairs, i.e., constitutional issues, voting behavior, the balance of power, and the effect of judicial review, among others. Political philosophy generates visions of the good social life, i.e. the ruling set of values and institutions that combine men and women together. Political philosophy is used to develop a political system.

The main focus of any political system should be how to deploy or limit public power to improve the survival of its people and enhance the quality of human life. The Declaration of Independence declared that people were entitled to: "Life, Liberty and the pursuit of Happiness." How do people pursue happiness in their lives? According to Charles Murray, the proper role of any political system is to maximize its citizens' ability to pursue happiness.[20]

There are many different schools of thought on how to accomplish this. The environment and the scope and limitations of the human mind at a particular time in history will shape any political system. The political system of our prehistoric ancestors was far different than the political systems of today. The answers given will reflect the knowledge and assumptions of their times. Each of us has a political philosophy concerning the best interests of our society, even though some may not think about what that is. Some questions to consider in developing a political philosophy would include: the role of government, the obligations of citizens to their government, individual rights, sovereignty, political liberty, and social justice. That philosophy may change as we get older, change our status, or by some other event that changes the way we see the world. Your view of society as a college student may be far different from the way you see things as a married person with three children, a job, and a mortgage.

A distinction must be made between political philosophy, which reflects the world outlook of successive theorists and which demands an appreciation of their historical settings, and a political system at any given period of time. While political philosophy is important in setting standards of judgment and defining constructive purposes for the use of public power, it is the political system in place at any given time that dictates what happens to people.

People have different political philosophies and unless you understand their political philosophy, you may be unable to find common ground in resolving conflicts. Although each person has his or her own political philosophy, some philosophies may be identifiable in the following groups:

a. Liberalism:

The term "liberalism" conveys two distinct positions in political philosophy, the one a pro-individualist theory of people and government, the second a pro-statist or what is better termed a "social democratic" concept. The former is often referred to as "classical liberalism," derived from the word "liberty," freedom, and toleration. The latter is often referred to as "modern liberalism," and accepts rights to entitlements such as health care and education. A modern liberal might say the state has a duty is to ensure a just and fair opportunity for all to compete and flourish in a civil society that may require state intervention. A classic liberal rejects state intervention. A modern liberal might say that poverty is not conducive to pursuing the contemplative life and support redistributive or welfare policies. A classical liberal believes people are neither born equal nor can they be made equal. Talents and motivation are distributed unequally across a population, and attempts to reduce men and women to the same status will imply a reduction in the ability or freedom of the more talented to act and to strive for their own progression. Both classical and modern liberals would agree that the government has a strict duty towards impartiality and should be neutral in its evaluation of the good life.

Classical and modern liberals express skepticism towards experts knowing what is in the best interest of others, and thus liberals tend to reject any interference in people's lives as unjustifiable and, from a utilitarian point of view, counter-productive. Life, for the liberal, should be led from the inside (self-oriented) rather than the outside (other-imposed). Modern liberals believe individuals ought to be provided with the resources to ensure that they live the good life as they see fit. The classical liberal asks who will provide those resources and to what age should people be deemed incapable of learning or striving by themselves. Despite differences over policy, liberals—of both the modern and classical strain—predominantly hold an optimistic view of human nature.

b. Conservatism:

This approach plays down the unifying or omniscient implications of liberalism and its unifying rationalism and accords institutions or modes of behavior that have weathered the centuries a greater respect than liberals. Politically, philosophical conservatives are cautious in tampering with forms of political behavior and institutions, and they are especially skeptical of whole scale reforms. They err on the side of tradition, because of a skeptical view of our human ability to redesign whole ranges of social values that have evolved over many generations; detrimental values will fall into disuses of their own accord. Conservatives believe that reason can be highly overestimated for it belongs to single individuals and to their own political motives, errors, and prejudices.

Conservatives are highly skeptical of power and peoples' desire to use it; they believe that power corrupts even the most freedom loving wielders. For conservatives, the value of institutions cannot always be examined according to the rational analysis of the present generation. This imposes a demand on conservatism to explain or justify the rationale of supporting historical institutions. Conservatives do not reject reform but are thoroughly skeptical of any present generation's or present person's ability to understand and hence to reshape the vast edifices of behavior and institutions that have evolved with the wisdom of prior generations. They are skeptical of large scale planning, whether it is constitutional or economical or cultural and are against socialists who become impatient with present defects. The conservatives counsel patience, not for its own sake, but because the vast panoply of institutions that are rallied against—including human nature—cannot be reformed without the most detrimental effects. Conservatives typically condemn revolutions and coups as leading to more bloodshed and violence than that which the old regime produced. Some conservatives argue that a modicum of redistribution is required to ensure a peaceful, non-revolutionary society. Whereas modern liberals justify redistribution on the grounds of providing an initial basis for human development, conservatives possess a pragmatic fear of impoverished masses rising up to overthrow the status quo. Conservatives typically possess a pessimistic vision of human nature.

c. Socialism:

The term "socialist" describes a broad range of ideas and proposals that are held together by an overarching tenet—the central ownership and control of the means of production—because central ownership is deemed more efficient and/or more moral. Socialists believe that capitalism (free-market conservativism or liberalism) is morally and politically flawed. Some socialists of the Marxist persuasion argue that socialism is the final historical era that supplants capitalism before proper communism emerges.

Central Ownership: socialists claim that the free market system (capitalism) should be replaced or reformed. Most argue for a radical redistribution of resources, usually to "workers." The state or some form of democratic institution should take over the running of the economy. In the face of a growing unpopularity of central planning, many socialists have preferred to concentrate on altering the presiding property relationships. They demand that companies be given to the workers rather than the exploitative capitalist classes. Resources, most socialists claim, need to be radically redistributed. Worker-controlled socialism supports worker owned and operated businesses, usually small-scale and run on a democratic basis. Legislative proposals that demand more discussion and agreement between management and staff are a reflection of such beliefs. The policy to give control to the workers presumes (a) the workers are a definable class deserving of a greater moral and hence political status than presently they enjoy, which ethically would have to be established, and (b) that the workers are permanently either employed or exploited. An individual can at the same time be an employer, an employee, a worker, and a capitalist. Since individuals can move between the economic classes, scientific precision is reduced and even abandoned.

The Moral Critique of Capitalism: The initial unequal distribution of talent, energy, skills, and resources is not something that socialists usually focus on. Rather, they comment on the historical developments that led to an unequal distribution of wealth in favor of some individuals or nations. War and exploitation by the powerful, they argue, resulted in an immoral distribution, which reformers would prefer to correct to build society on a more moral basis. Socialists often refer to the historical injustices that have kept the downtrodden and meek poor and oppressed as a justification for present reforms or critique of the status quo. Proposals are wide-ranging on how to redistribute resources and to ensure present and future generations are permitted to equal access to a specified standard of living or opportunities. Moderates overlap with left wing or social democratic liberals and pragmatic conservatives, who believe in the primacy of freedom, but with a modicum of redistribution to ensure that all children get a fair start in life. Socialists prefer collective action over individual action, or at least individual action that is supportive of group rather than personal or selfish values. Socialists have an optimistic vision of what we can be, perhaps not what we now are (exploited or oppressed), but what we are capable of once society is reformed along socialist lines.

d. Progressiveness:

This social and political philosophy is fundamentally opposed to the concentration of wealth and power in the hands of the few at the expense of the many. A progressive philosophy is opposed to corruption and oppression. Progressives fight for the vulnerable and underprivileged, i.e. workers, the sick and powerless, and every other minority group that is marginalized by existing power structures. Progressives believe in the fundamental equality of human beings. Discrimination is a form of oppression, and a movement cannot be egalitarian and against oppression while tolerating discrimination.

They are opposed to the mass privatization of goods and services that should remain public: healthcare, education, and other necessities for a decent life. Democracy is the constant pursuit of civic engagement and public involvement in the direction of society. Without democracy, the American principles of life, liberty, and the pursuit of happiness are unattainable. The progressive movement requires transparency and accountability. Big money must stay out of the political process so that the people can elect those who are best fit to serve all the people. The progressive movement supports freedom of the press so that the public is fully informed and elected officials are held accountable. The progressive movement seeks justice for all Americans. Solidarity is essential since human beings have shared interests, and progress is not possible unless people stand together on the issues that matter.

e. Anarchism:

A social and political system without a state or more broadly a society that is characterized by a lack of any hierarchical or authoritarian structures. The anarchist believes that the good life can only be lived without constraining or limiting structures. Any institution or morality that is inconsistent with the life freely chosen is to be attacked, criticized, and rejected. The crucial issue for anarchists is defining what constitutes genuinely artificial impediments and structures from those that are the product of nature or of voluntary activities. Anarchism emphasizes different aspects of the protracted leaderless society. Utopian versions look forward to a universal egalitarianism in which each is to count for one and no more than one, and accordingly each person's values are of equal moral and political weight. Libertarian thinkers who support the free market have proposed anarchic solutions to economic and political problems. They stress the voluntaristic nature of the market system as a moral as well as an efficient means of distributing resources, and accordingly condemn state failure to provide adequate resources, i.e., health care, education, police, and defense services. Public goods and services ought to be provided privately through the free market. Regardless of the political direction that the anarchist leans towards, collectivism or individualism, how the anarchic community is to be secured presents philosophical problems that demand a close regard to possible inconsistencies. Historicist anarchists believe that anarchy is the ultimate state that humanity is inevitably ascending towards.

Radical anarchists claim that the future can only be fought for, and any imposition of authority on an individual's actions is to be defended against. This extends to anarchists actively undermining, disrupting, and dismantling the apparatus of the coercive state. Those on the libertarian wing stress that only government coerces, whereas those more sympathetic to socialism's moral critique of capitalism emphasize the oppressive nature of multinational companies and of global capitalism. While some anarchists are pacifistic in their rejection of authority, others condone the use of violence to secure their freedom from external coercion. In common with modern liberals and with some socialists and conservatives, some branches of anarchism reject the material world and economic progress as innately valuable. Anarchists who rail against economic progress (or "global capitalism") as somehow limiting their choices seek alternative ends to their political utopia.

f. Environmentalism:

Beyond the traditional ethical disputes concerning the good life for human beings and what political situation would best suit our development, others take up an alternative conception of humanity and its relationship with the living world. This political philosophy does not concern itself with the rights of people or of society, but of the rights of the planet and other species. The political philosophies of liberalism, socialism, conservativism, and anarchism, and all of their variants, agree that the good life sought by political philosophy ought to be the good life for human beings. Their respective criticism of political practice and mores stem from a competing standard of what ought to constitute the good life. Environmentalism starts on a different premise. Human beings are not the center of our politics, nature is.

Environmentalism considers our place on earth as secondary to that of the natural world. In its weaker forms, environmentalism claims that human beings are custodians of nature, to which we must respect and show certain ethical and political obligations to the natural world. Environmentalism condemns the very existence of humanity as a blot on the landscape, as the perennial destroyer of all that is good.

Environmentalists distinguish themselves from conservationists who argue that landscapes or animals ought to be protected from extinction only if they are beneficial or pleasing to humanity in some form or other. Environmentalists reject such human-centered utilitarianism in favor of a broad ethical intrinsicism. Their theory is that all species possess an innate value independent of any other entity's relationship to them. Environmentalism extends rights to or duties towards other species, which range extended beyond those animals closest to natural and cultural human sympathies. Rats, insects, and snails have been championed by various lobbies seeking to protect animals from human incursions. Utilitarians of the traditional political schools may agree with such proposals as being useful for humanity for future generations, but environmentalists prefer to remove "human beings" from the equation and deposit inalienable rights on such non-human entities, regardless of their relationship to humanity. Since animals are not ethical beings, environmentalists have a difficult task explaining why a snail darter possesses a greater right to live on the planet than a human. Because we can reason and comprehend the import of our actions implies we are not to be trusted for we can willingly commit evil. An animal is amoral in that regard. It kills, eats other entities, adapts to its environment, breeds, and pollutes, but it possesses no conception of what it does. For the environmentalist, this accords non-human species a higher moral status. Animals act and react, and there is no evil in this, but people think, and therein lies the source of our immorality. From this premise, all human creations can be universally condemned as unethical.

These major theories provoke in turn a vast range of discussion and debate on the subtleties of such issues as the law, economy, freedom, gender, nationality, violence, war, rebellion, and sacrifice, as well as on the grander visions of our proper political realm and the criticism of present institutions from the local to the international level.

POLITICAL PARTIES IN THE UNITED STATES

The United States currently has two major political parties: (1) Democratic Party, (2) Republican Party, and three significant minor parties: (1) Libertarian Party, (2) Green Party, (3) Constitution Party. There are also a number of other minor political parties. Many citizens are not affiliated with any political party, but do share some of the ideas expressed by political parties. One may be a member of a political party and share some of the principles of that party, but may also share principles from one of the other parties. For example, if one is a member of the Democratic Party, he or she is likely to support a woman's right to choose an abortion, but not necessarily. A member of the Republican Party is likely to oppose abortion, but again, not necessarily. Each political party will have a platform that may change. A person can be an active member of a political party and agree with the entire platform, many of the positions, some of the positions, a few of the positions, or even one of the positions. A person may not be a member of any particular party but may lean toward a particular party when it comes to voting. Many people vote the candidate and not the party.

Democratic Party:

Core Principals: Cooperation is better than conflict. Unity is better than division. Empowerment is better than resentment. Bridges are better than walls. The economy has to work for everyone—an economy that grows incomes for working people, creates good-paying jobs, and puts a middle-class life within reach for more Americans. Spur more sustainable economic growth to create good-paying jobs and raise wages. Have more economic fairness, so the rewards are shared broadly, not just with those at the top. The economy should prioritize long-term investment over short-term profit-seeking. This rewards the common interest over self-interest, and promotes innovation and entrepreneurship. Today's extreme level of income and wealth inequality—where the majority of the economic gains go to the top one percent and the richest 20 people in our country own more wealth than the bottom 150 million—makes our economy weaker, our communities poorer, and our politics poisonous.

Race still plays a significant role in determining who gets ahead in America and who gets left behind. This must be fixed. A good education is a basic right of all Americans, no matter what zip code they live in. End the school-to-prison pipeline and build a cradle-to-college pipeline instead, where every child can live up to his or her God-given potential. Help Americans balance work and family without fear of punishment or penalty. Guarantee equal pay for women. Protect every American's right to retire with dignity. Greed, recklessness, and illegal behavior on Wall Street must be brought to an end. Wall Street must never again be allowed to threaten families and businesses on Main Street.

Protect citizens' right to vote, while stopping corporations' outsized influence in elections. End the broken campaign finance system, overturn the disastrous *Citizens United* decision, restore the full power of the Voting Rights Act, and return control of elections to the American people. Climate change poses a real and urgent threat to the economy, the national security, and the children's health and futures. Americans deserve the jobs and security that come from becoming the clean energy superpower of the 21st century. America must bring the world together and lead with principle and purpose. Alliances should be strengthened. The military should be the best-trained, best-equipped fighting force in the world. Everything must be done to honor and support veterans. Only the United States can mobilize common action on a truly global scale, to take on the challenges that transcend borders, from international terrorism to climate change to health pandemics.

Above all, Democrats are the party of inclusion. Respect differences of perspective and belief, and work together to move this country forward, even when there is disagreement. Do not merely seek common ground—strive to reach higher ground. America should be proud of its heritage as a nation of immigrants. Civil liberties must be protected. Civil rights, voting rights, women's rights, workers' rights, LGBT rights, and rights for people with disabilities must be guaranteed.[21]

Republican Party:

Core Principals: American is exceptional. The United States of America is unlike any other nation on earth, that America is exceptional because of its historic role—first as refuge, then as defender, and now as exemplar of liberty for the world to see. People are created equal, endowed by their Creator with inalienable rights of life, liberty, and the pursuit of happiness. The Constitution was written not as a flexible document, but as an enduring covenant, that the constitutional system—limited government, separation of powers, federalism, and the rights of the people—must be preserved uncompromised for future generations, that political freedom and economic freedom are indivisible.

When political freedom and economic freedom are separated—both are in peril; when united, they are invincible. People are the ultimate resource—and that the people, not the government, are the best stewards of the country's God-given natural resources. As Americans and as Republicans, peace must come through strength. Make America safe. Seek friendship with all peoples and all nations, but recognize and be prepared to deal with evil in the world.

America's standing in world affairs has declined significantly—enemies no longer fear America and its friends no long trust America. People want and expect an America that is the most powerful and respected country on the face of the earth. The men and women of our military remain the world's best.[22]

Libertarian Party:

Core Principals: The Libertarian Party, challenges the cult of the omnipotent state and defend the rights of the individual. All individuals have the right to exercise sole dominion over their own lives, so long as they do not forcibly interfere with the equal right of others. Governments throughout history have regularly operated on the opposite principle, i.e. the State has the right to dispose of the lives of individuals and the fruits of their labor. Even within the United States, all political parties other than the Libertarian Party grant to government the right to regulate the lives of individuals and seize the fruits of their labor without their consent. Where governments exist, they must not violate the rights of any individual: namely, (1) the right to life—the initiation of physical force against others must be prohibited; (2) the right to liberty of speech and action—all attempts by government to abridge the freedom of speech and press, as well as government censorship in any form must be opposed; and (3) the right to property—all government interference with private property, such as confiscation, nationalization, and eminent domain.

Since governments, when instituted, must not violate individual rights, all interference by government in the areas of voluntary and contractual relations among individuals must be opposed. People should not be forced to sacrifice their lives and property for the benefit of others. They should be left free by government to deal with

one another as free traders; and the resultant economic system, the
only one compatible with the protection of individual rights, is the
free market.[23]

Green Party:

Core Principals: The Green Party is a party of social and environmental justice, which supports a radical transformation of society for the
benefit of all, and for the planet. The threats to economic, social and
environmental wellbeing are part of the same problem, and solving
one of these crises cannot be achieved without solving the others.

Humankind depends on the diversity of the natural world for
its existence. Other species are expendable. The Earth's physical
resources are finite. People threaten the future if they try to live
beyond those means, so they must build a sustainable society that
guarantees the long-term future.

Every person, in this and future generations, should be entitled to
basic material security as of right. Actions should take account of the
well-being of other nations, other species, and future generations. A
healthy society is based on voluntary co-operation between empowered individuals in a democratic society, free from discrimination
whether based on race, color, gender, sexual orientation, religion,
social origin, or any other prejudice.

Emphasize democratic participation and accountability by ensuring that decisions are taken at the closest practical level to those
affected by them. Use non-violent solutions to conflict situations,
which take into account the interests of minorities and future generations in order to achieve lasting settlements. The success of a society
cannot be measured by narrow economic indicators, but should take
account of factors affecting the quality of life for all people: personal
freedom, social equity, health, happiness, and human fulfilment.

Electoral politics is not the only way to achieve change in society.
Use a variety of methods, including lifestyle changes, to help effect
progress. Provide those methods that do not conflict with other core
principles.[24]

Constitution Party:

Core Principals: Life for all human beings: from conception to natural death. Constrain the Government to its enumerated powers so it does not impede the Liberty of the People whom it serves. Each individual possesses the right to own and steward personal property without government burden.

Family is the bedrock of a healthy Society. It is imperative that government maintains a favorable position to the divinely instituted nuclear family, not one that leads to its destruction.

The Constitution and Bill of Rights are the bedrock of Liberty and the Supreme Law of the Land. The sole purpose of government, as stated in the Declaration of Independence, is to secure our unalienable rights given to us by the Creator. When Government grows beyond this scope, it is usurpation, and liberty is compromised. Major issues are best solved by a renewed allegiance to the original intent of the United States Constitution and the Bill of Rights.

The Constitution delegated few enumerated powers to the Federal Government, reserving all remaining powers to the States and the people. The federal republic was created by joint action of the several states. It has been gradually perverted into a socialist machine for federal control in the domestic affairs of the states. The federal government has no authority to mandate policies relating to state education, natural resources, transportation, private business, housing, health care, ad infinitum.

There should be no entangling alliances—via treaties, or any other form of commitment—which compromise the national sovereignty, commit America to intervention in foreign wars. Negotiation or ratification of any treaty, agreement, or partnership that would deprive United States citizens of their rights protected by the United States Constitution must be opposed. Any union whether political or economic, of the United States, Mexico, and Canada must be opposed. American participation in any form of world government organization, including any world court under United Nations auspices, must be opposed. Terminate United States membership in the United Nations, and its subsidiary organizations, and terminate U.S. participation in all so-called U.N. peace keeping operations; bar the United Nations, and its subsidiaries, from further operation, including raising of funds on United States territory.

The Constitution must be obeyed to prohibit the United States government from entering any treaty, or other agreement, which makes any commitment of American military forces or tax money, compromises the sovereignty of the United States, or accomplishes a purpose properly the subject of domestic law. The agreement establishing the proposed Free Trade Area of the Americas (FTAA) and any other such trade agreements, either bilateral or regional in nature, must be opposed.

All treaties must be subordinate to the Constitution, since the Constitution is the only instrument which empowers and limits the federal government. American troops must serve only under American commanders, not those of the United Nations or foreign countries.[25]

POLITICAL POLARIZATION

More in Common, a non-profit organization, sought to study the underlying causes of the political gridlock in America. The Hidden Tribes Project was launched in 2018 to better understand the forces that are driving Americans apart, and to galvanize efforts to address them. Its first report, Hidden Tribes: A Study of America's Polarized Landscape provided deep insights into the psychological drivers of polarization and the role of 'upstream' values and beliefs. This study identified an 'Exhausted Majority' of Americans fatigued by the polarized state of American society and eager for change. The study was undertaken to understand the core beliefs of Americans and explore how this understanding can be used, not to deepen polarization, but to bring people together. Their report aims to inform and support efforts to counter the forces of polarization and tribalism by fostering an understanding of the differences in core beliefs that underpin Americans' affiliations.[26]

The study identified five dimensions of deeply held core beliefs: (1) Tribalism and group identification—extent to which people identify with different groups based on nationality, gender, political party, ethnicity, and other factors; and their views on who is mistreated in American society; (2) Fear and perception of threat—extent to which people see the world as a dangerous place; (3) Parenting style and authoritarian disposition—basic philosophies regarding people's approach to parenting, which past research suggests may have important predictive power in explaining their attitudes towards more general public policies and authoritarianism; (4) Moral foundations—extent to which people endorse certain moral values or "foundations," including fairness, care, purity, authority, and loyalty; (5) Personal agency and responsibility—extent to which people view personal success as the product of individual factors (such as hard work and discipline) versus societal factors (such as luck and circumstance).

The study separated the population into seven tribes: (1) Progressive Activists; (2) Traditional Liberals; (3) Passive Liberals; (4) Politically Disengaged; (5) Moderates; (6) Traditional Conservatives; (7) Devoted Conservatives.

Progressive Activists (8%) have strong ideological views, high levels of engagement with political issues, and the highest levels of education and socioeconomic status. Their own circumstances are secure, which frees them to devote more attention to larger issues of justice in society around them. They have an outsized role in political discourse, even though they comprise a small portion of the total population. They are highly sensitive to issues of fairness and equity in society, particularly with regards to race, gender, and other minority group identities. Their emphasis on existing power structures leads them to be very pessimistic about fairness in America. They are uncomfortable with nationalism and ambivalent about America's role in the world. Their main concerns are climate change, inequality, and poverty.

Comparison to the average American:

- Three times more likely to say that people's outcomes are the result of "luck and circumstance"—75% v. 25%.

* Less likely to believe the world is becoming a "more and more dangerous place"—19% v. 38%.

* More than twice as likely to say that they never pray—50% v. 19%.

* Almost three times more likely to be "ashamed to be an American"—69% v. 24%.

* Eleven percent more likely to be white—80% v. 69%.

* Seven percent more likely to be between ages 18 and 29—28% v. 21%.

* Twice as likely to have completed college—59% v. 29%.

Traditional Liberals (11%) reflect the liberal ideals of the Baby Boomer generation. They maintain idealistic attitudes about the potential for social justice in America, yet they are less ideological than Progressive Activists. They are not as intolerant of conservatives. They have strong humanitarian values, and around half say that religion is important to them. Traditional Liberals are significantly more likely to say that people "need to be willing to listen to others and compromise." They are the most likely group, along with Progressive Activists, to handle conflict by "getting to the heart of the disagreement." Overall, Traditional Liberals respond best to rational arguments and are inclined to place more faith in the viability of American institutions, even if they are disillusioned with the country's current direction. Their main concerns are leadership and division in society.

Comparison to the average American:

* Eleven percent more likely to handle conflict by "getting to the heart of the disagreement"—68% v. 57%.

* Twelve percent more likely to say that "the people I agree with politically need to be willing to listen to others and compromise"—73% v. 61%.

- Seventeen percent more likely to say, "we need to heal as a nation"—77% v. 60%.

- Eight percent more likely to say that to be American it is very important to "believe in freedom and equality"—75% v. 67%.

- Eight percent more likely to be over the age of 65—28% v. 20%.

- Seven percent more likely to be white—76% v. 69%.

- Nineteen percent more likely to have graduated college—48% v. 29%.

Passive Liberals (15%) are weakly engaged in social and political issues, but when pushed they tend to have liberal views on social issues such as immigration, DACA, sexism, and LGBTQI+ issues. They are younger and have a higher proportion of females (59 percent) than any other segment. Unlike Progressive Activists and Traditional Liberals, they tend to feel isolated, even alienated, from their communities and the system at large. Passive Liberals are the least satisfied of all the segments. They are among the most fatalistic, believing that circumstances are largely outside of their own control. They are quite uninformed, consume little news media, and generally avoid political debates, partly from a general aversion to argumentation and partly because they do not know much about social and political issues. Their main concerns are healthcare, racism, and poverty.

Comparison to the average American:

- Fifteen percent less likely to say they have a "strong sense of home"—36% v. 21%.

- Six percent more likely to say they feel like a "stranger in my own country"—19% v. 13%.

- Twelve percent more likely to say the world is becoming a "more dangerous place"—50% v. 38%.

* Twice as likely to say "things have gotten worse for me personally in the last year"—32% v. 17%.

* Much less likely to be registered to vote—51% v. 72%.

* Much more likely to be African American—20% v. 12%.

* Seven percent more likely to be aged 18-29—28% v. 21%.

* Eight percent more likely to have not graduated from college—68% v. 60%.

* Four percent more likely to "avoid arguments"—86% v. 82%.

Politically Disengaged (26%) most resemble Passive Liberals in having lower levels of income and education and being less engaged in following current affairs. Fully 41 percent are making less than $30,000 per year, and approximately one in four have gone without enough food or without medical treatment. They differ from Passive Liberals by being more anxious about external threats and less open in their attitudes towards differences. They are the most likely to say that being white is necessary to be American and that people who hold other religious views are morally inferior. They are more concerned about the threat of terrorism and are quite closed to the view that Islamic and American values are compatible. They are practically invisible in local politics and community life, being one of the least likely groups to participate in political rallies or vote in local elections. They are also the least well-informed group on all measures of political knowledge. They are the most pessimistic about the possibility of reconciling differences between political factions. Overall, this makes the Politically Disengaged a difficult segment to reach and mobilize. Their main concerns are gun violence, jobs/ economy, and terrorism.

Comparison to the average American:

* Eight percent more likely to say that to fix America, we need a strong leader willing to break the rules—57% v. 45%.

* Nine percent more likely to believe the "differences between Americans are too big for us to work together"—32% v. 23%.

* Nine percent more likely to say that "being white" is important to being American—20% v. 11%.

* Nine percent more likely to make under $20,000 a year—26% v. 17%.

* More than twice as likely to not be involved in any community activity—78% v. 34%.

Moderates (15%) reflect the middle of the road of public opinion in America. They tend to be engaged in their communities, often volunteer, and are interested in current affairs, but uncomfortable with the tribalism of politics. They tend to be socially conservative. Religion plays an important role in their lives, but they reject extremism and intolerance. They strongly disapprove of Donald Trump as president and overwhelmingly believe that the country is headed in the wrong direction. They favored Democrats over Republicans in the 2018 midterm election by a margin of 4-3. They think that political correctness has gone too far. They dislike the activism and extremism of both progressives and conservatives. While they think feminism has gone too far, they also recognize sexual harassment as an important issue. They support the notion of sanctuary cities and want undocumented immigrants to have better treatment. They reject extreme policies such as building a border wall. They are worried about the state of America and feel that American identity is slipping away. They feel conflicted on certain social justice issues, including same sex marriage, and they are slower to embrace change. They tend to seek fewer radical solutions than Devoted or Traditional Conservatives. Their main concerns are division, foreign tensions, and healthcare.

Comparison to the average American:

* More likely to follow current affairs some or most of the time—80% v. 72%.

* Five percent more likely to agree that immigration is good for the country—61% v. 56%.

* Four percent more likely to say police are more violent toward African Americans than others—55% v. 51%.

* Nine percent more likely to believe that political correctness has gone too far—89% v. 80%.

* Six percent more likely to be over 45—60% v. 54%.

* Four percent more likely to have "some college"—27% v. 23%.

Traditional Conservatives (19%) value patriotism and America's Christian foundations. They believe Christian foundations are under threat from a liberal political culture that emphasizes diversity and devalues America's achievements. They believe in personal responsibility and self-reliance, and think that too much emphasis is given to issues of gay rights, sexual harassment, and racism. They have a clear sense of identity as American, Christian, and conservative, but they are not as strident in their beliefs as Devoted Conservatives. They are open to dialogue or compromise on a pathway to citizenship for undocumented immigrants brought here as children, and acknowledge that racist acts still persist in the United States. They are suspicious of the traditional media, yet they are more likely than any other group to feel that their voice is represented in American politics. Their main concerns are foreign tensions, jobs, and terrorism.

Comparison to the average American:

* Thirty-three percent less likely to say the country is rigged in favor of the rich and powerful—47% v. 80%.

* Almost twice as likely to feel that people like them have a say in politics—46% v. 24%.

* Eight percent more likely to say that "having two American parents" is a "very important" part of being American—23% v. 15%.

* Ten percent more likely to be white—79% v. 69%.

* Ten percent more likely to be older than 65—30% v. 20%.

* Similar education to average American.

Devoted Conservatives (6%) are the counterparts to the Progressive Activists, but at the other end of the political spectrum. They are one of the highest income-earning groups, and are happier and more content than most other Americans. They are highly engaged in social and political issues and think that religious liberty, abortion, and terrorism are especially important issues. They value patriotism and loyalty to the flag. They feel that traditional values are under assault and that Americans are being forced to accept liberal beliefs about issues such as immigration, racial inequality, Islam, and the role of women. They believe that American values are eroding rapidly, and they see themselves as defenders of those values. Their main concerns are immigration, terrorism, and jobs/economy.

Comparison to the average American:

* Almost twice as likely to list politics as a hobby—63% v. 35%.

* Three times more likely to strongly support a US-Mexico border wall—75% v. 24%.

* More than twice as likely to have donated to their place of worship—64% v. 24%.

* Almost three times more likely to strongly support a 'Muslim travel ban'—88% v. 31%.

- Twenty-four percent more likely to oppose compromise—63% v. 39%.
- Nineteen percent more likely to be white—88% v. 69%.
- Fourteen percent more likely to be older than 65—34% v. 20%—and much less likely to be born between 1985 and 2000—11% v. 27%.
- More likely to come from the South—45% v. 38%.

This study found that the most dramatic difference between the tribes is that which arises between the Progressive Activists and the Devoted Conservatives. Devoted Conservatives believe that individuals need to be raised to be obedient, well behaved, and hard-working. They take pride in the Judeo-Christian faith and American culture, and they believe that their traditional values can transform flawed individuals into people of self-discipline, character, and responsibility. Progressive Activists, who are at the opposite end of the spectrum, are skeptical of traditional authority and norms. They see those values as being established by socially dominant groups such as straight white men, for their own benefit. Progressive Activists seek to correct the historic marginalization of groups based on their race, gender, sexuality, wealth, and other forms of privilege.

The study calls them America's hidden tribes because what they have in common is a shared set of beliefs, values, and identities that shape the way they see the world, rather than visible external traits such as age, race, or gender. The study describes them as tribes because their behavior is often governed by a strong sense of shared identity and a collective adherence to core group principles. The study determined which people belonged in which hidden tribe by exploring the following political issues:

- Immigration, refugees, the border wall, DACA, sanctuary cities;
- American identity, patriotism;

* Shootings, terrorism, religion;
* Race, racism, social justice, white privilege;
* Gender, sexuality, sexism;
* Media, political discourse;
* Censorship, hate speech, political correctness and belief in conspiracy theories.

The people who conducted the study opined that many of today's most contentious issues are framed as us-versus-them identity-based struggles, as battles pitting men against women, American citizens against immigrants, Muslims against Christians, and African Americans against the police. In fact, these conflicts often stem from individuals' core beliefs on issues such as fairness, justice, privilege, and oppression. Today, America is deeply factionalized. Violent hate crimes are rising and Washington is gripped by a sense of permanent crisis regularly compared to that of the Watergate era. This reflects America's profound polarization, in which any and every issue can be channeled into an us-versus-them conflict between warring factions, and where partisan ends justify any means.

It is difficult to break this cycle of polarization. Tribal outrage works as a business model for social media, cable television, and talk radio. It succeeds where redistricting has shifted the political contest from the center ground in general elections to the mobilized base in primary campaigns. The well-documented result is that growing numbers of Americans are segregated into echo chambers where they are exposed to fewer alternative ideas, and fed a constant stream of stories that reinforce their tribal narratives. Over time, this environment spawns increasing extremism, as start-up initiatives from political campaigns to new media outlets seek to out compete established players through ideological purity and aggression. Scientists and researchers have made strides in their understanding of human nature and psychology. This knowledge, combined with the powerful platforms and tools of social media, can be used for good or for ill.

Today, millions of Americans go about their lives with inaccurate perceptions of each other. Partisan media consistently elevates the most extreme representations of "them," whether they are liberals, conservatives, immigrants, Evangelicals, Muslims, gun owners, gun control advocates, or any other group central to America's deepening tribal conflicts. This creates a false impression that outliers are somehow representative of the majority. The intolerance for the other is a grave threat to our democratic system, as political actors cast off the restraints of convention and even the rule of law, with a ruthless determination to crush the other side no matter the cost. The report has shown that despite America's profound polarization, the middle is far larger than conventional wisdom suggests, and the strident wings of progressivism and conservatism are far smaller. Progressive Activists are not representative of most liberal Americans; Devoted Conservatives are not representative of most conservative Americans. Most Americans are appalled by our politics, but many are also conditioned by it.

The forces that are driving polarization and social fracturing are profoundly powerful: from rising inequality and economic insecurity to the media echo chambers and the bewildering pace of social and demographic change. All this is happening against a backdrop of fears of crime and terrorism, which further heighten people's perception of threat and accelerate their retreat into their tribal identities.

The same sense of frustration and distrust that is undermining Americans' ability to communicate with their fellow citizens is also reflected in their relationship to the news media. Approximately two-thirds of Americans believe that "most mainstream media are biased in their coverage." This includes media coverage of immigrants (64%), urban areas (67%), police shootings (65%), sexual assault (62%), sexism (66%), and Muslims (65%). This perception of bias is consistently lowest among Traditional Liberals (about 1 in 3 sees bias across these issues) and highest among Devoted Conservatives (about 9 in 10 see bias across these issues). The subject on which people are most likely to perceive bias is the subject of immigration, where 97 percent of Devoted Conservatives claim inaccurate reporting from the mainstream media.

Americans are highly critical of the partisan cable networks, such as conservative Fox News and liberal MSNBC. Negative perceptions of those networks are more than twice as intense as positive ones. Fox News is perceived to be somewhat or very honest by 40 percent of the public, including 87 percent of Devoted Conservatives. In contrast, 98 percent of Progressive Activists believe Fox News is dishonest, and 88 percent say it is "very dishonest." Similarly, MSNBC is rated as at least "somewhat honest" by 41 percent of the public, including 72 percent of Traditional Liberals and 67 percent of Progressive Activists. On the other hand, it is deemed "very dishonest" by 74 percent of Devoted Conservatives. These negative views align with the conviction of the wing segments that their political opponents' network will "report false stories if it benefits them." For example, 95 percent of Progressive Activists believe this about Fox News, while 87 percent of Devoted Conservatives believe this about MSNBC.

Social media has intensified the environment of tribalism as it tends to polarize those who are most engaged in public debates. Fringe or extreme perspectives can enter mainstream debate far more easily in the digital era since there are fewer information gatekeepers. Where trust in traditional media has declined, false information can spread widely and information can be micro-targeted to specific audiences. The algorithms that give priority to certain types of content on social networks tend to foster expressions of moral outrage, thereby contributing to the polarization of debate. Social norms are being eroded by repeated exposure to behaviors and commentary that, in other settings, might be subject to social sanction.

The high level of internal agreement among Progressive Activists and Devoted Conservatives may in part be explained by their online presence. In an increasingly tribalized social media environment, those who express sympathy for the views of opposing groups may experience backlash from their own cohorts. That backlash, in the form of negative feedback on social networking sites, is often expressed in much stronger terms than it would be in a face-to-face encounter. Those who witness this process learn not to deviate from group norms, especially on polarizing issues of identity and belonging.

The study suggests that tribalism has contributed to a loss of objectivity in reporting, as some news outlets have pursued a business model that fosters polarization, while others have increasingly substituted opinion writing for investigative journalism. This has contributed to a loss of faith in news outlets. Public awareness of disinformation efforts has further diminished trust online. The dynamics of social media have intensified partisanship and tribalism, especially among the most engaged population segments. The filter bubbles and echo chambers of social media restrict people's exposure to alternative views and elevate the loudest, more extreme voices. This has helped to enforce similar ways of thinking and behaving within the most engaged wing groups, while discouraging others from engaging at all.

This environment of weak trust in sources of information is complicated by concerns over the culture of outrage and offense that many associate with tribalization and political correctness. These concerns are often expressed most strongly by those in the middle groups. The 'wing segments' differ from the majority of Americans in diminishing either the seriousness of concerns about political correctness, or diminishing the seriousness of concerns about hate speech. In contrast, the Exhausted Majority of Americans is concerned about both. Effective communication at both the national and the personal level requires an atmosphere of trust and objectivity. Tribalism destroys trust and objectivity, and replaces them with competing loyalties. The context of a low-trust news environment and a tribalized social media creates significant obstacles for communicating across the ideological divide. Although the patterns of communication are becoming entrenched, the study suggests that many Americans want to move beyond division. This creates an opportunity for new initiatives that seek to create trust and connection across the lines of difference and bring Americans together around what unites them rather than what divides them.

Chapter 9

WORK AND
LEGAL CONFLICTS

For many people, their job is the single most important aspect of their lives. As much as a third of our lives can be spent working. Our job provides the means for us to obtain the necessities of life and some financial security. Our job supports our dreams of having families, homes, education, entertainment, and hobbies. Most of us rely on a job to provide health insurance, disability coverage, and manage pension contributions for our retirement. Social connections at the workplace become important to us. Our work provides us with self-esteem and self-worth. Unfortunately, millions of American workers lose their jobs every year.

This may come as a surprise, but in 49 states, an employer can fire you for good reason, bad reason, or no reason at all. It may sound un-American, but that is the law in this country. Your employer can one day decide he or she no longer wants you around. Workers can be "downsized," "laid off," or "reorganized" out of their jobs. Thousands will be fired, with or without "cause." Some workers will be forced to resign because of intolerable working conditions. If you work for someone else—and most of us do—sooner or later either you or someone you care about will lose his or her job. Not all work related conflicts involve terminations. Many conflicts involve work environments, personality clashes, and other related issues. There are a number of ways of resolving disputes in the workplace. The most expensive, time-consuming,

and least-effective method is a lawsuit. It is important for employers and employees to realize that they share mutual interests. All
employers should foster an environment that respects and values
their employees. The cooperation between the employer and its
employees benefits everyone.[27]

While lawsuits are time consuming and expensive. There may be
times when you have no better alternative and will have to resort to
the courts for a resolution. When you do file your lawsuit, look to
alternative dispute resolution processes at your earliest opportunity.

Harvard law professor Frank Sander, in his speech at the 1976
Roscoe Pound Conference, urged American lawyers and judges to
re-imagine the civil courts as a collection of dispute resolution procedures tailored to fit the variety of disputes that parties bring to
the courts. Professor Sander's speech drew attention to alternatives
to traditional dispute resolution that he argued would better serve
disputants and society than traditional adversarial processes. These
issues would include many legal disputes ranging from the family, to
the schoolyard, to workplaces and sales transactions, to community
decision-making, among others. These alternative forms of dispute
resolution are called alternative dispute resolution (ADR). Some
refer to the "A" in ADR as "appropriate" rather than "alternative."
Advantages of ADR include efficiency, flexibility and tailoring of
outcomes, party empowerment, legitimacy, and participation of the
parties. Some use ADR for privacy, since court is generally a public
process. Some use ADR to avoid setting of precedents, since court
decisions may set a precedent for future cases. As a result of ADR, civil
caseloads have declined significantly over the past decades in many
jurisdictions. At the same time, there has been a dramatic decrease
in the fraction of civil cases reaching trial. Federal courts are now
required by law to offer some form of ADR, and many state courts
require parties to attempt to resolve their cases through mediation
before they can obtain a trial date.

The American Bar Association lists the following dispute resolution processes:

Arbitration—a private process where disputing parties agree that one or several individuals can make a decision about the dispute after receiving evidence and hearing arguments. Arbitration differs from mediation because the neutral arbitrator has the authority to make a decision about the dispute. The arbitration process is similar to a trial in that the parties make opening statements and present evidence to the arbitrator. Arbitration can usually be completed more quickly and is less formal than a trial. Often the parties do not have to follow state or federal rules of evidence and, in some cases, the arbitrator is not required to apply the governing law. After the hearing, the arbitrator issues an award. Some awards simply announce the decision (a "bare bones" award), and others give reasons (a "reasoned" award). The arbitration process may be either binding or non-binding. When arbitration is binding, the decision is final, can be enforced by a court, and can only be appealed on very narrow grounds. When arbitration is non-binding, the arbitrator's award is advisory and can be final only if accepted by the parties.

Case Evaluation—a non-binding process in which parties to a dispute present the facts and the issues to be determined to an experienced neutral case evaluator. The case evaluator advises the parties on the strengths and weaknesses of their respective positions, and assesses how the dispute is likely to be decided by a jury or other adjudicator. The parties may then use this feedback to help reach a mutually agreeable resolution.

Collaborative Law—an out-of-court settlement process where parties and their lawyers try to reach an agreement satisfying the needs of all parties. The parties agree to provide all relevant information. If the parties engage in contested litigation, their Collaborative lawyers cannot represent them in court. The process typically involves "four-way meetings" with the parties, the lawyers, and other professionals such as neutral financial specialists, communications coaches, child specialists, or appraisers.

Cooperative Practice—the parties and their lawyers begin the case with a common commitment of creatively settling all issues. They go to court only if they cannot reach a reasonable settlement. They use an agreement describing how the negotiation process will work. If the parties do not settle, the lawyers can continue to represent them. The process is flexible and can be as formal or informal as desired. The cooperative negotiation agreement may be oral or written. The process typically involves "four-way meetings" with the parties and lawyers, though some negotiation may be directly between the law-yers or parties when appropriate. The agreement may provide for a "cooling off" period before the parties can go to court (except in an emergency). If parties and lawyers cannot reach agreement, they may hire a mediator to help resolve disagreements. The process may take place before a case is filed in court or while a court case is pending. In some places, the court may support the process.

Divorce Coaching—a flexible, goal-oriented process designed to support, motivate, and guide people going through divorce to help them make the best possible decisions for their future, based on their particular interests, needs, and concerns. Divorce coaches have different professional backgrounds and are selected based on the specific needs of the clients. Some divorce coaches are financial planners, mental health professionals, lawyers, or mediators who have experience dealing with divorcing clients.

Facilitation—a process in which a trained individual assists a group of two or more people to discuss issues addressed by the group. This may include assistance in defining and analyzing issues, developing alternatives, and executing the agreed upon solutions. A facilitator can help to enhance communication, consensus building, and decision-making among individuals in a variety of settings, including community, corporate, educational, and family groups.

Family Group Conference—a meeting between members of a family and members of their extended kinship group. At this meeting, the family becomes involved in making a plan to stop the abuse or other ill treatment between its members. Family Group Conferencing involves family and friends in resolving the abuse rather than leaving the decision-making entirely in the hands of the legal authorities and service providers. All participants are given a great deal of preparation, support and protection so that all family members can be both safe and informed in having a say in the decision-making.

Mediation—a private process where a neutral third person called a mediator helps the parties discuss and try to resolve the dispute. The parties have the opportunity to describe the issues, discuss their interests, understandings, and feelings; provide each other with information and explore ideas for the resolution of the dispute. While courts can mandate that certain cases go to mediation, the process remains "voluntary" in that the parties are not required to come to agreement. The mediator does not have the power to make a decision for the parties, but can help the parties find a resolution that is mutually acceptable. The only people who can resolve the dispute in mediation are the parties themselves. Mediation can proceed in a number of ways. Most mediations start with the parties together in a joint session. The mediator will describe how the process works, will explain the mediator's role, and will help establish ground rules and an agenda for the session. Generally, parties make opening statements. Some mediators conduct the entire process in a joint session. Other mediators will move to separate sessions, shuttling back and forth between the parties. If the parties reach an agreement, the mediator may help reduce the agreement to a written contract, which may be enforceable in court.

Mini-Trial—a private, consensual process where the attorneys for each party make a brief presentation of the case as if at a trial. The presentations are observed by a neutral advisor and by representatives (usually high-level business executives) from each side who have authority to settle the dispute. At the end of the presentations, the representatives attempt to settle the dispute. If the representatives fail to settle the dispute, the neutral advisor, at the request of the parties, may serve as a mediator or may issue a non-binding opinion as to the likely outcome in court.

"Multi-Door" Program—a concept, which envisions one courthouse with multiple dispute resolution doors or programs. Cases are referred through the appropriate door for resolution. The goals of a multi-door approach are to provide citizens with easy access to justice, reduce delay, and provide links to related services, making more options available for dispute resolution.

Neutral Fact-Finding—a process where a neutral third party, selected either by the disputing parties or by the court, investigates an issue and reports or testifies in court. The neutral fact-finding process is particularly useful for resolving complex scientific and factual disputes.

Parenting Coordination—a process used in cases where parents have significant conflict about their parenting arrangements and have difficulty resolving their conflicts themselves. The parenting coordinator (PC) is either appointed by a court or hired privately by parents to work out problems in implementing a parenting plan. The goal of the process is to reduce conflict between parents that harms their children.

Pro Tem Trial—a process similar to other civil trials, but the parties choose their own trial date and the court appoints an attorney to serve as a temporary (Pro Tem) judge for the trial. The pro tem judge has all the same powers of a regular judge, and will make a decision based on the evidence and arguments presented during the trial. Each side must follow the same rules and legal procedures as parties who have a trial in the courthouse. There is no option for a jury trial. The parties must provide their own court reporter. Depending on court rules, the decision of the Pro Tem judge may be appealable in the public courts.

Private Judging—a process where the disputing parties agree to retain a neutral person as a private judge. The private judge, who is often a former judge with expertise in the area of the dispute, hears the case and makes a decision in a manner similar to a judge. Depending on court rules, the decision of the private judge may be appealable in the public courts.

Settlement Conference—a meeting in which a judge or magistrate assigned to the case presides over the process. The purpose of the settlement conference is to try to settle a case before the hearing or trial. Settlement conferencing is similar to mediation in that a third party neutral assists the parties in exploring settlement options. Settlement conferences are different from mediation in that settlement conferences are usually shorter and typically have fewer roles for participation of the parties or for consideration of non-legal interests.

Summary Jury Trial—a process where attorneys for each party make abbreviated case presentations to a mock six member jury (drawn from a pool of real jurors), the party representatives, and a presiding judge or magistrate. The mock jury renders an advisory verdict. The verdict is frequently helpful in reaching a settlement, particularly where one party has an unrealistic assessment of the case.

WORK CONFLICTS

A work conflict includes any type of conflict that takes place within a workplace or among workers and/or managers and/or customers and/or other third parties, potentially including conflicts between employees in or out of work hours. It is a broad concept that includes several types of conflicts that are normally treated separately, including employment conflicts and labor-management conflicts. Beyond those two subtypes, however, a work conflict may not involve the employer as a party; a work conflict may be between two or more employees.

There is hardly anyone in the work force who has not been exposed to a workplace conflict at one time. Few understand the intricate distinctions regarding types of workplace conflicts. The rights American workers now have were not all established at once, but over decades, and the resulting patchwork of laws, regulations, and agencies can be very confusing. A basic understanding of how labor law and employment law have developed, of why they are separate concepts, and of the different mediation and arbitration procedures that now exist to streamline the handling of large numbers of cases, can help anyone better understand how the workplace works.

As an example, a successful new product is selling well, and its maker is running the factory an additional four hours a day Monday through Friday as required overtime for all employees. For the fourth Saturday in a row, the same three employees are called in for yet more overtime. If one of them objects about the perceived unfairness of being singled out for unwanted overtime, and gets into a heated argument with a supervisor, while the other two have no objection, this would be described by many as a "work" conflict. If the reason the employee gives for believing he was singled out is related to race, color, sex, sexual orientation, religion, national origin, age, or another protected category, this would often be viewed as an "employment" conflict—whether or not the employee was ultimately found correct in that perception. And if all three employees went to management together to complain about being selected for the additional overtime, this could constitute "concerted activity," which is related to union activity that would make the event more appropriately described as a form of labor-management conflict.

Work conflicts can cause an employee to act out of interests that are divergent from those of his or her employer, supervisors, or coworkers. Conflicts can also arise with customers or other third parties. With the wide range of cultural diversity in today's workforce, conflicts are inevitable unless you work in a job that completely segregates you from contact with other people.

Workplace conversations, memos, and presentations require a basic set of communication skills, which may be automatic and require minimal thought to perform. When dealing with personality conflicts, it is necessary to consciously focus on specific communication skills that can actually resolve the problem. Major issues must be overcome when dealing with personality conflicts at work in order to preserve a productive environment.

The Five Most Common Types of Conflicts in the Workplace:

(1) **Interdependence:** Having to rely on someone else's cooperation in order to get your job done. For example, a member

of your sales team is constantly late inputting monthly figures, causing you to be late producing a sales report.

(2) Differences in Style: Your preferred way of getting the job done is different from that of your co-worker or supervisor. For example, you like to complete a task as quickly as possible (task-oriented), but your co-worker wants to get everyone's input on how the job should get done (people-oriented).

(3) Background or Other Differences: Conflicts occur because of differences in educational backgrounds, personal experiences, ethnic heritage, culture, religion, gender, race, sexual orientation, disability status, military status, age, or political ideology.

(4) Leadership Differences: Differences in how leaders relate to their employees can confuse and irritate them by having to shift back and forth between different styles. For example, one leader is more open and inclusive, while the other is more directive.

(5) Personality Clashes: These types of conflict can be the most volatile and are usually fueled by emotion involving a perception about someone else's motives and character. For example, a team leader openly criticizes a team member for being late and views him or her as being lazy and disrespectful. The team member on the other hand sees the team leader as out to get him or her because he or she is not a favored employee.

If you do not get along with a co-worker, it is inevitable that a dispute will occur. Learn to listen and ask questions to get to the root of the problem and work together to make things right. If your worst enemy is working on a project with you, use it as an opportunity to come together. By sharing a positive work experience, you may be able to dissipate bad feelings.

Watch your written communications and emails, which can be taken the wrong way if not carefully worded. Avoid sarcasm or using capitals with excessive exclamation points, which is known as screaming in an email. Avoid petty email exchanges. Learn to try to talk things out face to face. In extreme situations, resolving conflict may involve a third party mediator. Experienced human resources advisors are trained to deal with these types of conflicts and at some point, it may be necessary to get them involved.

LEGAL CONFLICTS

A legal conflict is any dispute that can be filed and resolved in a court of law. Not every conflict can be resolved in court. Civil cases are claims in which private citizens (or companies) sue each other in court to resolve a dispute.

In most civil cases, the judge or jury makes a decision about which side wins based on a standard called "preponderance of the evidence." This means that to win your side of the story is more likely than not believed by the judge or in a case tried to a jury, by the jury. It does not mean that one side brought in more evidence than the other side. It means that one side's evidence was more believable than the other side.

In some cases, the standard for reaching a decision is "clear and convincing evidence." This means that, for you to win, you have to prove that your version of the facts is highly probably or reasonably certain, or "substantially more likely than not."

When using the court to decide the dispute or conflict, the parties are giving a third party, the court and/or a jury, the power to determine the outcome.

There are a number of different kinds of cases that can be filed in civil court:

Small claims cases for amounts typically less than $10,000, which are lawsuits between individuals where lawyers are not involved in the process.

General civil cases, usually involving suing someone for money in disputes over things like torts, contracts, consumer disputes, or damage to property.

Family law cases such as divorce, child support, child custody, and adoptions.

Landlord/tenant cases, where a landlord is trying to evict a tenant from a rental property or a tenant that has moved out is trying to get more of his or her security deposit back from the landlord.

Probate cases are generally about caring for people and their personal affairs (like wills) and conservatorships for people who cannot care for themselves or handle their own finances.

Juvenile cases deal with children under the age of 18 and are separated into two main categories: juvenile delinquency (for minors who have broken a criminal law) and juvenile dependency (for children who have been removed from the home or care of their parents).

Civil law covers all cases that do not involve the breaking of criminal laws and is divided into four main types, i.e., torts, contract law, family law, and property law.

Torts

A tort is an act or omission that gives rise to injury or harm to another and amounts to a civil wrong for which courts impose liability. The primary aims of tort law are to provide relief to injured parties for harms caused by others, to impose liability on parties responsible for the harm, and to deter others from committing harmful acts. Torts can shift the burden of loss from the injured party to the party who is at fault or better suited to bear the burden of the loss. Typically, a party seeking redress through tort law will ask for damages in the form of monetary compensation. Less common remedies include injunctions and restitution.

Common law and state statutory law defines the boundaries of tort law. Judges, in interpreting the language of statutes, have wide latitude in determining what actions qualify as legally cognizable wrongs, which defenses may override any given claim, and the appropriate measure of damages.

Torts fall into three general categories: (1) intentional torts (*e.g.,* intentionally hitting a person); negligent torts (*e.g.,* causing an accident by failing to obey traffic rules); and strict liability torts (*e.g.,* liability for making and selling defective products. Intentional torts are wrongs that the defendant knew or should have known would result in harm through his or her actions or omissions. Negligent torts occur when the defendant's actions were unreasonably unsafe. Unlike intentional and negligent torts, strict liability torts do not depend on the degree of care that the defendant used. In strict liability cases, courts focus on whether a particular result or harm was caused by something that was inherently dangerous, like using dynamite, or housing a dangerous animal.

There are a number of specific torts, such as trespass, assault, battery, negligence, products liability, and intentional infliction of emotional distress. Other separate areas of tort law include nuisance, defamation, invasion of privacy, and a category of economic torts.

Contract Law

Contracts are promises that courts will enforce. Contract law is generally governed by the state common law (case law rather than laws created by statutes). General overall contract law is common throughout the country. Some specific court interpretations of a particular element of the contract may differ in some states. If a promise is breached, the law provides remedies to the harmed party, often in form of monetary damages, or in limited circumstances, in the form of specific performance of the promise made.

The basic elements required for the agreement to be a legally enforceable contract are: mutual assent, expressed by a valid offer and acceptance; adequate consideration; capacity; and legality. In some states, element of consideration can be satisfied by a valid substitute. Possible remedies for breach of contract include general damages, consequential damages, reliance damages, and specific performance.

Contracts arise when a duty comes into existence, because of a promise made by one of the parties. To be legally binding as a contract, a promise must be exchanged for adequate consideration. There are two different theories or definitions of consideration: Bargain-for-Exchange theory of Consideration and Benefit-Detriment theory of consideration. (1) Under the Benefit-Detriment theory, an adequate consideration exists only when a promise made to the benefit of the promisor or to the detriment of the promisee, which reasonably and fairly induces the promisor to make a promise for something else for the promisee. Promises that are purely gifts are not considered enforceable because the personal satisfaction the grantor of the promise may receive from the act of generosity is normally not considered sufficient detriment to constitute adequate consideration; (2) Under Bargain-for-Exchange theory of consideration, adequate consideration exists when a promisor makes a promise in return for something else. Here, the essential condition is that the promisor was given something specifically to induce the promise being made. The Bargain for Exchange theory is different from the Benefit-Detriment theory because the focus in bargain for exchange theory is on the parties' motive for making the promises and the parties' subjective mutual assent, while in benefit-detriment theory, the focus is on an objective legal detriment or benefit to the parties.

Family Law

Family law deals with legal issues involving family relationships, such as adoption, divorce, and child custody. States have the right to determine "reasonable formal requirements" for marriage, including age and legal capacity. Likewise, state laws govern the various rules and procedures for divorce and other family law matters.

Property Law

There are two types of property: real and personal. Most of the legal concepts and rules associated with both types of property are derived from English Common Law. Modern law has incorporated many of these concepts and rules into statutes, which define the types and rights of ownership in real and personal property.

Personal property, also referred to as movable property, is anything other than land that can be the subject of ownership, including stocks, money, notes, patents, and copyrights, and intangible property.

Real property is land and ordinarily anything erected on, growing on, or affixed to it, including buildings and crops. The term is also used to declare any rights that issue from the ownership of land. The terms real estate and real property generally refer to land. The term land, in its general usage, includes not only the face of the earth but also everything of a permanent nature over or under it, including minerals, oil, and gases.

The difference between real property and personal property is ordinarily easily recognizable. The character of the property, however, can be altered. Property that is initially personal in nature becomes part of realty by being annexed to it, such as when rails are made into a fence on land.

In certain cases the intention or agreement of the parties determines whether property that is annexed retains its character as personal property. A landlord and tenant might agree that the new lighting fixture the tenant installs remains the tenant's property after the expiration of the lease.

Personal property can be divided into two major categories: tangible and intangible. Tangible property includes such items as animals, merchandise, and jewelry. Intangible property includes such rights as stock, bonds, patents, and copyrights.

Possession is a property interest under which an individual to the exclusion of all others is able to exercise power over something. It is a basic property right that entitles the possessor to continue peaceful possession against everyone else except someone with a superior right. It also gives the possessor the right to recover personal property (often called chattel) that has been wrongfully taken, and the right to recover damages against wrongdoers.

To have possession, an individual must have a degree of actual control over the object, coupled with an intent to possess the object and exclude others from possessing it. The law recognizes two types of possession: actual and constructive.

Actual possession exists when an individual knowingly has direct physical control over an object at a given time, like a piece of jewelry. Constructive possession is the power and intent of an individual to control a particular item, even though it is not physically in that person's control. An individual who has the key to a bank safe-deposit box containing a piece of jewelry that she owns is said to be in constructive possession of the jewelry.

Property may be further classified as either private or public. Private property is that which belongs to one or more persons. Public property is owned by a country, state, or political subdivision, such as a Municipal Corporation or a school district.

Chapter 10

TERRITORIAL AND ENVIRONMENTAL CONFLICTS

When our ancestors were hunter-gatherers, they were at the mercy of their environment. If the environment was not suitable, their only option was to move to a more hospitable territory. Territorial issues were local and insignificant. Early humans had to find their own food. A large part of each day was spent gathering plants and hunting or scavenging animals. The earliest record of recognizably modern humans appear in the fossil record at Omo Kibish in Ethiopia, around 200,000 years ago. According to the genetic and paleontological record, many modern humans left Africa in significant numbers between 60,000 and 70,000 years ago.

Human-caused environmental issues became significant about 12,000 years ago, when humans learned how to control the growth and breeding of certain plants and animals. This discovery led to farming and herding animals, activities that transformed Earth's natural landscapes. first locally, then globally. As humans invested more time in producing food, they settled down. Villages became towns, and towns became cities. With more food available, the human population began to increase dramatically. Our species has been so successful that it has inadvertently created a turning point in the history of life on Earth. Throughout history, people and societies have adjusted to changes in climate with varying degrees of success. Earth's climate has been relatively stable for the past 12,000 years and this stability has been crucial for the development of modern civilization and life as we know it. Human actions are now destroying habitats, endangering the lives of future generations, and threatening life on our planet.

The territorial issues were much less complicated when the Earth had fewer human inhabitants. Population growth has had a dramatic impact on territorial issues. Some theorize that territoriality is a genetically fixed form of behavior, which has evolved in most species, including our own. Others point to evidence indicating a lack of rigid territoriality in many contemporary hunting and gathering groups has been viewed as supporting the argument that humans are not by nature territorial.

Most anthropologists who have studied the issue opine that a territorial system occurs under conditions of high density and predictability of critical resources. If a resource is so abundant that its availability or rate of capture is not limited to a population, then there is no benefit to be gained by its defenses and territoriality is not expected to occur. With relatively scarce but still predictable resources, large home ranges with some degree of overlap would be expected. With unpredictability of resources, a territorial tie to a fixed area is not economically defendable, and the degree of movement in foraging over a large area must increase (nomadism). Depending on the average density of the resources within a patch, unpredictable resources are most efficiently exploited by communal sharing of information (high average density) or by a high amount of dispersion (low average density). This simplified correlation between resource distributions and foraging strategy provides a general framework for explaining the occurrence (or nonoccurrence) of territoriality.

Due to the human population, territorial and environmental conflicts have now become the most difficult to resolve. This book provides only a brief introduction to the issues and problems we face regarding territorial and environmental conflicts.

Remember, these conflicts, like all conflicts, are resolved most effectively by meeting the needs of the parties.

TERRITORIAL CONFLICTS

Territorial conflicts on a global scale are a recent and growing problem because of climate change and limited resources.[28]

A territorial conflict may be defined as a disagreement over the possession and/or control of land between two or more territorial entities. Territorial disputes are often related to the possession of natural resources such as rivers, fertile farmland, mineral, or oil resources; although, the disputes can also be driven by culture, religion, and ethnic nationalism.

Territorial disputes may be caused by vague and unclear language in a treaty that established the original boundary. These disputes are a major cause of wars and terrorism as states try to assert their sovereignty over a territory through invasion, and non-state entities try to influence the actions of politicians through terrorism. International law does not support the use of force by one state to annex the territory of another state. The United Nations Charter states in part: "All Members shall refrain in their international relations from the threat or use of force against the territorial integrity or political independence of any state, or in any other manner inconsistent with the Purposes of the United Nations."

Territorial disputes occur when official representatives of one country make explicit statements claiming sovereignty over a specific piece of territory that is claimed or administered by another country. These disputes lead to militarized conflict more frequently than other types of diplomatic disputes involving maritime, river, identity, economic, cultural, or natural resources. A majority of interstate wars have been fought between countries embroiled in one or more territorial disputes. Countries who share contiguous borders are more likely to fight wars with each other than non-contiguous states, especially if they have disagreements over specific pieces of territory. Territory valued because of natural resources, religious sites, or historical homeland claims, generates more violence. Wars can spread across geographic boundaries. Territorial disputes can be resolved successfully with peaceful conflict management tools such as arbitration and adjudication through international courts. State borders have become more difficult to violate in recent decades because of the emergence of a norm of territorial integrity. The general decline in territorial conquest stems in part from increasing economic interdependence among countries. While disputes over traditional land borders have decreased over time, other types of territorial disputes have become more prevalent, such as competition over maritime resources in areas around islands or homeland areas.

Border disputes are notoriously difficult to resolve. International law does not contain a clear, prioritized set of norms—established through international conventions or jurisprudence—for determining national sovereignty over territory with competing factual claims (e.g., based on cultural, ethnic, historical, religious, and other political, economic, and social factors). Governments are unwilling to "lose" boundary disputes since they might suffer political consequences as well as loss to national interests. Border disputes often flare up after they become linked with important economic or social interests. Disputed territories may contain important natural resources, such as hydrocarbon, mineral reserves, or water sources; provide access to the sea or shared terrestrial resources, such as grazing areas; or be a strategic location. Such areas may be subject to irredentist claims based on historical or cultural factors or demands for self-determination by their inhabitants. Competition for contested or shared resources has become more intense in recent years due to economic developments, such as higher commodity prices, and environmental changes, such as overutilization of agricultural land, overgrazing, and desertification, as well as regional and global climate change. It is unlikely that increasing stresses among states resulting from these factors can be successfully resolved using traditional legal methods, particularly adjudication.

The same factors that make it difficult for parties involved in a border dispute to reach agreement often also make them unwilling to submit their dispute to international adjudication or arbitration. Such proceedings tend to focus on issues of sovereignty, and the parties to a dispute may fear losing their claims or being forced to undertake unpleasant concessions. In many cases judicial or arbitral awards of territory have not been implemented by the losing side. Two distinctions between approaches to the resolution of border disputes form the basis for a matrix of approaches.

The first distinction is between binding and nonbinding procedures, with the former encompassing adjudication and arbitration and the latter including "good offices" or facilitation. Utilizing the services of international leaders or eminent persons for conciliation and mediation. Mediation is distinguished from arbitration in that the resulting award must be accepted by the parties to the dispute. Nonbinding international means of resolving disputes allow for participation of the parties throughout the process of dispute resolution.

The second distinction is between approaches based primarily on law and those that permit the dispute resolution agent or panel to explore alternative approaches based on equity and natural justice. Depending on their terms of reference, arbitrators may be granted the power to make an award on this basis. Even the International Court of Justice, under its statute, may decide cases ex aequo et bono (i.e., based on equity and welfare) at the request of the parties. Nevertheless, parties to a territorial dispute may be unwilling to submit their competing claims to arbitration or adjudication. The International Court of Justice has limited capacity to resolve factual issues related to equity.

International adjudicative and arbitral bodies usually emphasize the legal determinants of a territorial dispute. They can consider equitable factors, either directly at the request of the parties, or in order to apply the relevant law most reasonably and fairly under the circumstances.

Other approaches to territorial disputes, including conciliation and other forms of facilitation by third parties, may be more attractive, although they too may be resisted by states with weak claims but strong political interests. Conciliators, facilitators, and mediators have greater flexibility to design outcomes that are oriented primarily toward reaching a conclusion that might be satisfactory to both sides in a boundary dispute. What is often needed to resolve a territorial conflict is to devise a "no lose" (non–zero sum) solution. It is difficult for judges and arbitrators to achieve such a result, since they are usually required to take a legalistic approach, remaining strictly within the terms of the submitted case (in adjudications) or mandate of the parties (arbitrations). Conciliators and other facilitators have the ability to be more responsive, yet may still have difficulty identifying workable approaches.

The three primary legal factors establishing sovereignty over territory are treaties, recognized historical boundaries, and evidence of effective control. The prominence of territorial conflicts derives from their nature, magnitude, and intensifying factors. Ethnic conflict and third-party involvement are the most important intensifying factors. The likelihood of violent conflict results from how the antagonists view territory. War is likely to erupt when an ethnic minority demands sovereignty over its territory, but the state views its territory as indivisible. Violence is most likely to occur when the settlement pattern of the minority makes it the majority in particular regions. Contests over territory by population groups are likely to lead to enduring internal rivalries that lead to protracted and violent conflict. A military victory by one side, an intense period of fighting, or a lengthy period of peace reduce the chances for a recurrence of violence.

States are generally willing to pursue reasonable, functionalist approaches to interstate conflicts over territory, including cooperative and facilitated methods of dispute resolution. Many border issues remain unresolved for long periods, during which the absence of the important international institution of defined and recognized borders tends to retard national development due to adverse effects on investment and trade. Cooperative regulation of shared resources, such as fresh water, and terrestrial commons, in areas where human activities occur, including pastoral and agricultural uses, intermingle without definite entitlements, is a peaceful method of resolving some territorial conflicts.

Except where arbitration or adjudication has previously been agreed to, the most flexible approaches to the resolution of border disputes combine elements of the nonbinding methods and equitable approaches to problem solving. Focusing on the practical elements of a territorial dispute, including the resources and other issues at stake, as well as how to address them in a way that is acceptable to the parties while avoiding legal issues related to sovereignty can be a successful strategy. Many cooperative approaches to resource and border issues have been implemented by states on an agreed basis or as a result of dispute resolution assistance.

Such approaches include: joint management and exploitation of contested or shared resources, including hydrocarbon reserves or fishery stocks; joint regulation, or cooperative sharing, of contested and/or shared resources, such as grazing rights or water supplies; negotiated access to the sea for landlocked states or through territorial waters for neighboring states; agreed rights of transit for states with noncontiguous territories; and/or commitments to respect the cultural, historical, or social heritage, as well as political autonomy of national minorities.

ENVIRONMENTAL CONFLICTS

The environment is the circumstances, objects, or conditions which surround us. The complex of physical, chemical, and biotic factors such as climate, soil, and living things, that act upon an organism or an ecological community and ultimately determine its form and survival.

The effect that humans have on the environment is becoming more evident. Human actions are destroying habitats and endangering the lives of future generations. Our environment is changing rapidly. These major environmental challenges are:

Overpopulation: The number of inhabitants on the planet leads to most of the other environmental problems.

Air Pollution: Air that is essential for life is being contaminated by gases and poisons discharged by businesses, manufacturing plants, mining, animal agriculture, and transportation. This causes acid rain that adversely affects aquatic ecosystems, plants, and animals. Excess use of nitrogen can disrupt ecosystems, primarily through overstimulation of plant and algae growth, which damages the marine population.

Water Pollution: Waste from industrial, human, and agricultural activities pollute the water that is used by humans, animals, and plants.

Soil and Land Pollution: Human activities like mining, littering, deforestation, industrial, construction, and agricultural activities using man-made chemicals cause degradation of the earth's surface, which in turn has an adverse effect on plant and animal life. Woodlands create oxygen, which help manage temperature and precipitation. Wooded areas are being lost on a regular basis because people need homes, food, and materials. Deforestation results in loss of habitat for many species, placing many at risk and leading to large-scale extinction.

Ocean Problems: Acid rain has increased ocean acidification. Overfishing depletes fish stocks. Marine debris, any human-made solid material that is disposed of or abandoned on beaches, leads to the ocean. Marine debris, including plastics, paper, wood, metal and other manufactured materials is found on beaches worldwide and at all depths of the ocean. Marine life mistake floating trash for food; if ingested, it can choke them or block their digestive systems. Large debris, such as old fishing gear and nets, can kill animals by strangulation or prevent them from performing vital activities such as swimming or diving. Plastic trash smaller than 5mm (microplastic) poses an additional threat because it adsorbs toxic chemicals, including DDT and PCBs, which can cause cancers, weaken the immune system, and make animals more susceptible to diseases. Ocean acidification, overfishing, and marine debris cause a polluted and unbalanced ocean, severely affecting natural ecosystems in the process. It also has negative effects on coastal communities that rely on fishing and tourism to support their economies.

Waste: Even the proper disposal of waste can create substantial problems. Cleaning up litter is very expensive. Landfills are huge garbage dumps that make the city look ugly and produce toxic gases that are fatal to plant and animal life. Landfills are generated due to large amount of waste that is generated by households, industries, and healthcare centers. Medical waste is a bio-hazard. The waste can include needles, syringes, gloves, tubes, blades, blood, and body parts.

Loss of Biodiversity: Continued human activities and expansion has led to lowered biodiversity. Deforestation, overpopulation, pollution, and global warming cause habitat loss. A lack of biodiversity means that future generations will have to deal with an increase in the vulnerability of plants and animals, which will lead to less food and fewer sources of fresh water. A decrease in biodiversity will have a pronounced impact on climate change, pollution, and on ecosystems.

Ozone Layer Depletion: Ozone depletion is caused by the release of chemicals, primarily chlorine and bromide, into the atmosphere. A single atom of either has the potential to destroy thousands of ozone molecules before leaving the stratosphere. Ozone depletion results in more ultraviolet B-rays reaching the Earth's surface. This radiation has been linked to skin cancer and eye disease, and affects plant life on land and sea.

Urban Sprawl: The continued expansion of urban areas into traditionally rural areas has increased air and water pollution.

Natural Resource Depletion: Non-renewable resources are limited. The depletion of these resources will lead to an energy crisis. Chemicals emitted by many natural resources are strong contributors to climate change.

Climate Change: The majority of the issues previously listed contributes to global warming and climate change. Statistics created by NASA state that global temperatures have risen by 1.7 degrees Fahrenheit since 1880, which reduces the Arctic ice. Climate change will impact deforestation, water supplies, oceans, habitation, seasons, and ecosystems. Climate change creates severe weather patterns: droughts; heavy downpours; flooding; increase in intensity, frequency, and duration of the strongest storms (Category 4 and 5); increase in frequency and intensity of winter storms; increase intensity and frequency of tornadoes, hail, and damaging thunderstorm winds; and increase in frequency and intensity of heat waves of abnormally hot weather lasting days to weeks.

Nuclear Issues: Radioactive waste contains radioactive substance and is a by-product of nuclear power generation. Radioactive waste is extremely toxic and can have devastating effects on the lives of the people living nearby, if not disposed of properly. Radioactive waste is harmful for humans, plants, animals, and the surrounding environment. The proliferation of nuclear weapons is an existential threat to not only life on Earth but to the Earth itself.

Global warming induced by greenhouse gases emitted by human activities can cause conflicts in at least two ways:

First, erratic, unfavorable weather and climate could affect migration. In recent years refugees, the neediest subcategory of migrants, have numbered around 10 million annually. Studies attribute rather few refugees directly and solely due to environmental disasters and shortages of resources, but some scientists warn of the growing potential for these factors to increase human migration.

Second, inequitable or apparently inequitable means to reduce carbon emissions, especially from coal and oil could occur. Conflict might arise between the rich, developed countries and the poorer ones.

We live in an interdependent world. No longer can isolated communities afford to think of one another as fundamentally separate.

The Covid-19 pandemic is a drastic illustration of the interconnection of all life on earth. Today, whatever happens in one region eventually affects many other areas. The United Nations Environment Programme coordinates the organization's environmental activities and assists developing countries in implementing environmentally sound policies and practices. According to the World Health Organization (WHO) climate change is impacting human lives and health. All populations will be affected by climate change. By the late 21st century, climate change is likely to increase the frequency and intensity of drought on a regional and global scale. Extreme weather is occurring much more frequently with devastating results. Floods are increasing in frequency and intensity, and the frequency and intensity of extreme precipitation will continue to increase throughout the current century. Humans have created these environmental problems and only humans can solve them. They will not solve themselves.

Part Three

SOLUTIONS TO CONFLICTS

"One of the things I learned when I was negotiating was that until I changed myself, I could not change others."

—Nelson Rolihlahla Mandela

Chapter 11

METHODS FOR RESOLVING CONFLICTS

C onstructive conflict resolution is the process where people with different positions on issues arrive at mutually acceptable solutions through collaborative problem solving. Satisfying the needs of the parties is at the heart of successful conflict resolution. The two parts to any conflict resolution are: (1) The substance of the conflict—what are the issues; (2) The process—what methods will be used.

There are many ways to resolve conflicts. Direct negotiation between the parties is usually the easiest, quickest, and most efficient method; however, direct negotiations are not always successful.

When direct negotiations are not successful, many organizations have a roster of neutrals providing alternative dispute resolution services for individuals and organizations. Community mediation provides low-cost, community-based services. It provides a forum for dispute resolution at the earliest stage of conflicts and an alternative to the judicial system at any stage of a conflict. Community mediation offers constructive processes for resolving differences and conflicts between individuals, groups, and organizations. It is an alternative to avoidance, destructive confrontation, prolonged litigation, or violence. It gives people in conflict an opportunity to take responsibility for the resolution of their dispute and control of the outcome. Community mediation is designed to preserve individual interests while strengthening relationships and building connections between people and groups.

The National Association for Community Mediation (NAFCM) supports the maintenance and growth of community-based mediation programs and processes, providing people in conflict an opportunity to resolve their conflicts constructively. You can find a community mediation center near you by going on the NAFCM website and clicking on their Member Locater.[29]

One innovative organization, The Arbinger Institute, delivers training, consulting, coaching, and digital tools to help individuals and organizations change mindset, transform culture, accelerate collaboration, resolve conflict, and sustainably improve results. Their theory is that self-deceptive attitudes are the ethical, affective, and cognitive bases of all types of human unhappiness. These attitudes include despising what we find ourselves repeatedly doing; feeling overcome by, and helpless in the face of, abuse; and suffering from enmity, bitterness, vengeance, or fear. Every emotion or mood in which we feel provoked, used, victimized, disturbed, or in some manner overcome prevents us from reaching our goals. Such attitudes express the conflictedness, defensiveness, anxiety, or compulsivity, which lies at the heart of the misery suffered by those who hold such attitudes. The root cause of most organizational problems is that employees often unknowingly work with an inward mindset, focusing on their own needs, challenges, and objectives without an awareness of their impact on others. Organizations can only resolve internal problems and achieve breakthrough results by maximizing the extent to which their employees work with an outward mindset, taking into account their impact on others and focusing on the needs of the entire organization. With an outward mindset, organizations are far better prepared to address their challenges and achieve superior results. The Arbinger Institute helps individuals, teams, and organizations move from the default self-focus of an inward mindset to the results-focus of an outward mindset. Through training, coaching, consulting, and a suite of implementation tools, they enable organizations and their people to achieve results that are only possible with an outward mindset.[30]

The Internet is dramatically changing how we interact with one another. It has brought us Online Mediation Techniques and E-Mediation that can be a completely automated online dispute resolution system with no interaction from a third party.

The use of reliable Big Data will replace guesses, conventional wisdom, and shoddy correlations with what actually works. Big Data is information that will play a more significant role in conflict resolution. The more information you have, the more you understand the nature of hidden biases, the more likely you will find a solution that will satisfy the needs of the parties. To guard against the dangers of always using Big Data for making decisions, the following protections should be used:

First is openness: making available the data and algorithm underlying the prediction that affects an individual.

Second is certification: having the algorithm certified for certain sensitive uses by an expert third party as sound and valid.

Third is disprovability: specifying concrete ways that people can disprove a prediction about themselves.[31]

In addition to Big Data, using algorithms will be an effective method for resolving conflicts in the future. One innovative company, iCan Systems Inc., developed automated decision systems that support collaborative formal negotiations between multiple decision makers with conflicting objectives. Eight intelligent algorithms implemented at a secure neutral site on the Internet power a suite of Smartsettle platforms. The Smartsettle approach turns adversaries into collaborators and guides them to agreement more quickly, efficiently, and cost-effectively than possible by any other means. The algorithms typically operate in this order:

Single Negotiating FrameworkSM (SNF) establishes the context for the negotiations and any conditions that will apply once agreement has been reached.

Comprehensive Preference AnalysisSM (CPA) enables the system to learn the underlying priorities and interests of the parties.

Visual Blind BiddingSM (VBB) enables the parties to submit both open and secret offers in a way that helps parties reach agreement quickly.

Reward Early EffortSM (REE) distributes the overlap in a way that discourages holding back and motivates collaboration.

Automatic Deal-CloserSM (ADC) resolves a small gap impasse in a more intelligent and fair way than the traditional split the difference.

Fairness Enhancing NormalizationSM (FEN) adjusts satisfaction scales in order to make fair comparisons among all the parties.

Maximize the Minimum GainSM (MMG) analyses comprehensive preferences to uncover and fairly distribute hidden value after a Baseline agreement has been reached.

Expert Neutral Deal-CloserSM (END) integrates neutral intervenors in a safe way, but only as a last resort in order to guarantee a collaborative outcome.

iCan has built two platforms to support a wide range of conflict types. Smartsettle ONE is used when the conflict can easily be reduced to two parties and one issue, such as a financial settlement. For conflicts that involve more than one issue and multiple parties, Smartsettle has a more advanced system called Infinity that can model the problem, manage preference information, and quickly optimize solutions. Smartsettle Infinity supports an unlimited number of quantitative or qualitative issues between any number of parties in any combination of real-time and asynchronous negotiations, whether face-to-face or over great distances, anywhere on Earth.[32]

Private mediation is another method available to the parties. The mediator facilitates the resolution of the parties' disputes by supervising the exchange of information and the bargaining process. The mediator helps the parties find common ground and deal with unrealistic expectations. The mediator may also offer creative solutions and assist in drafting a final settlement. The role of the mediator is to interpret concerns, relay information between the parties, frame issues, and define the problems.

There are three basic mediation styles: (1) Facilitative; (2) Evaluative; (3) Transformative. Depending on the conflict, one style may be more effective than another style. Sometimes, all three styles may be used in a single mediation, depending on the parties, the mediator, and the issue or issues that need to be resolved.

Facilitative mediation seeks to have the parties reach an agreement based on the underlying needs and interests of the parties. The mediator will ask questions to validate and normalize parties' points of view; search for interests underneath the positions taken by parties; and assist the parties in finding and analyzing options for resolution. The facilitative mediator does not make recommendations to the parties, give advice or render an opinion as to the outcome of the case, or predict what a court would do in the case. The mediator is in charge of the process, while the parties are in charge of the outcome. The mediator will predominantly hold joint sessions with all parties present so that the parties can hear each other's points of view, but will hold private sessions or caucuses regularly to learn more about their underlying interests or needs and help create mutually satisfactory options.

Evaluative mediation is a process modeled on settlement conferences held by judges. An evaluative mediator assists the parties in reaching resolution by pointing out the weaknesses of their cases, and predicting what a judge or jury might do. An evaluative mediator might make formal or informal recommendations to the parties. Evaluative mediators are concerned with the legal rights of the parties rather than their needs and interests. They meet most often in separate meetings with the parties and their attorneys, practicing "shuttle diplomacy." They help the parties and attorneys evaluate their legal position and the costs against the benefits of pursuing a legal resolution rather than settling in mediation. The evaluative mediator structures the process, and directly influences the outcome of mediation. The parties are most often present in the mediation, but the mediator may meet separately with the attorneys and with the parties and their attorneys. There is an assumption in evaluative mediation that the mediator has substantive expertise or legal expertise in the substantive of the dispute. Most evaluative mediators, because of the connection between evaluative mediation and the courts and because of their comfort level with settlement conferences, are attorneys.

Transformative mediation is based on the values of "empowerment" of each of the parties as much as possible, and "recognition" by each of the parties of the other parties' needs, interests, values, and points of view. The potential for transformative mediation is that any or all parties or their relationships may be transformed during the mediation. Transformative mediators meet with parties together, since only they can give each other "recognition." In transformative mediation, the parties structure both the process and the outcome of mediation, and the mediator follows their lead.

There are other more formal methods of resolving disputes such as med-arb or arb-med. In med-arb, a mediation-arbitration hybrid, parties first reach agreement on the terms of the process itself. Unlike most mediations, the parties typically agree in writing that the outcome of the process will be binding. Next, they attempt to negotiate a resolution to their dispute with the help of a mediator. If the mediation ends in an impasse, or if issues remain unresolved, the process is not over. At this point, parties can move on to arbitration. The mediator can assume the role of arbitrator (if qualified to do so) and render a binding decision, either on the case as a whole or on the unresolved issues. Alternatively, an arbitrator can take over the case after consulting with the mediator.

In arb-med, another type of mediation, a trained, neutral third party hears disputants' evidence and testimony in an arbitration; writes an award but keeps it from the parties; attempts to mediate the parties' dispute; and unseals and issues the previously determined binding award if the parties fail to reach agreement. The process removes the concern in med-arb about the misuse of confidential information, but keeps the pressure on parties to reach an agreement. The arbitrator/mediator cannot change the previous award based on new insights gained during the mediation.

THE BETTER WAY

There is little we can do alone; however together, there is little we cannot do. We have the ability to shape our world and solve problems when they occur. Most forms of life survive only if they can adapt to their environment. We have the ability to adapt our environment to our needs. Resolving conflicts through war and violence is not inevitable but can lead to the destruction of the human race.

Empathy is an emotional skill that can help resolve conflicts that may appear intractable. Empathy is first and foremost an emotional skill. There are six essential aspects of empathy:

1. **Emotion Contagion**: Sense that an emotion is occurring in another or that an emotion is expected from you.

2. **Empathetic Accuracy**: Accurately identify and understand emotional states, thoughts, and intentions in yourself and others.

3. **Emotion Regulation**: Develop the ability to understand, regulate, and work with your own emotions.

4. **Perspective Taking**: Put yourself in the place of others, see things through their eyes, and accurately sense what they may be feeling and thinking so that you can understand what they might want or need.

5. **Concern for Others**: Feel emotions with others, accurately identify those emotions, regulate them in yourself, and take the perspective of others. Your concern will help you engage with them in a way that displays your care and compassion.

6. Perspective Engagement: Make decisions based on your empathy and respond in a way that works for others.

Emotions help you learn, decide, behave, interact, and relate to yourself and others. Your emotional awareness is a key aspect of your capacity to accurately identify and work with the emotions, thoughts, and intentions of others. Emotions are your empathetic entrée into understanding yourself and others more deeply. A list of sixteen emotional categories will give you a working vocabulary and set of tools to understand emotions emphatically, as nuanced and reliable action-requiring responses to very specific stimuli:

ANGER: Anger arises to address challenges to your positions, ideas, interpersonal boundaries, or self-image. The task is to restore your interpersonal boundaries without violating the boundaries of others. Questions: What must be protected? What must be restored?

APATHY AND BOREDOM: Apathy or boredom is a protective mask for anger and arises in situations when you cannot or probably should not express your anger openly. Questions: What is being avoided? What must be made conscious?

GUILT AND SHAME: Shame arises to moderate your behavior and ensure that you do not hurt, embarrass, or dehumanize yourself or others. Questions: Who has been hurt? What must be made right?

HATRED: Hatred is a very powerful emotion that arises when there are things you cannot accept in yourself and demonize in others. Questions: What is unacceptable? What must be done?

FEAR: Fear arises to orient you to change, novelty, or possible hazards, and focuses on the present moment and your immediate surroundings. Question: What action should be taken?

WORRY AND ANXIETY: Worry and anxiety arise to help you organize, plan for, and complete your tasks. Questions: What triggered this feeling? What really needs to get done?

CONFUSION: Confusion is a mask for fear and anxiety, and it arises when you are overwhelmed by change, novelty, or too many tasks. Questions: What is my intention? What action should be taken?

JEALOUSY: Jealousy arises in response to challenges that may destabilize your connection to love, mate retention, or loyalty, and can come from external sources, from an internal lack of self-worth, or both. Questions: What has been betrayed? What must be healed and restored?

ENVY: Envy is a response to challenges that may destabilize your connection to material security, resources, or recognition, and can come from external sources, internal lack of self-worth, or both. Questions: What has been betrayed? What must be made right?

PANIC AND TERROR: Panic and terror arises when your life is directly and immediately threatened, and you can fight, flee, or freeze. During the emergency the best response is to listen to your body. Do not think; just react to your instincts. Questions (for post-traumatic stress disorder)—What has been frozen in time? What healing action must be taken?

SADNESS: Sadness arises when it is time to let go of something that is not working. Questions: What must be released? What must be rejuvenated?

GRIEF: Grief arises when something has been irretrievably lost or when someone has died. Questions: What must be mourned? What must be released completely?

SITUATIONAL DEPRESSION: Situational depression arises when some aspect of your life is already unworkable or dysfunctional. Questions: Where has my energy gone? Why was it sent away?

HAPPINESS: Happiness arises to help you look forward to the future with hope and delight.

CONTENTMENT: Contentment arises to help you look toward yourself with pride and satisfaction.

JOY: Joy arises when you feel a blissful sense of expansiveness and connection to others, to ideas, or to experiences.

When you know what emotions you are dealing with, it is much easier to communicate with people and be truly empathic. Emotions are always true because they are always responding to emotionally evocative stimuli; however if the stimuli are not valid, they may not be right. If you act on an emotion evoked by stimuli that are not valid, you might do something misguided or injurious. For example, you might think your neighbor is intentionally being noisy to annoy you, and you yell. It may turn out that the neighbor was yelling for another reason. When dealing with an emotionally evocative stimulus, identify the emotion and feeling it invokes, act on the information the emotion provides, or decide not to act because the stimulus is invalid.

In dealing with feelings and attitude, Professor Albert Mehrabian of UCLA identified three aspects of face-to-face communication: (1) body language, (2) voice tonality, and (3) words spoken. He studied how people derive meaning when a speaker says one thing but means another. If the speaker sends a mixed message, the listener will rely on cues to determine true meaning: 55% of impact is determined by body language, i.e., postures, gestures, and eye contact; 38% by the tone of voice; and 7% by the content or the words spoken.

Each of us is motivated to act to satisfy a need. We have physiological needs such as air, water, food, shelter, and sleep, and we have psychological or emotional needs that motivate us to take action. A conflict is created when our needs are not satisfied. Each of us has hidden biases that may make it difficult to understand our own needs and the needs of others. The most effective resolution of any conflict is the one that best satisfies the needs of all the parties.

Use these principles when resolving conflicts:

1. Know the difference between facts and opinions;

2. Understand your filtering system;

3. What you know and what you do not know. You know the words spoken and their impact on you, but you do not know the speaker's intent;

4. People are egocentric; it is difficult to change a person's perception or opinion;

5. There are three parts to verbal communication: (a) The words spoken; (b) the body language; (c) the tone of voice;

6. Listen and strive to understand the speaker's point of view. Be sure the speaker understands your point of view. Listen without making judgments or assumptions;

7. Understand the conscious, subconscious, and unconscious levels of the mind; be aware of biases;

8. There may be a hidden, unspoken message that the speaker may not be aware of;

9. Conflicts arise from past events; solutions are made in the present;

10. Both parties must have a genuine interest in resolving the conflict.

The parties seeking to resolve any conflict must have a common understanding of the disputed issues. Without that common understanding, the parties will be unable to resolve their conflict.

If one of the parties does not want to find a resolution, the party who wants a resolution must act to change the recalcitrant party's attitude or some other event will have to occur.

Japan's refusal to surrender to the United States in World War II is a drastic example of one's failure to find a solution. Only after the United States dropped two atomic bombs on Hiroshima and Nagasaki killing over 100,000 people, causing millions of dollars in destruction of property, and injuring over a million people, did the United States and Japan work out a resolution that ended the war.

If a conflict has a legal basis, you can resort to the courts for resolution; however, many conflicts have no legal basis, and the court option is not available. Even if a court action is available, it may not be a viable option for legal based conflicts because of the time, the expense, and the uncertainty of the outcome.

FILTERING INFORMATION

Each person has a unique mental filtering system, which provides a perspective on the world. This system consists of our genetic makeup and personality (nature) and is expanded by our life experiences (nurture). We grow up in families, communities, and within a geographic location that influences our value system and opinions. While many of these values and opinions are appropriate, our filtering system may include conscious and subconscious biases and prejudices.

Our filtering system is so ingrained that we think everyone sees the world as we do. This is not the case. Many of our beliefs are so deeply held that we think of them as facts rather than opinions. Our opinions may have no rational basis. Since our beliefs are so ingrained, we tend to look for information that confirms this information. If we do encounter a person or experience that challenges our belief system, we view that person or experience as an anomaly rather than rethink this aspect of our belief system.

Neuro-Linguistic Programming describes the fundamental dynamics between mind (neuro) and language (linguistic) and how their interplay affects our body and behavior (programming). Neuro-Linguistic Programming encompasses the three most influential components involved in producing human experience: *neurology, language,* and *programming.* The neurological system regulates how our bodies function; language determines how we interface and communicate with other people; and our programming determines the kinds of models of the world we create. When you are in negotiations working to resolve any conflict, understanding Neuro-Linguistic Programming can be helpful.

As human beings, we never know reality. We only know our perceptions of reality. We experience and respond to the world primarily through our sensory representational systems. It is not realty, but rather our 'neuro-linguistic' maps of reality that determine how we behave and give those behaviors meaning. It is generally not reality that limits us or empowers us, but rather our map of reality.

Systemic processes take place within and between human beings and their environment. Our bodies, our societies, and our universe form an ecology of complex systems and sub-systems all of which interact with and mutually influence each other. It is not possible to completely isolate any part of the system. Such systems are based on certain 'self-organizing' principles and naturally seek optimal states of balance or homeostasis.

You need to distinguish between the reality you create internally and that which you receive externally through your senses. Emotions are action-requiring neurological programs. Decision-making is the emotional process of attaching value and meaning to data.

We are programmed to believe that when someone, particularly one in authority, tells us something is wrong with us, it must be true. Do not react to negative comments. Do not take it personally. Focus on how to resolve the conflict in a way that will meet both your needs and the needs of the person or persons you are in conflict with.

There are three steps to being an effective negotiator: (1) know the outcome you want; (2) be flexible in your behavior; (3) have enough sensory experience to know when you get the responses you want.

If you tell a child, "Don't fall down," in order to understand what you said, he has to access some representation of "falling down." That internal representation will usually result in the behavior that the parent is trying to prevent. If you give positive instructions like, "Be careful, pay attention, and move slowly," the child will access representations that will help him cope with the situation.

The response you get is the meaning of your communication to the listener. If you are not getting the result you want, change what you are doing. You have to clearly distinguish between outside influences, and how you are interpreting that at the unconscious level and contributing to it by your own internal state.

When someone uses a word like guilt or depression or grief, you need to understand what the internal process is for that person. If they make themselves feel guilty with eidetic images, you can have them change the image to constructed ones. If the responses are not the ones you want, what you are doing is not working. If you do not change your behavior, the same response is likely to occur again. If you change your behavior, something else may happen. Einstein is often credited with saying, "The definition of insanity is doing the same thing over and over again, but expecting different results."

The halo effect is a cognitive bias that may cause us to believe that our perspective is the correct one. People that agree with us are right. The demonizing effect will cause us to believe that those who disagree with us are not only wrong, but morally bad. We attribute positive traits to people who agree with us and negative traits to people who disagree with us.

Although people generally act in their own self-interest, they may not be aware of this due to a perceptual bias. People act in ways they perceive is in their own best interests, although it may not be in their best interests. The perceptual bias may cause them to perceive something as beneficial, when it is actually harmful.

Although smoking is in fact harmful, many people perceive it as pleasurable. People continue to smoke because they are addicted, they underestimate the risk, or because they perceive the pleasure of smoking outweighs the risks.

DISTINGUISHING FACT FROM OPINION

Opinions may be rational or irrational, sound or unsound, and are changeable. It is essential to distinguish between facts and opinions. Facts never change; however, opinions can change. Everyone is entitled to an opinion. No one is entitled to his or her own version of the facts. A fact is something that is always true and can be tested or proved. An opinion is someone's view or perspective about a subject. Arguments can contain both facts and opinions. You need to distinguish facts from opinions in order to make a sound judgment about the information you are receiving.

A statement of fact expresses only what happened, or what can be proven as true by objective criteria. A statement of opinion expresses an attitude, a view, a judgment, or a conclusion that may be true or false. To determine whether a statement is a fact or an opinion, you can use the five questions designed by Darrell Huff in *How to lie with statistics:*[33] (1) Who Says So? (2) How Does He Know? (3) What's Missing? (4) Did Somebody Change the Subject? (5) Does It Make Sense?

FUNDAMENTALS OF CONFLICT RESOLUTION

Conflicts are resolved when the parties have a genuine interest in finding a solution. All necessary parties (sometimes referred to as stakeholders) must be involved in the negotiations. The needs of the parties have to be sufficiently satisfied. Sometimes the parties do not fully understand their own needs; and sometimes their needs change during the course of negotiations. There is generally more than one option that will satisfy the needs of the parties. Always look for the option that will best satisfy the needs of the parties.

The method used to resolve a conflict depends on the nature of the conflict. Simple conflicts, like deciding what to eat, may be easy to resolve. Other conflicts, like the conflict in the Middle East, are extremely difficult to resolve. The method you use to decide what to eat will not be the same methods you would use to resolve the conflict in the Middle East.

All conflicts are resolvable if the parties have a genuine interest in finding an effective solution.

The following steps will be useful for resolving many conflicts:

First, identify the nature of the conflict. What are the parties trying to accomplish? What are the issues that need resolution? A conflict is created in the past. The solution to that conflict is created in the future.

Second, create a positive environment. Have a positive attitude as you approach issues honestly and openly. Chose a time that is best for all parties involved, i.e., when no one is feeling pressed to move on or pressured in other ways. Pick a place where all parties feel comfortable. Remember that positive conflict resolution benefits both parties. Working together helps solve conflicts. Keep in mind the long-term relationship. Positive conflict resolution will improve that relationship.

Third, treat the conflict as a joint problem. A difference of opinion provides an opportunity to work together to find a workable solution. Do not attack each other. Separate the problem from the people. Think of shared needs. You need each other to successfully resolve conflicts. You need to meet both your needs as well as the other person's needs. Individuals often share needs in common. Recognize that there may be some emotional issues.[34] People can become fixated on resolving the conflict only as it suits them. Blaming, name-calling, or antagonizing the other person is not likely to result in a positive resolution. A calm, rational approach is more likely to result in a constructive resolution.

Fourth, focus on underlying needs or issues rather than positions. Positions are generally based on underlying needs. What are you trying to accomplish? Respect the other person's perspective. People are generally motivated by their perceived self-interest. Listen and respond with empathy. Ask open-ended questions to better understand the other person's position. Do not be judgmental. Use active listening skills. Encourage the other person to speak about the conflict from his perspective. Do not agree or disagree. You are trying to learn about the other party's underlying interests or motives. Use reflective listening skills by clarifying, by paraphrasing, and by summarizing what the other person is saying. Focus on the positive. If the other person uses negative words, reframe the words into positive words. If the situation gets too emotional, take a timeout. By careful listening, you may find a solution that serves the interests of both parties. Give the other person a chance to tell his side of the conflict completely. Learn how the other person feels. Each party's perspective has to be heard and understood.

Fifth, create options that can satisfy the needs of both parties. Think of as many different solutions to the problem as you can. List the options before discussing the value of any particular option. The more options you have, the more likely you are to find one that will satisfy both parties. There may be more than one option that will satisfy the needs of both parties. Look for shared interests and common ground. To paraphrase Albert Einstein, "We cannot solve problems by using the same kind of thinking we used when we created them."

Sixth, use objective standards. An agreement should provide a constructive solution to the conflict that meets shared goals and needs. Mutual benefit agreements should give you lasting solutions to specific conflicts.

Conflict can trigger strong emotions that can lead to hurt feelings, disappointment, and discomfort. These emotions can cause irreparable rifts and resentments. When conflict is resolved in a healthy way, we increase our understanding of one another, builds trust, and strengthens our relationship. Differences of opinion or disagreements are essential for human progress. Without these differences, we would still believe that the Earth was flat, that evil spirits caused disease, and that witches cast evil spells. Our perceptions of the world are often erroneous.

Encourage the free exchange of ideas. A distinction must be made between questioning, criticizing, and denigrating an idea, belief, or opinion. When we criticize or denigrate someone's idea, belief, or opinion, that person may view this as a personal attack. When we question someone else's idea, belief, or opinion, we are often met with resistance. Some people with strongly held beliefs may not accept someone questioning those beliefs. How receptive would you be if someone questioned your deeply held beliefs?

Do not expect to change someone else's idea, belief, or opinion. A change will occur only when that person decides that the idea, belief, or opinion held is no longer valid or rational.

When a conflict arises, often the best course of action is to use respectful negotiations to resolve the disagreement. The goals of negotiation: (1) produce a solution that all parties can agree to; (2) work as quickly as possible to find this solution; (3) improve, not hurt, the relationship between the groups in conflict.

Negotiating a resolution can do the following: (1) help you understand more about those whose ideas, beliefs, and backgrounds may be different from your own. In order to resolve a conflict, you need to look at the conflict from the other person's point of view and learn more about the other person's perspective and motivations; (2) ensure that your relationship with the other person continues and grows. When you achieve peace, you create allies. Successful negotiations pave the way for smooth relationships in the future; (3) find peaceful solutions to difficult situations.

Some important principles to keep in mind:

Listen to what people have to say. Their opinions are important to understand, because their opinions may be the source of the conflict. Recognize what is important to them. Recognizing does not mean agreeing. We talk to teach. We listen to learn.

All necessary parties must participate, because participants have a stake in the resolution. They will want to find a constructive solution. Do not react to emotional outbursts.

Dr. Marshall Rosenberg, in his transformative book, *Nonviolent Communication: A Language of Life,* sets forth a four-step process in fostering compassionate or empathetic communication for meeting the needs of the parties without making judgments, blaming, or finding fault.[35] Dr. Rosenberg describes this as nonviolent communication. This process involves the following steps:

1. Differentiate observation from evaluation, carefully observe what is happening free of evaluation, and specify behaviors and conditions that are affecting you;

2. Differentiate feeling from thinking, identify and express internal feeling states in a way that does not imply judgment, criticism, or blame/punishment;

3. Connect with the universal human needs/values (e.g. sustenance, trust, understanding) that are being met or not met in relation to what is happening and how you are feeling; and

4. Request what you would like clearly and specifically stating what you do want (rather than what you do not want), and that is truly a request and not a demand (i.e. do not attempt to motivate, however subtly, out of fear, guilt, shame, obligation, but rather out of willingness and compassionate giving).

Four-Step Nonviolent Communication in Action	
Clearly expressing how I am without blaming or criticizing.	Empathically receiving how you are without blaming or criticizing.
OBSERVATIONS	
1. What I observe (see, hear, remember, imagine, free from my evaluations) that does or does not contribute to my well-being: *"When I (see, hear)..."*	1. What you observe (see, hear, remember, imagine, free from your evaluations) that does or does not contribute to your well-being: *"When you see/hear..."* (sometimes unspoken when offering empathy)
FEELINGS	
2. How I feel (emotion or sensation rather than thought in relation to what I observe: *"I feel..."*	2. How you feel (emotion or sensation rather than thought) in relation to what you observe: *"You feel..."*
NEEDS	
3. What I need or value (rather than a preference, or a specific action) that causes my feelings: *"... because I need/value..."* Clearly requesting that which would enrich my life without demanding.	3. What you need or value (rather than a preference, or a specific action) that causes your feelings: *"... because you need/value..."* Empathically receiving that which would enrich your life without hearing any demand.
REQUESTS	
4. The concrete actions I would like taken: *"Would you be willing to...?"*	4. The concrete actions you would like taken: *"Would you like...?"* (Sometimes unspoken when offering empathy)

Compassionate Communication is a twelve-step process, developed by Newberg and Waldman, which can lead to intimacy, cooperation, and trust.[36] The first six steps of this process are preparatory, and are done before you engage another person in a conversation in the following order: (1) relax; (2) stay present; (3) cultivate inner silence; (4) increase positivity; (5) reflect on your deepest values; (6) access a pleasant memory. These steps create an inner state of intense awareness and calm. The next six steps in the process include: (7) observe nonverbal cues, such as, the other person's tone of voice, facial expressions, and body gestures, to tell what the person may be thinking and feeling. When you engage in dialogue, adhere to the following strategies: (8) express appreciation; (9) speak warmly; (10) speak slowly; (11) speak briefly; (12) listen deeply.

Impediments to listening deeply include daydreaming (thinking about unrelated topics when someone is speaking), debating (having an inner argument about what is being said), judging (letting negative views influence you), problem solving (yearning to give unasked-for advice), pseudo listening (pretending to be a good listener), rehearsing (planning what you want to say next), stage hogging (redirecting the conversation to you), defensive listening (taking everything personally, and avoidant listening (blocking out what you do not want to hear).

All of us are motivated to act to meet our perceived needs. The physiological needs required for human survival include: (1) Air; (2) Water; (3) Food; (4) Shelter; (5) Sleep. In addition to these essential physiological needs, there are many other human needs.[37] Every conflict involves a need that is not being satisfied. Satisfy the need, and you resolve the conflict.

These needs might include:

AUTONOMY: choosing dreams, goals, values; freedom; independence; space; spontaneity.

CONNECTION/INTERDEPENDENCE: acceptance; affection; appreciation; belonging; cooperation; communication; companionship; compassion; consideration; emotional safety; empathy; inclusion; intimacy; love; mutuality; nurturing; respect/self-respect; safety; security; stability; support; to know and be known; to see and be seen; to understand and be understood; trust; warmth.

HONESTY: authenticity; creativity; integrity; meaning; presence; self-worth.

MEANING: awareness; challenge; clarity; competence; consciousness; contribution; creativity; discovery; efficacy; effectiveness; hope; learning.

PHYSICAL/EMOTIONAL WELL-BEING: movement/exercise; sexual expression; safety

PLAY: joy; humor; fun; laughter.

PEACE: beauty; communion; ease; equality; harmony; inspiration; order.

Feelings that can arise when your needs are not satisfied:

AFRAID: apprehensive; dread; foreboding; frightened; mistrustful; panicked; petrified; scared; suspicious; terrified; wary; worried.

ANNOYED: aggravated; dismayed; disgruntled; displeased; exasperated; frustrated; impatient; irritated.

ANGRY: enraged; furious; incensed; indignant; irate; livid; outraged; resentful.

AVERSION: animosity; appalled; contempt; disgusted; dislike; hate; horrified; hostile; repulsed.

CONFUSED: ambivalent; baffled; bewildered; dazed; hesitant; lost; mystified; perplexed; puzzled; torn.

DISCONNECTED: alienated; aloof; apathetic; bored; cold; detached; distant; distracted; indifferent; numb; removed; uninterested; withdrawn.

DISQUIET: agitated; alarmed; disconcerted; disturbed;

perturbed; rattled; restless; shocked; startled; surprised; troubled; turbulent; turmoil; uncomfortable; uneasy; unnerved; unsettled; upset.

EMBARRASSED: ashamed; chagrined; flustered; guilty; mortified; self-conscious.

FATIGUE: beat; burnt out; depleted; exhausted; lethargic; listless; sleepy; tired; weary; worn out.

PAIN: agony; anguished; bereaved; devastated; grief; heartbroken; hurt; lonely; miserable; regretful; remorseful.

SAD: depressed; dejected; despair; despondent; disappointed; discouraged; disheartened; forlorn; gloomy; heavy hearted; hopeless; melancholy; unhappy; wretched.

TENSE: anxious; cranky; distressed; distraught; edgy; fidgety; frazzled; irritable; jittery; nervous; overwhelmed; restless; stressed out.

VULNERABLE: fragile; guarded; helpless; insecure; leery; reserved; sensitive; shaky.

YEARNING: envious; jealous; longing; nostalgic; pining; wistful.

Feelings that may arise when your feelings are satisfied:

AFFECTIONATE: compassionate; friendly; loving; open hearted; sympathetic; tender; warm

CONFIDENT: empowered; open; proud; safe; secure.

ENGAGED: absorbed; alert; curious; engrossed; enchanted; entranced; fascinated; interested; intrigued; involved; spellbound; stimulated.

EXCITED: amazed; animated; ardent; aroused; astonished; dazzled; eager; energetic; enthusiastic; giddy; invigorated; lively; passionate; surprised; vibrant.

EXHILARATED: blissful; ecstatic; elated; enthralled; exuberant; radiant; rapturous; thrilled

GRATEFUL: appreciative; moved; thankful; touched.

HOPEFUL: expectant; encouraged; optimistic.

INSPIRED: amazed; awed; wonder.

JOYFUL: amused; delighted; glad; happy; jubilant; pleased; tickled.

PEACEFUL: calm; clear headed; comfortable; centered; content; fulfilled; mellow; quiet; relaxed; relieved; satisfied; serene; still; tranquil; trusting.

REFRESHED: enlivened; rejuvenated; renewed; rested; restored; revived.

Understanding and meeting the needs of the parties is an effective way to resolve the conflict.

VERBAL ATTACKS

In resolving conflicts, always attack the problem not the person. If you are verbally attacked, you have to be prepared. Know that you are under attack. Know what kind of attack. Learn how to make your defense fit the attack and how to follow through.

Most verbal attacks contain presuppositions or hidden messages. A presupposition has a hidden meaning that a native speaker of a language knows is part of a sequence of that language, even if not overtly present in the sequence.

Examples of verbal attacks with presuppositions:

a) *"If you really* loved me, you would not go golfing."
Presupposition: "You don't really love me."

b) *"Don't you even care* about me"
Presupposition: "You don't really care about me."
"You should care about me. It's wrong not to."
"Therefore, you should feel rotten."

c) *"Even* a man should be able to understand this."
Presupposition: "There is something wrong with being a man."
"It is simple to understand."
"You should feel guilty and stupid."

d) *"Everyone understands* why you are having a hard time doing this job."
Presupposition: "You are having a hard time doing the job."
"Everyone knows about the problem, so there is no point in trying to hide it or deny it.

e) "A person who *really* wanted to resolve this case would agree to this term."
Presupposition: "You don't really want to resolve this case."

f) *"Why don't you* want me to be happy."
Presupposition: "You don't want me to be happy."
"You have the power to make me happy, but are not willing to use it."

HIDDEN MESSAGES

People generally express five common verbal behavior patterns according to Virginia Satir:[38]

1. **Blamer**—finds fault, name calls, and is ripe with criticism;

2. **Computer**—intellectualizes and shows little emotion;

3. **Distracter**—brings up irrelevancies to take the focus away from the issue;

4. **Placater**—apologetic, tentative, and self-effacing (sometimes appears like a martyr);

5. **Leveler**—engages in honest, direct, clear communication.

These verbal behavior patterns differ depending on whether you are talking to your child, your significant other, or your boss. When people communicate, there are hidden messages. For example, when a person says, "If you really loved me, you would go the movies with me."

Presupposition or Hidden Message: "You do not really love me."

Another example: "If you really loved me, you would want to go to the movies with me."

Presupposition or Hidden Message: "You do not really love me." "You have the power to control your feelings if you want to but you choose not to."

If you go to the movies in the first example, you have "proved" that you really love the other person. In the second example, you are hopelessly trapped. Whether you go to the movies or not, you will feel guilty. If you go to the movies, you will feel guilty because you wish you were not going. If you do not go, you will feel guilty because you are not going.

Another example: "Even you should be able to follow this argument."

Presupposition or Hidden Message: "The argument is simple." "You are stupid."

Another example: "Everyone understands why you are having a hard time agreeing to these terms."

Presupposition or Hidden Message: "You are having a hard time agreeing to the terms." "Everyone knows about it." "You should agree to the terms."

Another example: "A person who has serious emotional problems can't be expected to cope with the work load here like the other employees do."

Presupposition or Hidden Message: "You have serious emotional problems." "The work load is reasonable." "You can't handle the workload."

Another example: "Why don't you ever want to help me?"

Presupposition or Hidden Message: "You don't want to help me." "You have the ability to help me, but choose not to." "You don't care enough about me to want to help."

Another example: "Some bosses would object to having an employee come in five minutes late every day."

Presupposition or Hidden Message: "It's wrong to come to work late." "I'm not like other bosses—I'm superior to them by letting you come to work late." "I have the power to fire you for not coming to work on time." "You should feel guilty for coming to work late." "You should feel grateful."

These are the steps you can take in responding to verbal attacks.

Identify the Satir behavior mode: (1) Identify the presupposition(s) or hidden messages in the statement(s); (2) Respond with a neutral request for information about the presupposition; (3) Maintain a neutral tone; (4) Do not get angry, hurried, or upset; (5) Do not talk in the first person; (6) Talk in abstractions and generalities; (7) Be calm and relaxed.

Chapter 12

OVERCOMING CHALLENGES TO CONFLICT RESOLUTION

U sing logical arguments can be helpful in resolving conflicts. One needs to distinguish logical from illogical arguments. Is the argument rational and logical or does it contain faulty reasoning? Evidence must be organized in a coherent manner in the form of premises. The premises not only must lead to a conclusion, but also must be true. When dealing with true premises, the evidence must be truly and fairly represented in the premises, and the premises that represent the evidence must be clear and intelligible.

ILLOGICAL ARGUMENTS

Illogical arguments may be used to support one's position. By challenging illogical arguments, you are in a much better position to resolve conflicts on a rational basis. What form of argument is being made to persuade you, deductive, inductive, or abductive reasoning?

Deductive reasoning works from general information to a specific prediction. The process involves following one or more factual statements (i.e. premises) through to their logical conclusion. In a deductive argument, if all the premises are true, and the terms correctly applied, then it holds that the conclusion will also be true. Aristotle gives us the classic example of deductive reasoning:

(a) All men are mortal (First premise).

(b) Socrates is a man (Second premise).

(c) Therefore, Socrates is mortal (Conclusion).

Here, the conclusion is true because the second premise defines Socrates as part of the subset "men," where the first premise stipulated all men are mortal. Note the progression from a general statement to a specific conclusion.

Inductive reasoning is a form of inferential reasoning in which a set of particular observations leads to a general statement. This is an example of a basic form of inductive reasoning, with a premise based on concrete data and a generalized conclusion:

All the swans I have seen are white (Premise).

Therefore, all swans are white (Conclusion).

In this example, the conclusion is actually wrong—there are also black swans. This is a "weak" argument. You can make the conclusion stronger, by making it more probable:

All the swans I have seen are white (Premise).

Therefore, most swans are probably white (Conclusion).

Common types of inductive reasoning would include:

Generalized: It uses premises about a sample set to draw conclusions about a whole population, such as the swan example above.

Statistical: This form uses statistics based on a large and random sample set, and its quantifiable nature makes the conclusions stronger. For example, "95% of the swans I have seen on my global travels are white, therefore 95% of the world's swans are white."

Bayesian: This method adapts statistical reasoning to take into account new or additional data. For example, location data might allow a more precise estimate of the percentage of white swans.

Analogical: Shared properties between two groups are also likely to share some further property. For example, "Swans look like geese and geese lay eggs, therefore swans also lay eggs."

Predictive: This type of reasoning draws a conclusion about the future based on a past sample. For instance: "There have always been swans on the lake in past summers, therefore there will be swans this summer."

Causal inference: This includes a causal link between the premise and the conclusion. For example, "There have always been swans on the lake in summer, therefore the start of summer will bring swans onto the lake."

Abductive reasoning goes from observation to a hypothesis that accounts for the reliable data and seeks to explain relevant evidence. For example, the lawn is wet. If it rained last night, it is not surprising that the lawn is wet. By abductive reasoning, the possibility that it rained last night is reasonable. However, abducing rain last night from the observation of the wet lawn can lead to a false conclusion. In this example, dew, lawn sprinklers, or some other process may have resulted in the wet lawn, even in the absence of rain. Lawyers often use abductive reasoning to convince jurors to draw reasonable inferences from known facts. Science tends to follow the rule known as Occam's Razor, where the simplest explanation is likely to be the correct one. For example, a researcher might observe the phenomenon of increasing levels of violence shown by children. Further research may show that this tends to occur more in societies where violence is prevalent on television. Abductive reasoning would lead the researcher to propose the most obvious hypothesis, 'If children are exposed to more violence on TV, they are more likely to exhibit violent behavior as adults.' This is probably the simplest hypothesis and is an excellent starting point for research. It is not necessarily correct, as other factors may contribute or cause rising violence, but it is the 'best explanation.' Further research may show that there are other factors.

It is important to understand the difference between cause and effect and correlation. Correlation is a statistical measure of the degree to which two variables are related to each other. It can take any value from –1 to 1. A perfect correlation exists when one variable changes perfectly with another. A perfect negative correlation exists when one variable changes perfectly opposite the other. A correlation of 0 exists when two variables are completely unrelated. A correlation shows only that two (or more) variables are linked, not that one causes the other. Correlation does not imply causation. A correlation is also useful in that it provides an estimate for how much of the variability in the observations is caused by the two variables being tracked. For example, a correlation of .78 between height and weight indicates that 78 percent of the differences in weight across individuals are linked to differences in height. The statistic does not tell us what the remaining 22 percent of the variability is attributed to—additional experimentation would need to be conducted, but one could assume other factors such as diet, genetics, exercise, and so on are part of that 22 percent.

A cause and effect relationship occurs when an event (the cause) makes another event occur (the effect). Natural phenomena are complicated and intertwined, making it difficult to establish a natural order. For example, in an experiment to study the effects of depression upon alcohol consumption, researchers find that people who suffer from higher levels of depression drink more, and announce that this research shows that depression drives people to drink. Is this necessarily the case? Depression could be the cause that makes people drink more, but it is equally possible that heavy consumption of alcohol, a depressant, makes people more depressed. With that example, an alcoholic drink manufacturer could use the second interpretation to claim that alcohol is not a factor in depression and that the responsibility is upon society to ensure that people do not become depressed. An anti-alcohol group could claim that alcohol is harmful and use the results to lobby for harsher drinking laws. The same research leads to two different interpretations. A correlation does not establish a cause and effect relationship.

If you understand what an illogical argument is, you are in a much better position to refute it and move to a resolution based on a more objective basis. Some of the more common illogical arguments may be categorized in the following manner:

Faulty Generalizations

Information and principles, when expressed in language, take the form of generalizations. If a generalization claims "all" or "none," then even one counter instance makes it false. The two most common forms of faulty generalizations are jumping to conclusions and selecting the cases.

The fallacy of generalization found from too few cases results in drawing a conclusion on the basis of experience with particulars, which are insufficient for the size of the unit examined.

Example: Frank, who is white, works with one black employee who constantly comes to work late. He says, "All black people are lazy." Frank does not know any other black people.

Some people have an impulse to suppress the counter instances; consciously or unconsciously, they vitiate the evidence by selecting only a part of it. They look exclusively for evidence that will support an idea, with the result that they over-look any opposing evidence.

Example: Chinese students are diligent. The college professor states, "I had three Chinese students in my class, and they were all hard workers." The number is far too small to permit anything but the hastiest generalization.

Faulty Casual Generalization

People speak of one event causing another, when actually the two events belong to two classes as per the following rule: Every event of the first class is closely followed by an event of the second class. The rule implies that if lightening causes thunder, then every flash of lightening will be followed by a peal of thunder. If we accept the generalization that lightening causes thunder, any atmospheric electrical display, such as the Northern lights, will not be classified as lightening, unless it is followed by thunder.

Example: Some people argue that the ultimate cause of war is human aggression. As long as human beings are aggressive, there will be wars. Therefore, world peace organizations and disarmament programs are doomed to failure. The word "ultimate" presumably means the cause behind the proximate cause. The cause of a war victim's death may be injuries to vital organs caused by a bullet from a gun. "The cause" here refers to the war.

Assuming the Cause: "Post Hoc Reasoning

Post hoc means "after this." Paired constructions of causes and effects have in common that the effects follow the causes. This is a necessary feature, but it is by no means a sufficient one for constructing the classes of causes. The word refers to assuming without proof that a prior event explains a subsequent occurrence. Magic, superstitions, and political debates are all examples of post hoc reasoning.

Example: A student studies European wars and notices that in the years preceding the outbreak of wars there was an increase of arms among the warring nations. He states his thesis: "increased arms appear as one of the major causes of European wars." The increase of arms and the outbreak of war may both be the effects of the same cause or causes. Friction and tension between nations can result in increased arms and war, but increased arms are not the cause of war.

Faulty Analogy

An analogy is the assertion that things, which resemble each other in some aspects, will resemble each other in some further aspects. Faulty analogy results either when there is the assumption that shared properties will continue indefinitely in new members or when it is highly probable there will be other shared property in a class so wide that there is only a low initial probability of finding any other shared properties. Stereotyping is a type of faulty analogy. Stereotyping consists in lumping together all types of individuals and treating them as a unit, because they share one or more common characteristics.

Example: A real estate broker tells a colleague, "This deal is a sure thing because the buyer is a musician, and everybody knows musicians are easy to work with." Later the broker confessed to his colleague, "The deal fell through because the musician knew more about property value than I did." All musicians know something about music, after that they are not a "harmonious" group.

Composition and Division

The fallacy of composition is related to faulty analogy. The assumption is that what holds true for each member of a class standing alone will hold true for all members of the class taken together. The fallacy of division assumes that what holds true for all members of a class is necessarily true for each alone.

Example: A requirement that everyone have a college education will benefit society. Not everyone may benefit from a college education. There are many occupations that benefit society that do not require a college education, but require other forms of training, such as work in a trade, acting, or athletics.

The All-or-Nothing Mistake

Although truth can be a matter of black and white, more often there are gray areas. Where a situation requires a relative judgment, it is inaccurate to make an all or nothing proposition. Where there is no demand for an immediate decision, impatient individuals commit a fallacy when they cut through complex situations as if everything has to be decided by a simple yes or no.

Example: You cannot treat these union workers kindly. The only way to convince them is to give them nothing.

That attitude could lead to a strike that could have been avoided.

The False Dilemma

In a false dilemma, the speaker represents the situation as offering only undesirable alternatives when the facts do not warrant it. One of the given alternatives may be neutral or even desirable. More often an unstated alternative exists, which is at least neutral, so the false dilemma turns out to be no dilemma at all.

Example: A farmer can never expect to earn much money. Either the farmer raises a bumper crop and finds the price is low, or the price is high with a meager crop to sell. This dilemma is false since it overlooks the possibility of government subsidies and price supports, as well as other factors. Refuting a false dilemma by pointing out an additional possibility that is not undesirable is called "going around" or "between the horns of the dilemma." Refuting a false dilemma by pointing out that one of the alternatives is not undesirable is called, "taking the dilemma by the horns."

Unnecessary Vagueness

When the meaning of words is unclear, it creates confusion. To say that a person pursues the good is vague. We do not know what "the good" means. Value terms are examples of terms that resist reduction.

Example: "Give to the United Fund. You can deduct it from your income tax." Without such vagueness advertising would be impossible. "Take it off your income tax" can, in law, mean only "take it off your income before computing the tax, if you use the long form and not the standard deduction for charity." However, you are not supposed to think of that.

Over-Precision

When an attempt is made to be too precise, the argument may become arbitrary and artificial.

Example: A museum tour guide says that a dinosaur is 100,000,005 years old because when he started working there five years ago, an expert told him it was one hundred million years old.

Word Magic

The existence of a name does not guarantee the existence of any corresponding entity. The use of such terms as "destiny" and "faith" provides no clue for reduction and strongly suggests hypostatization of entities. Such use is commonly called word magic. Word magic is that instance of reification, and there is no alternative non-metaphysical interpretation and where the construction cannot be verified or falsified.

Example: Peter, a docile follower of the party line, states, "the dialectic of the class struggle requires the inevitable over throw of capitalism." If "dialectic" means the clash of opposing political and economic classes, then the outcome will be decided by the course of events and the strength of the interests involved. If "dialectic" means the resolution of apparently opposed propositions, this will be a logical exercise, irrelevant to the world of political and economic struggle. Finally, if "dialectic" means some underlying principal of historical development, then it is another magical abstraction, and there is no point in producing evidence from history, since none is relevant.

Emotive Language: "Colored Words"

The most common of all fallacies is playing on emotion to color the case and distract from a close scrutiny of the issue. Language has great emotive power. Certain names of emotions have the power to evoke and decree the states they refer to. The descriptions of some emotions or moods also convey attitudes toward them.

Example: A commentator says, "there is no point listening to him, he is a liar and a fraud." "Liar" and "fraud" are highly emotional words. They describe and denounce the person speaking as someone who is untrustworthy.

Ceremony or Setting: Pomp and Circumstance

The same words uttered by the President before a joint session of Congress and by an acquaintance because of the difference in setting, have entirely different penetrating power. The President's argument is no better than that of your acquaintance and the same words vary in effectiveness with the setting.

Example: Frank and his wife stop to hear a street orator. "Let's go," Frank says to his wife, "he would make more of an impression on me if he had a shave." Frank may be expressing a reluctance to consider argument from such a source. As expressed, his reluctance is an instance of reliance on setting, if we can regard a stubbed chin as a setting for a speech.

Appeal to Authority: "Ipse Dixit" Or "He Says So!"

It is entirely proper that authorities be called on for information. An authority is personally reliable in the same way that anybody else is as long as these conditions are met:

1. The authority is telling the truth as he sees it or there's no reason to suppose he is lying.
2. The authority is disinterested or there's no reason to suppose him swayed by bias.
3. The authority is conscientious or there's no reason to suppose that he has not been attentive to the problem and diligent in gathering data.

An authority must be qualified as an expert in the field in which he or she is cited. Expert qualifications include the following: the authority is clearly identified; the authority has professional standing; the qualifications of experts are properly judged, not by laymen, but by follow experts; the authority is current; the authority is expressing an opinion within the field of his or her special competence; the authority in the opinion cited must hold representative views in his or her field where there is controversy; and it is not proper to cite one side without acknowledgement of the other.

In summary, an appeal to authority is proper when the problem is technical and the expert cited is qualified and reliable. Otherwise, the appeal may be suspect. At best the speaker may not realize what is required for a proper appeal to authority; at worst, he may be trying to give his opinion a weight it would not have without the aid of great names or unidentified "expert opinion."

Example: A senator argues, "George Washington warned against entangling foreign alliances. Invited on all sides to international adventures, we should remember the wisdom of the father of our country."

While George Washington was considered astute in his own time, it would be inappropriate to apply opinions he held in 1798 as proper for the present world situation.

Appeal to Tradition of Faith: "Tried and True"

There are two main types of improper appeal to tradition or faith. The first occurs when the discussion concerns ways and means for implementing a group's basic decision. The improper appeal to the basic decisions of a group occurs when the group questions the basic decision itself. When a proposal to change a policy, to modify a traditional practice, or recast a fundamental objective is under discussion by the membership group, it is clearly circular to attack the proposal as undermining the established order.

Example: Paul is reading the Congressional Record for 1919. He discovers the debates concerning the entrance of the United States into the League of Nations and reads the following statement by Senator George: "I am an isolationist and intend to remain one. The Wilsonites are subversive of the American tradition, a tradition hallowed by our great founder and by thirteen decades of American history."

Isolationism was a basic decision of American policy prior to 1919. Those men (the "Wilsonites") who favored joining the League of Nations in 1919 were challenging the soundness of the tradition itself in the light of World War I. Such a challenge is always subversive: It is a proposal to "subvert" a tradition. Calling Wilson's followers subversive was stating that they were challenging the tradition with an emotional suggestion that it was wrong.

Impressing by Large Numbers: "Get on the Band Wagon"

Large numbers constitute a sort of pseudo authority. Though it is pleasant to conform, to go along, and to ride a bandwagon, truth is not always democratic. Just because many or most people believe something is true does not make it true. The authority of many numbers commonly amounts no more than mere suggestion or unquestioning acceptance of tradition. "What everybody knows" is not necessarily true, for once "everybody" knew that the earth was flat, that Monarchs ruled by divine right, that evil spirits caused disease.

Example: A salesman representing a perfume manufacturer tells a prospective customer, "Fifty thousand women can't be wrong." Unfortunately, the world presents a daily spectacle of tens of millions of individuals holding wrong beliefs and consequently following disastrous results to their social and individual welfare.

Popular Passions: "Ad Populum Appeals"

Prejudice is an opinion held without reasonable grounds. It takes the form of a decided preference for or against something. It is often presumed that the strongest bias people have toward their own self-interest, especially its economic and social interests. Whatever threatens the audience's self-interest is a likely area of negative prejudice. The appeal "Ad Populum" or "to the people" is characteristic of addresses to the uninformed. The person who uses racial or religious hatred, the agitator who stirs passions by pointing to the evils of welfare without acknowledging any of its benefits, the demigod who recalls any proposal he does not like as "communist," is either relying on popular passion or invoking the self-interest of the crowd.

Example: In talking about Mexican immigrants, President Trump said, "They are not our friend, believe me. They're bringing drugs. They're bringing crime. They're rapists. And some, I assume, are good people." This appeal to popular passions is commonly known as "name calling." This device is stock in trade for demigods. The essence of name-calling is reliance on prejudicial terminology to invoke popular passion. Inflection of the voice or contacts of epithet can make a name like "immigrants" into a term of abuse.

Damming the Origin: "Condemning the Source"

The opposite of regarding argument as established through an appeal to authority, is the fallacy of origin, that is, rejecting an argument due to its undesirable source.

Example: At a town meeting a speaker said, "I believe in looking a gift horse in the mouth. The largest landowner in town is offering to donate a site for the new high school. I prefer to choose our own site and pay a fair price for it."

The speaker wants to reject the offer because he distrusts the landowner.

Personal Attacks: "Ad Hominem"

Damming an opponent is a common method of damming the source. Personal attacks are effective because it is difficult to credit a person who has been tarred and feathered. Character assassinations are the easiest to construct and the hardest to combat. This may be the reason personal attacks are so commonly made.

Example: A foreman is fired by his employer. He gives a newspaper interview charging unfair labor practices at his company. The company official states, "The foreman is sore about being fired. He is a troublemaker and was once convicted of embezzlement." The reference to the foreman as a "troublemaker" can be dismissed as a vague personal charge designed to create prejudice. His alleged spite and previous dishonesty bear on his reliability and should be considered as character evidence. Such evidence can justify refusing to accept his story without further confirmation. The idea of "not accepting" is not equivalent to "rejecting." The foreman may be telling the truth, even if he is a vindictive person. What needs to be determined is whether the unreliable foreman was telling the truth on this occasion. This can only be done by seeking more evidence about the facts. Those who adopt the simple solution of reasoning to themselves, "the foreman is a rascal, so we will disregard everything he says," are the victims of prejudice.

Forestalling Disagreement

The fallacy here lies in the attempt to make an opponent or an audience unwilling to meet the argument. Many expressions, such as "it is obvious," "everybody knows," "clearly," "as anyone can see," are designed to convince the audience that it is not necessary to think about the problem.

Example: "It is obvious that unless scientific research is subsidized, the whole country will suffer." Whether or not "the whole country will suffer" is what the speaker should be trying to prove. "It is obvious" is a mild attempt to forestall disagreement.

Creating Misgivings:
"Where there is Smoke there is Fire"

The lingering suspicion that follows on unfounded charges of immorality, corruption, or disloyalty, is notoriously hard to resolve. It is a paradox that the more wild and damaging the charges, the more likely they are believed. People reason that nobody would say such a terrible thing unless it was true, at least partially true.

Example: "They are saying the Mayor's attorneys bought land when they got the tip that the freeway was going through there."

Self-Righteousness

Lip service, paying verbal homage to one thing when actually doing or advocating something different. Everyone, in some degree, believes in the worth and justice of his own motives and interests. Righteous intentions do not necessarily lead to truth and neither interest nor motives have any necessary relationship to the justice of the case.

Example: A dictator says, "We have done all that we can to keep the peace. This morning our army will march on foreign soil, and we will right the wrongs that we have too long endured. Our hands are clean. Our aim is justice." The dictator appeals to the audience's willingness to believe in the justice and the nobility of their own cause. Millions of people convinced of the rightness of the cause when it coincides with their self-interest or what they are persuaded to believe is their self-interest. This is a tribute to cultural conditioning, the efficiency of distorting the news, and the human weakness for assuming that one's own motives and interests must be noble and just.

Finding the "Good" Reason

Finding the "good" reason is the process of selecting a fact that is creditable or, at least not discreditable, and proposing it as the explanation of one's actions.

Example: A student explains his failure at calculus. "The teacher was terrible."

There are a number of possible explanations for the student's failure: he did not study, the course was too advanced for his background, the student is not bright. For the purpose of rationalization, the student wants a reason that would be respectable.

Wishful Thinking

Wishful thinking can lead to fake expectations. Self-interest often leads us to refuse to look for evidence that we do not want to face.

Example: On a balmy spring afternoon, Salesman Frank is tired of soliciting prospects. "There are a lot of good contacts to make at the golf course, and besides I need a rest." He takes the afternoon off. There should be no surprise when his sales drop.

Special Pleading: "Having it Both Ways"

One-sided pleading becomes special pleading when you "have it both ways." You find the reasons where your advantage lies, but refuse to apply the same principle to yourself that you apply to others. Anybody who has something to gain may ignore or twist the facts to his own advantage.

Example: A real estate broker shows a friend a large parking lot that he has recently acquired to accommodate his salespersons' cars. "It is a good investment. It will save time and money for my employees." Shortly after, the city purchased land for a parking lot to accommodate municipal employees. The land values are comparable, and the parking facilities equally congested in the two areas. "Another instance of extravagance in the City Hall," protests the real estate broker. Unless the real estate broker can point out significant differences between the two situations, what is a "good investment" for one employer would hardly be "extravagant" for another.

Lip Service

All of us are restrained by the taboos current in our particular society or culture. The pressure that society exerts to make individuals conform to its beliefs and ideals is generally sufficient to prevent all but a few individuals from openly disagreeing with the current notion. An individual may support an ideal such as racial equality without questioning the depth of his belief until he is called upon to put it into public practice. Lip service can be a smoke screen conscientiously created, e.g., one who proclaims his support of sexual taboos that he clandestinely violates. This person has made the passage from lip service to flagrant hypocrisy. It is not a difficult passage. The majority of people on occasion, intentionally or otherwise, say one thing and do another.

Example: A speaker at a veteran's organization declares: "Democracy must be alert against government by special interest and pressure groups. The legislator should listen to the farmer, the business person, the veteran, but he must decide for the good of all." The speaker explains how he is supporting a bill that greatly extends benefits for veterans. "Your Congressman won't be against this bill if he gets a lot of letters from you!" Though it is fashionable to deprecate "special interests and pressure groups," few speakers can resist the temptation to appeal to such groups whenever opportunity offers and the question concerns their own self-interest.

SATISFYING NEEDS

Everything we do we do to satisfy a need. Hidden biases prevent us from fully, understanding our needs. It is even more difficult to understand the needs of others. When needs are not met, emotional and psychological problems develop. Even "normal" people may resort to violence when their needs are not met. By understanding and satisfying the needs of the parties, we can resolve our conflicts constructively, reduce violence, and create a more cooperative world. The inability to find common ground can lead to destructive conflicts. The better you understand these biases, the more likely you are to fashion an effective resolution that will satisfy the needs of the parties.

Maslow's Hierarchy of Needs is an excellent model for understanding human motivation. Maslow's theory is that human beings are motivated by a hierarchy of needs. The order is flexible based on external circumstances or individual differences. Most behavior is multi-motivated, that is, simultaneously determined by more than one need.

Maslow describes five needs in the ascending order:

Level 1: Biological and Physiological: air, food, water, shelter, warmth, sex, sleep.

Level 2: Safety: protection from elements, security, order, law, stability.

Level 3: Love and Affiliating: friendship, intimacy, trust, receiving and giving affection and love, being part of a group (family, friends, work).

Level 4: Esteem: esteem for oneself (dignity, achievement, independence) and the desire for reputation or respect from others (e.g., status, prestige).

Level 5: Cognitive: knowledge and understanding, curiosity, exploration, need for meaning and predictability.

The following levels were added later:

Level 6: Aesthetic: appreciation and search for beauty, balance, form.

Level 7: Self-Actualization: realizing personal potential, self-fulfillment, seeking personal growth and peak experiences.

Level 8: Transcendence: helping others to achieve self-actualization.

Understanding whether striving to achieve a particular need or aim is 'fun' can provide a basis for identifying a Maslow driver within a given behavior, and determining where a particular behavior fits into the model.

In order to relate a particular 'doing it for fun' behavior in the Hierarchy of Needs, we have to know what makes it 'fun' (i.e., rewarding) for the person. If a behavior is 'for fun', then consider why it is 'fun' for the person. Is the 'fun' rooted in 'belongingness,' or is it from 'recognition', i.e., 'esteem'? Or is the fun at a deeper level, from the sense of self-fulfillment, i.e., 'self-actualization'?

If you apply this approach to any behavior that does not seem to fit the model, it will help you to see where it does fit. The common interpretation of Maslow's theory suggests that once a need is satisfied the person moves onto the next level; however, a strict application of this interpretation can produce a rigid analysis. People's motivations are more complex. While it is broadly true that people move up (or down) the hierarchy levels, depending what is happening to them in their lives, it is also true that most people's motivational 'set' comprises elements of all motivational drivers. Self-actualizers (level 7) are mainly focused on self-actualizing, but still must eat (level 1) and socialize (level 3). Homeless people whose main focus is food (level 1) and finding shelter (level 2) can still be concerned with social relationships (level 3), how their friends perceive them (level 4), and even the meaning of life (level 7). Maslow's theory is a guide, which requires some interpretation and thought. It can be useful in understanding, explaining, and managing human behavior.

Professor Manfred F. Max-Neef, in his book *Human Scale Development*, classifies fundamental human needs into nine categories: subsistence, protection, affection, understanding, participation, recreation (in the sense of leisure, time to reflect, or idleness), creation, identity, and freedom.[39] According to Professor Max-Neef, every human being, in every culture, over every generation, on every continent has these categories of needs. The expression of these needs may take on different phenotypes and appear different depending on the person. "Inborn needs are responsible for our individual and group survival as a species and continue to play a significant role in the evolution of human society. Fundamental human needs are finite, few, and classifiable. These needs are the same in all cultures and in all historical periods. What changes, both over time and through cultures, is the way or the means by which the needs are satisfied."

Some needs overcome others. A child may choose to be with an abusive parent because it fulfills the need of belonging. A person's top two or three needs will determine the course he takes as he moves to satisfy them. People meet needs differently at different times. Some people express the need for connection by thriving on "one-on-one attention" in their relationships with others, while others prefer group relationships. At a party, some people find one person and chat in one corner, while others will hang out with a group talking and socializing. Some require more empathy from those they are in a relationship with than from others. Some people can be invigorated by being with friends and crowds, while others prefer time alone time for reflection.

Sleep is something that everybody needs. Some people need a specific number of hours of sleep per day to function properly. Without those hours, they become irritable, angry, and stressed. Others manage with less sleep without visible effects. Self-awareness is important, so that a person can organize his life to have the amount of sleep he needs to function effectively.

Needs can be defined according to the existential categories of being, having, doing, and interacting. From these dimensions, a 36 cell matrix can be filled with examples of satisfiers for those needs:

Fundamental Human Needs	Being (qualities)	Having (things)	Doing (actions)	Interacting (settings)
Subsistence	physical and mental health	food, shelter, work	feed, clothe, rest, work	living environment, social setting
Protection	care, adaptability, autonomy	social security, health systems, work	co-operate, plan, help	social environment, dwelling
Affection	respect, generosity, sensuality	friendships, family, relation with nature	share, make love, express emotions	privacy, intimate spaces
Understanding	curiosity, intuition	literature, policies, teachers	analyze, study, investigate	schools, families, communities
Participation	receptiveness, dedication	responsibilities, duties, work, rights	cooperate, dissent, express opinions	associations, parties, temples, neighborhoods
Leisure	imagination, tranquility, spontaneity	games, parties, peace of mind	day-dream, remember, cooperate, relax	landscapes, intimate spaces
Creation	imagination, curiosity, inventiveness	abilities, skills, work, techniques	invent, build, design, compose, interpret	spaces for expression, workshops, audiences
Identity	sense of belonging, self-esteem, consistency	language, work, religions, customs, values, norms	know oneself, grow, commit oneself	places one belongs to, everyday settings
Freedom	autonomy, passion, self-esteem, open-mindedness	equal rights	dissent, choose, run risks, develop awareness	anywhere

There are a number of ways to satisfy these needs. Satisfiers have different characteristics: they can be violators or destroyers, pseudo satisfiers, inhibiting satisfiers, singular satisfiers, or synergic satisfiers. Certain satisfiers, promoted as satisfying a particular need, in fact inhibit or destroy the possibility of satisfying other needs: e.g., formal democracy, which is supposed to meet the need for participation, often disempowers and alienates, commercial television, which satisfies the need for recreation, interferes with understanding and creativity. When essential needs are not met, they give rise to emotional and psychological problems. Understanding human needs and meeting them in yourself and in others is an effective way of resolving conflicts.

CONFLICT STYLES AND LEARNING MODES

The Thomas-Kilmann Conflict Mode Instrument (TKI)[40] helps individuals discover which of five conflict-handling styles—competitive, collaborative, compromising, avoiding, and accommodating—is their preferred mode:

Competitive: People take firm stands, and know what they want. They usually operate from a position of power, such as their position, rank, expertise, or persuasive ability. This style can be useful in an emergency when a decision needs to be made fast, when the decision is unpopular, or when defending against someone who is trying to exploit the situation. It can leave people feeling bruised, unsatisfied, and resentful when used in less urgent situations.

Accommodating: A willingness to meet the needs of others at the expense of one's own needs. The accommodator often knows when to acquiesce, but can be persuaded to surrender a position even when it is not warranted. This person is not assertive and is highly cooperative. Accommodation is appropriate when the issues matter more to the other party or when peace is more valuable than winning.

Avoiding: Evade the conflict entirely by delegating controversial decisions, accepting default decisions, and avoiding hurt feelings. This can be useful when victory is impossible, the controversy is trivial, or someone else is better positioned to solve the problem.

Compromising: Find a solution that will partially satisfy everyone if everyone is prepared to give up something. Compromise is useful when: the cost of conflict exceeds the cost of losing ground; equal strength opponents are at a standstill; a deadline is looming.

Collaborative: Meet the needs of all people involved. This process involves bringing together a variety of viewpoints resulting in a solution that meets the needs of all the parties. This is the style to use whenever possible

People may use one or more of these styles depending on the situation. Know your style, and the style used by the party in conflict with you.

In addition to negotiating styles, different learning modes impact both our understanding of the information being conveyed to us, and the information we are seeking to convey to the other person. Knowing the person's learning mode will help you to convey the information more effectively.

Visual Learners: They need to see the speaker's body language and facial expression to fully understand the information. They think in pictures and learn best from visual displays, such as diagrams, illustrated textbooks, videos, flipcharts, and handouts. They are likely to take detailed notes.

Auditory Learners: They learn best through verbal discussions: talking things through and listening to what is said. They interpret the underlying meanings by listening to verbal tone, pitch, and speed. Written information may have little impact.

Tactile/Kinesthetic Learners: They learn through moving, doing, and touching: They learn best through a hands-on approach. Sitting for long periods of time is difficult, as they become distracted by their need for activity and exploration.

Maximum impact is gained when information is geared to the other person's learning mode. When you receive information in the learning mode best suited to you, you have a better understanding of the other person's issues.

LANGUAGE

There is no consensus when humans (or their ancestors) first used language. Estimates range from about two million (2,000,000) years ago, during the time of Homo Habilis, to as recently as forty thousand (40,000) years ago, during the time of Cro-Magnon man. Today, there are more than 6,000 distinct languages spoken worldwide. People speaking the same language may place different meanings on the same word, phrase, or sentence.

People need to understand each other when they communicate. Any word has only the meaning we agree to give it. For example, a pen is an object that we agree to call a pen. It is much more difficult to reach agreement on the meaning of a word like "affirmative action." Some people think "affirmative action" is discriminatory because it provides unfair preferences to a class of people, while others think that "affirmative action" is a necessary correction for past discriminatory practices. Your view may be influenced by whether you were benefited or were penalized by "affirmative action."

Language communicates ideas and expresses feelings. It describes how we perceive the world around us. Understanding words differently leads to misunderstandings; therefore, it is critical to understand each other as we communicate. The denotation of a word has a specific meaning, i.e., distinct from an implied or associated idea; the dictionary definition. The connotation of a word is an idea or feeling that a word invokes in addition to its literal or primary meaning. These word meaning differences can lead to conflicts.

There are three competing goals every time we communicate: (1) a task goal—get the job done; (2) a relational goal—do not do unnecessary damage to the relationships between you and others by your message; (3) An identity management goal—make your communication project the image that you want.

Active listening skills can resolve these conflicts by understanding what the person means when he or she uses language to convey information. Be an active listener. Rephrase what you hear as a question: "Let me see if I am following you. You're saying that... Have I got that right?"

Speak about yourself, not the other party. For example, you might say, "I feel angry when you treat me like a child," rather than "Don't treat me like a child!" Be concrete, but flexible. Speak about your interests, not about your position. Avoid making judgments. Ask questions and gather information. Your goal is to find a solution that will benefit all parties. Find a way to make their decision easy. Make them feel that the solution is theirs, not yours. It is more likely that they will accept the solution if they have a stake in it.

What if the other person is more powerful and influential or refuses to meet or talk with you? If you have already decided on your best alternative, you can walk away at any time. Think about alternatives to a negotiated resolution. Even if you are in a weaker position, have all the available information when making a decision.

What if the other person refuses to budge from his or her position? Treat that position as a real possibility. Ask questions. Listen to the arguments. Understand his interests, wants, or needs. Learn to accept criticisms of your ideas. The more information you have, the more likely you will find a satisfactory resolution for both parties.

Whenever there is a conflict or a misunderstanding between two parties, assume that both parties played some role in creating the situation. Test any assumption by looking at the available facts at the time. As you gather additional information, your assumption may change if the new facts warrant this.

Each side usually thinks they are right, and the other side is wrong. Parties may assess fault and blame to one another, which can escalate the conflict. The parties may use words with negative connotations. Instead of using the word "misunderstanding," one side may use the word "misrepresentation." Now, instead of a simple misunderstanding, we have a full-blown conflict that could continue to escalate as each side continues to use more words with negative connotations. You are more likely to reach resolution if you assume that each side played a role in the misunderstanding. Parties can learn from each other, if they use neutral words.

REFRAMING

Negative emotions or feelings can pose an impediment to resolving your conflict. Reframing negative emotions into a positive course of action can lead to effective solutions.

REFRAME YOUR THINKING		
Possible Emotion	**Maladaptive Response**	**Reframing Statement**
Anger (I'm mad at my boss because he won't talk to me directly)	Acting out (mopping, complaining, yelling, being irritable)	It's up to me to get the feedback I need.
Anxiety (I don't know what will happen)	Brooding (withdrawal, avoiding)	Finding out can open up new opportunities for me.
Fear of Confrontation (I don't want to do this)	Procrastination (canceling meetings with boss)	Taking the initiative puts me in charge and gives me power.
Fear of Reprisal (If I speak up, will I be fired, demoted?)	Denial (I don't need any feedback. I'm doing just fine)	I need to know how I'm doing.
Hurt (Why did he say I wasn't trying hard?)	Irritability (silence, plotting to get even)	I can pay attention to what he said even though I feel hurt.
Defensiveness (I'm better than he says)	Acting out (You can bet I'm not going to his stupid meeting, or if I go, I won't pay attention)	Being defensive prevents me from hearing what was said and improving the situation.
Sadness (I thought he liked me)	Withdrawal (being quieter than usual, feeling unmotivated)	Whether I'm liked has nothing to do with doing my job well.
Fear of Change (How will I ever be able to do everything he wants me to do?)	Denial (keep doing things the same way as before)	I need to change to keep my job.

Ambivalence (Should I stay or should I go?)	Passivity. (waiting for someone else to solve the problem)	What really serves my interests best? I need to be proactive.
Resignation (I have to leave)	Resistance to change. (It's too hard to look for another job.)	I'll be much happier working elsewhere.

INDIVIDUAL DIFFERENCES

When dealing with conflict, it is essential to understand individual differences. While each person is unique, there are many characteristics that are considered universal. Some of these characteristics would include: abstraction in speech and thought; beliefs in supernatural/ religion, death, disease, fortune, and misfortune; choice making (choosing alternatives); classification; means of dealing with conflict; cooperation; culture; daily routines; decision making; distinguishing right and wrong; division of labor by age and sex; dominance/submission; emotions; empathy; facial expressions; fairness (equity); good and bad distinguished; government; interpreting behavior; judging others; language; law; likes and dislikes; male and female differences; moral sentiments; music; myths; preference for own children and close kin (nepotism); reciprocity; resistance to abuse of power, to dominance; risk-taking; rites of passage; rituals; sanctions; semantics; sex; shame; shelter; roles; taboos; trade; violence; weapons.[41]

People who have serious psychological issues present a challenge. Psychologists estimate that about 1% of the population can be classified as psychopaths. They demonstrate addictive behavior, criminality, personality disorders, and impaired mental development. Characteristics of this population include the inability to control impulses or to delay gratification, the failure to learn from experience, disrespect for authority and the rights of others, and the failure to anticipate consequences. Their reality is so different from the norm that peaceful resolution of conflicts with them may not be possible.

The Dark Triad personality consists of three traits:[42] (1) Machiavellianism: a tendency to be manipulative and deceitful, to focus on self-interests, and exploit others to achieve their goals, which usually stems from a lack of respect or disillusionment for others; (2) Narcissism: an egotistical preoccupation with self. Narcissists appear charming, but have extreme difficulty in developing close relationships; (3) Psychopathy: a reflection of shallow emotional responses. The lack of emotions results in high stress tolerance, low empathy, and little guilt.

Along with narcissism and psychopathy, Hughes includes paranoia as a serious problem in his groundbreaking book, *Disordered Minds*.[43] According to the American Psychiatric Association, paranoid personality disorder is more prevalent in males and affects 2.3 to 4.4 percent of the general population. People with paranoid personality disorder are generally characterized as having a long-standing pattern of pervasive distrust and suspiciousness of others. They usually believe that other people's motives are suspect or even malevolent and assume that other people will exploit, harm, or deceive them without evidence to support this belief. While it is fairly normal for everyone to have some degree of paranoia about certain situations in their lives (such as worry about pending layoffs at work), people with paranoid personality disorder take this to an extreme. They are generally difficult to get along with and often have problems with close relationships. Their excessive suspiciousness and hostility may be expressed in overt argumentativeness, in recurrent complaining, or by quiet, apparently hostile aloofness. Although they may appear to be objective, rational, and unemotional, they more often display hostile, stubborn, and sarcastic expressions. They have an excessive need to be self-sufficient, have a strong sense of autonomy, and need to have a high degree of control over those around them. They are often rigid, critical of others, and unable to collaborate. They have great difficulty accepting criticism.

Although most people have some degree of the traits identified by the Dark Triad and paranoia, it is only the very extreme of these traits that are problematic, and when these traits interfere with normal functioning.

CORE VALUES

Core values are traits or qualities that represent an individual's deeply held beliefs and fundamental driving forces. These are beliefs that are formed often subconsciously or unconsciously and may form the basis for your decision-making process.

Our minds are wired to avoid pain and seek pleasure. The survival of the human species depends on it. Although we share many core values, some are more important to us than others. Religious beliefs may be very important to some people but not very important to others.

The following is a list of some common core values: Achievement; Appearance; Authority; Challenge; Communication; Community; Competence; Courage; Creativity; Dependability; Diversity; Empathy; Environment; Equality; Excellence; Fairness; Family; Flexibility; Forgiveness; Freedom; Friendship; Happiness; Hard work; Health; Honesty; Independence; Individuality; Integrity; Justice; Knowledge; Love; Loyalty; Obedience; Optimistic; Patience; Peace; Persistence; Pessimistic; Power; Prosperity; Rationality; Recognition; Religion; Risk-taking; Self-control; Self-Respect; Security; Simplicity; Sincerity; Spiritual Growth; Strength; Success; Teamwork; Tolerance; Trust; Wisdom.

Know your core values and understand that your core values may differ from other people. Although core values differ, you can still find common ground by working together. Remember core values may have different meanings to different people. Your concept of fairness as a core value would not necessarily have the same meaning to the other person.

What are your ten most important core values? What are the ten most important core values of the other person you are in conflict with? Are these core values reconcilable?

Some things to consider:

What are your moral absolutes?

What do you believe in?

What really matters to you?

What values help govern how you live your life?

How do you define right from wrong?

What values will help you build strong relationships?

What values do you want to pass on to your children?

Sometimes conflicts arise where the core values are so different that it appears that the conflict cannot be resolved. At one time, no one thought that Apartheid in South Africa could ever be resolved peacefully, but it was. As Nelson Mandela once said, "It always seems impossible until it's done." Conflicts that appear intractable can be resolved.

As Mahatma Gandhi said, "Your beliefs become your thoughts. Your thoughts become your words. Your words become your actions. Your actions become your habits. Your habits become your values. Your values become your destiny." To paraphrase Dr. King, "We must learn to live together as brothers [and sisters] or perish together as fools."

Concluding Thoughts

Conflict in human interactions is inevitable and occurs when people have different ideas for resolving a conflict, each convinced that his approach is the best or only way. You now have the information and tools you need to resolve conflicts effectively despite differences in core values, gender, race, religion, culture, national origin, age, and sexual orientation.

Your focus should be on resolving the conflict and maintaining a positive relationship with the other party. While conflict may feel uncomfortable, it allows you to recognize difficult situations, synthesize diverse perspectives, and ensure reasonable solutions. Understanding and using the concepts in this book will enhance your ability to resolve conflicts successfully.

Express your opinion in a neutral way when you disagree with the other party. It is s not necessary for someone else to be wrong for you to be right. Engage the other party in collaborative problem solving, not confrontation. Where there is disagreement, treat this as an option, not an insult to your intelligence. Ask open-ended questions to learn more about the other party's position. Demonstrate that you are open to new ideas and finding an effective solution. If you disagree with a proposed course of action, learn the basis for the suggestion. When you understand the reasoning behind the proposal, you may find another way to accomplish the same goal. When both sides have a genuine interest in resolving the conflict, they can work together to find solutions that will best satisfy their needs. Do not lose sight of your objective, i.e., the resolution of the conflict.

While the most effective way to resolve conflicts is for the parties to work together, there will be times when this does not happen. If an impasse occurs, find and use a skilled mediator to help resolve your conflict. Mediation is a voluntary process, and you can enter or withdraw from the process at any time. You have the right to information about the process, options, and resources prior to consenting to participate. The parties define the issues, needs, solutions, and the outcome of the process. The parties have the right to have a mediator who is impartial and neutral and treats the parties fairly. All the information provided to the mediator is kept within the mediation process and cannot be used in any subsequent proceeding.

What you should look for in a mediator:

1. **Rapport**. The ability to develop rapport—a relationship of understanding, empathy, and trust—with each of the disputing parties is a key skill. A sense of rapport can encourage parties to communicate fully with the mediator, often providing the information needed to help the parties reach a mutually acceptable resolution.

2. **Creativity**. By understanding each party's interests, a mediator can generate creative solutions that can satisfy each party. Novel solutions can result when parties focus on interests. The mediator's ability to suggest options that acknowledge feelings, perceptions, and hurts that might otherwise block meaningful and fair resolution is a vital skill.

3. **Patience**. The parties need the time to fully express emotions and ideas, while at the same time focusing intently on the primary task—dispute resolution. If the parties have a genuine interest in resolving the conflict, the patience of the mediator can be the difference between impasse and resolution.

4. **Knowledge**. Substantive knowledge of the area of law involving the disputed issues increases the mediator's

ability to help the parties find a solution. If the conflict involves employment issues, the mediator should have expertise in employment law.

How to use the mediator effectively:

1. **Solicit the mediator's opinion**. The mediator's private conversations with each party can lead to a settlement framework that will satisfy everyone involved. Some mediators volunteer settlement ideas; others do not. Ask the mediator for suggestions regarding your own settlement proposal. This not only assists you in identifying a proposal that would suit you, but also takes advantage of the mediator's knowledge of the other side's interests. You should avoid making a proposal the other side will find offensive.

   Example: Initially, you plan to demand $5.5 million on a $6.5 million employment claim and gradually reduce your demand to $1 million. Instead of conveying the initial demand, ask for the mediator's opinion. The mediator might say: "The other side thinks your current $6.5 million claim is outrageous. An opening proposal of $5.5 million could make serious negotiations impossible." The mediator might suggest that you make an initial demand of $3.5 million to point out that you moderated your claim substantially. The mediator could then suggest that if the other side's next offer is similarly moderate, each side will have demonstrated a good-faith desire to settle. Although you are under no obligation to accept the mediator's advice, recognize that the private conversations with the other side gives the mediator considerable knowledge about the other side's interests. Taking advantage of that knowledge could lead to a settlement sufficient to satisfy your client.

2. **Share your great ideas with the mediator.** When talks
   heat up, negotiators can develop negative opinions about
   each other. If you think the other side was not bargaining
   in good faith, this can lead to skepticism about their position—a tendency that psychologists call reactive devalua-
   tion. Skepticism can impede a reasonable resolution. Use
   the mediator to help overcome this obstacle. If the mediator believes your plan is fair and has merit, the mediator
   may help you present it in a way that minimizes the other
   side's skepticism.

3. **Take a reality test.** An unrealistic view of your position
   can be a barrier to settlement. If you fail to understand the
   other side's interests or priorities, you could be waiting for
   concessions that never come. Use the mediator to bolster
   your position by asking for the mediator's views: "How
   likely is the other side to concede? How likely are we to
   prevail in court?" A mediator's experience and neutrality
   is given special status.

Understand the sources of conflicts. This will lead to effective ways of dealing with conflicts while maintaining positive relationships. You can successfully deal with different
types of conflicts by asking yourself two questions. First,
what am I trying to resolve? Second, what method will
best satisfy the needs of the parties? When you look at the
conflict as a joint problem to solve, you move from "win-
lose" to "win-win." Focus on a resolution that satisfies the
needs of the parties, and you will reach common ground.

CONFLICT RESOLUTION ASSESSMENT QUESTIONNAIRES

Core Value Assessment

CORE VALUE ASSESSMENT TEST

1. **Determine your core values.** From the list below, choose and write down every core value that resonates with you. Do not overthink your selection. As you read through the list, simply write down the words that feel like a core value to you personally. If you think of a value you possess that is not on the list, write it down.

Abundance	Dedication	Kindness	Professionalism
Acceptance	Dependability	Knowledge	Punctuality
Accountability	Diversity	Leadership	Relationships
Achievement	Empathy	Learning	Reliability
Adventure	Encouragement	Love	Resilience
Advocacy	Enthusiasm	Loyalty	Resourcefulness
Ambition	Ethics	Making a Difference	Responsibility
Appreciation	Excellence	Mindfulness	Responsiveness
Attractiveness	Expressiveness	Motivation	Security
Autonomy	Fairness	Optimism	Self-Control
Balance	Family	Open-Mindedness	Selflessness
Being the Best	Friendships	Originality	Simplicity
Benevolence	Flexibility	Passion	Stability
Boldness	Freedom	Performance	Success
Brilliance	Fun	Personal Development	Teamwork
Calmness	Generosity	Proactive	Thankfulness
Caring	Grace	Professionalism	Thoughtfulness

Challenge	Growth	Quality	Traditionalism
Charity	Flexibility	Recognition	Trustworthiness
Cheerfulness	Happiness	Risk Taking	Understanding
Cleverness	Health	Safety	Uniqueness
Community	Honesty	Security	Usefulness
Commitment	Humility	Service	Versatility
Compassion	Humor	Spirituality	Vision
Cooperation	Inclusiveness	Stability	Warmth
Collaboration	Independence	Peace	Wealth
Consistency	Individuality	Perfection	Well-Being
Contribution	Innovation	Playfulness	Wisdom
Creativity	Inspiration	Popularity	Zeal
Credibility	Intelligence	Power	
Curiosity	Intuition	Preparedness	
Daring	Joy	Proactivity	
Decisiveness			

2. **Group all similar values together from the list of values you just created.** Group them in a way that makes sense to you, personally. Create a maximum of five groupings. If you have more than five groupings, drop the least important grouping(s). See the example below.

Abundance	Acceptance	Appreciation	Balance	Cheerfulness
Growth	Compassion	Encouragement	Health	Fun
Wealth	Inclusiveness	Thankfulness	Teamwork	Happiness
Security	Intuition	Thoughtfulness	Spirituality	Humor
Freedom	Kindness	Mindfulness	Well-being	Inspiration
Independence	Love	Passion	Stability	Joy
Flexibility	Success	Enthusiasm	Simplicity	Optimism
Peace	Open-Mindedness	Achievement	Fairness	Playfulness

Diversity	Trustworthiness	Cleverness	Power	Adventure
Quality	Relationships	Motivation	Reliability	Warmth

3. **Choose one word within each grouping that represents the label for the entire group.** Again, do not overthink your labels – there are no right or wrong answers. You are defining the answer that is right for you. See the example below – the label chosen for the grouping is bolded.

Abundance	**Acceptance**	Appreciation	Balance	Cheerfulness
Growth	Compassion	Encouragement	Health	Fun
Wealth	Inclusiveness	Thankfulness	Teamwork	**Happiness**
Security	Intuition	Thoughtfulness	Spirituality	Humor
Quality	Kindness	Mindfulness	Well-being	Inspiration
Independence	Love	Passion	**Stability**	Joy
Flexibility	Success	Enthusiasm	Simplicity	Optimism
Peace	Open-Mindedness	**Achievement**	Fairness	Playfulness
Quality	Trustworthiness	Cleverness	Power	Adventure
Diversity	Relationships	Motivation	Reliability	Warmth

4. **Add a verb to each value** so you can see what it looks like as an actionable core value, For example:

Experience growth.
Seek acceptance in the community.
Work for achievement.
Promote stability.
Multiply happiness.

5. **Finally, write your core values in order of priority in your planner**, so they are available as an easy reference when you are faced with decisions. For example:

1. Seek acceptance in the community.
2. Promote stability.
3. Work for achievement.
4. Multiply happiness.
5. Experience growth.

——— TEN DOMAIN CORE VALUE ASSESSMENT ———

Professor Shalom Schwartz of Hebrew University has identified ten broad core value domains that are universal and fairly comprehensive:

POWER: Social status and prestige, control or dominance over people and resources

ACHIEVEMENT: Personal success through demonstrating competence according to social standards

HEDONISM: Pleasure or sensuous gratification for oneself

STIMULATION: Excitement, novelty, and challenge in life

SELF-DIRECTION: Independent thought and action - choosing, creating, exploring

UNIVERSALISM: Understanding, appreciation, tolerance, and protection for the welfare of all people and for nature

BENEVOLENCE: Preservation and enhancement of the welfare of people with whom one is in frequent personal contact

TRADITION: Respect, commitment, and acceptance of the customs and ideas that traditional culture or religion provide

CONFORMITY: Restraint of actions, inclinations, and

impulses likely to upset or harm others and violate social expectations or norms

SECURITY: Safety, harmony, and stability of society, of relationships, and of self

The scale measures the degree to which you value each of ten domains that Professor Schwartz has found across many cultures. Values are defined as "desirable, trans-situational goals, varying in importance, that serve as guiding principles in people's lives." The idea behind the scale is that there is an internal order and structure to values. Using various statistical techniques, Professor Schwartz has found that the ten basic human values show a pattern of relationships.

CORE VALUE RANKING

To determine your core values, rate each value on a scale of 1 to 10, with one being the most important to ten being the least important.

_____Fairness	_____Patriotic
_____Honesty	_____Convictions about specific issues
_____Tolerance	_____Commitment to your mate
_____Courage	_____Commitment to each other as a family
_____Integrity	_____Happiness
_____Forgiveness	_____Honor
_____Peace	_____Flexibility
_____Environment	_____Perspective
_____Challenge	_____Recognition
_____Self-Acceptance, Self-Respect	_____Learning
_____Knowledge	_____Freedom
_____Adventure	_____Influence

_____Creativity	_____Decisiveness
_____Personal Growth	_____Quality
_____Inner Harmony	_____Hard work
_____Spiritual Growth	_____Responsiveness
_____Belonging, Connected	_____Purposefulness
_____Diplomacy	_____Diversity
_____Teamwork	_____Strength
_____Helping	_____Cleverness
_____Communication	_____Success
_____Friendship	_____Equality
_____Consensus	_____Harmony
_____Respectfulness	_____Humor
_____Tradition	_____Empathy
_____Security	_____Patience
_____Stability	_____Risk-taking
_____Neatness	_____Simplicity
_____Self-control	_____Obedience
_____Perseverance	_____Independence
_____Rationality	_____Financial growth
_____Health	_____Effectiveness
_____Pleasure, Play	_____Dependability
_____Excellence	_____Trust
_____Prosperity	_____Beauty
_____Family	_____Loyalty
_____Appearance	_____Profitability
_____Intimacy	_____Clarity
_____Justice	_____Love
_____Community	_____Hope
_____Competence	_____Sincerity
_____Achievement	_____Wisdom
_____Religious beliefs, God	_____Reliable
_____Intellectual Status	_____Consistent
_____Recognition	_____Efficient
_____Authority	_____Innovative

_____Power   _____Creative

_____Competition   _____Fun-loving

_____Social-minded   _____Optimistic

_____Persistence

When you are done ranking those core values, take your Top Ten, and then rank your Top Ten, from 1 to 10. Those ten are your core values.

EMPATHY QUESTIONNAIRE

Answer "Yes" or "No" to the following statements:

___I need to know how others are feeling.

___I tend to avoid conflict because I do not want to hurt others.

___People and their relationships and interactions are interesting to me.

___I do not need to see others' faces to read their emotions.

___I am drawn to situations of injustice and how to alleviate suffering.

___I often mimic the mannerisms, accents, and body language of others without meaning to.

___I tend to think about interpersonal issues by imagining myself in the place of those involved.

___I have an easy time reading between the lines, under the surface, and behind the obvious.

___I feel beauty palpably and it creates a sense of delight.

___Interpersonal conflict, even when it does not involve me personally, is painful to me.

___I do not like black-and-white polarization; the truth is usually in the middle.

___When I make a social blunder, I get upset and work hard to make things right again.

___I feel the emotions of others viscerally.

___I can sense and identify multiple simultaneous emotions in myself and others, and in interactions between others.

___ I can sense and identify the relative intensity of multiple simultaneous emotions in myself and others, and in interactions between others.

___I consider the needs and feelings of others in decisions I make, often to the point of ignoring my own needs and feelings.

___I love to watch interactions, especially when the people are unaware of me.

___I enjoy drama, movies, interesting television show, and well-told stories.

___I enjoy well-written literature.

___I love to play with and interact lovingly with people.

___I have an easy, natural ability in one or more art forms.

___I have a good sense of humor.

___I relate well with shy people.

___I relate well with children.

___I relate well with animals.

___In an emergency, I can focus on what is important and provide assistance.

___I often feel tender, protective feeling toward others-even complete strangers.

___Art, music, and literature touch me very deeply.

___I am very sensitive to foods and tend to respond markedly to dietary changes.

___I have an intense capacity to focus on activities that delight and engage me.

___When in conflict with others, I tend to talk to third parties to sort out the issues that led to the conflict.

___I enjoy talking and thinking about interpersonal issues and social structures.

___I have a rich interior life, and I enjoy being alone with my thoughts and ideas.

___I often need to get away from others and recharge my emotional batteries.

___I am sensitive to things like sounds, colors, textures, shapes, and spatial relationships between objects.

___I am able to stay present (for myself and others) in the face of intense emotions like grief, rage, and despair.

___I tend to physically feel the emotions of others in my own body, especially when others are unwilling or unable to admit to feeling them.

___I enjoy thinking about, searching for, and finding the perfect gift for others.

___I regularly feel alongside others their emotions and concerns.

___I tend to approach problems tangibly, using my hands and body as I think about the issues involved.

___I gesture a great deal when I communicate, and my face is often very animated.

___With those closest to me, I tend to rely on gestures and eye contact (rather than words) during conversations.

___I am very aware of the personal space of others.

Scoring Your Answers:

1-20 "yes" responses: If you answered "yes" to twenty or fewer of these questions, you can consider yourself low in empathy.

21-32 "yes" responses: This midrange of "yes" responses places you in the just right spot where your empathy is neither too hot nor too cool.

33-44 "yes" responses: This number of "yes" responses places you in the high empathy category. This hyper-empathy may make it difficult for you to create effective boundaries, work gracefully with emotions, and use self-regulation when you are overwhelmed.

MORAL FOUNDATIONS QUESTIONNAIRE

Part 1. When you decide whether something is right or wrong, to what extent are the following considerations relevant to your thinking? Please rate each statement using this scale:

[0] = not at all relevant (This consideration has nothing to do with my judgments of right and wrong)

[1] = not very relevant

[2] = slightly relevant

[3] = somewhat relevant

[4] = very relevant

[5] = extremely relevant (This is one of the most important factors when I judge right and wrong)

___1. Whether or not someone suffered emotionally.

___2. Whether or not some people were treated differently than others.

___3. Whether or not someone's action showed love for his or her country.

___4. Whether or not someone showed a lack of respect for authority.

___5. Whether or not someone violated standards of purity and decency.

___6. Whether or not someone was good at math.

___7. Whether or not someone cared for someone weak or vulnerable.

___8. Whether or not someone acted unfairly.

___9. Whether or not someone did something to betray his or her group.

___10. Whether or not someone conformed to the traditions of society.

___11. Whether or not someone did something disgusting.

___12. Whether or not someone was cruel.

___13. Whether or not someone was denied his or her rights.

___14. Whether or not someone showed a lack of loyalty.

___15. Whether or not an action caused chaos or disorder.

___16. Whether or not someone acted in a way that God would approve of.

Part 2. Please read the following sentences and indicate your agreement or disagreement using the following scale:

[0]	[1]	[2]	[3]	[4]	[5]
Strongly disagree	Moderately disagree	Slightly disagree	Slightly agree	Moderately agree	Strongly agree

___17. Compassion for those who are suffering is the most crucial virtue.

___18. When the government makes laws, the number one principle should be ensuring that everyone is treated fairly.

___19. I am proud of my country's history.

___20. Respect for authority is something all children need to learn.

___21. People should not do things that are disgusting, even if no one is harmed.

___22. It is better to do good than to do bad.

___23. One of the worst things a person could do is hurt a defenseless animal.

___24. Justice is the most important requirement for a society.

___25. People should be loyal to their family members, even when they have done something wrong.

___26. Men and women each have different roles to play in society.

___27. I would call some acts wrong on the grounds that they are unnatural.

___28. It can never be right to kill a human being.

___29. I think it is morally wrong that rich children inherit a lot of money while poor children inherit nothing.

___30. It is more important to be a team player than to express oneself.

___31. If I were a soldier and disagreed with my commanding officer's orders, I would obey anyway because that is my duty.

___32. Chastity is an important and valuable virtue.

To score the MFQ yourself, you can copy your answers into the grid below. Then add up the 6 numbers in each of the five columns and write each total in the box at the bottom of the column. The box then shows your score on each of 5 psychological "foundations" of morality. Scores run from 0-30 for each foundation (Questions 6 and 22 are just used to catch people who are not paying attention. They do not count toward your scores).

Question #	Your Response	Question #	Your Response	Question #	Your Response	Question #	Your Response	Question #	Your Response	Question #	Your Response
1		2		3		4		5		6	
7		8		9		10		11			
12		13		14		15		16			
17		18		19		20		21		22	
23		24		25		26		27			
28		29		30		31		32			
Harm / Care		Fairness / Reciprocity		In-group / Loyalty		Authority / Respect		Purity / Sanctity			

The average politically moderate American's scores are: 20.2, 20.5, 16.0, 16.5, and 12.6. Liberals generally score a bit higher than that on Harm/care and Fairness/reciprocity, and much lower than that on the other three foundations. Conservatives generally show the opposite pattern.[1*]

1* The Moral Foundations Questionnaire (MFQ-30, July 2008) by Jesse Graham, Jonathan Haidt, and Brian Nosek. For more information about Moral Foundations Theory, scoring this form, or interpreting your scores, see: www. MoralFoundations.org. To take this scale online and see how you compare to others, go to www.YourMorals.org

Negotiating Style Assessment

THOMAS-KILMANN CONFLICT MODE

Competitive: People who tend towards a competitive style take a firm stand, and know what they want. They usually operate from a position of power, drawn from things like position, rank, expertise, or persuasive ability. This style can be useful when there is an emergency and a decision needs to be made fast, when the decision is unpopular, or when defending against someone who is trying to exploit the situation selfishly. However, it can leave people feeling bruised, unsatisfied and resentful when used in less urgent situations.

Accommodating: This style indicates a willingness to meet the needs of others at the expense of the person's own needs. The accommodator often knows when to give in to others, but can be persuaded to surrender a position even when it is not warranted. This person is not assertive but is highly cooperative. Accommodation is appropriate when the issues matter more to the other party, when peace is more valuable than winning, or when you want to be in a position to collect on this "favor" you gave. However, people may not return favors, and overall this approach is unlikely to give the best outcomes.

Avoiding: People tending towards this style seek to evade the conflict entirely. This style is typified by delegating controversial decisions, accepting default decisions, and not wanting to hurt anyone's feelings. It can be appropriate when victory is impossible, when the controversy is trivial, or when someone else is in a better position to solve the problem. However, in many situations this is a weak and ineffective approach to take.

Compromising: People who prefer a compromising style try to find a solution that will at least partially satisfy everyone. Everyone is expected to give up something, and the compromiser also expects to relinquish something. Compromise is useful when the cost of conflict is higher than the cost of losing ground, when equal strength opponents are at a standstill, and when there is a deadline looming.

Collaborative: People tending towards a collaborative style try to meet the needs of all people involved. These people can be highly assertive but unlike the competitor, they cooperate effectively. This style is useful when you need to bring together a variety of viewpoints to get the best solution; when there have been previous conflicts in the group; or when the situation is too important for a simple trade-off.

THOMAS-KILMANN CONFLICT MODE QUESTIONNAIRE

Consider situations in which you find your wishes differing from those of another person. How do you usually respond to such situations?

There are several pairs of statements describing possible behavioral responses. For each pair, please circle the "A" or "B" statement, which is most characteristic of your own behavior. In many cases, neither the "A" nor the "B" statement may be very typical of your behavior, but please select the response which you would be more likely to use.

When done answering, transfer your answers to the scoring sheet, and sum up each of the columns.

1. A. There are times when I let others take responsibility for solving the problem.

   B. Rather than negotiate the things where we disagree, I stress things where we both agree.

2. A. I try to find a compromise solution.

   B. I attempt to deal with all of another's and my concerns.

3. A. I am usually firm in pursuing my goals.

   B. I might try to soothe the other's feelings and preserve our relationship.

4. A. I try to find a compromise solution.

   B. I sometimes sacrifice my own wishes for the wishes of the other person.

5. A. I consistently seek the other's help in working out a solution.

   B. I try to do what is necessary to avoid useless tensions.

6. A. I try to avoid creating unpleasantness for myself.

   B. I try to win my position.

7. A. I try to postpone the issue until I have had some time to think about it.

   B. I give up some points in exchange for others.

8. A. I am usually firm in pursuing my goals.

   B. I attempt to get all concerns and issues immediately out in the open.

9. A. I feel that differences are not always worth worrying about.

   B. I make some effort to get my way.

10. A. I am firm in pursuing my goals.

    B. I try to find a compromise solution.

11. A. I attempt to get all concerns and issues immediately out in the open.

    B. I might try to soothe the other's feelings and preserve

our relationship.

12. A. I sometimes avoid taking positions, which would create controversy.

   B. I will let another have some of their positions if they let me have some of mine.

13. A. I propose middle ground.

   B. I press to get my points made.

14. A. I tell another my ideas and ask them for theirs.

   B. I try to show him the logic and benefits of my position.

15. A. I might try to soothe the other's feelings and preserve our relationship.

   B. I try to do what is necessary to avoid tension.

16. A. I try not to hurt the other's feelings.

   B. I try to convince the other person of the merits of my position.

17. A. I am usually firm in pursuing my goals.

   B. I try to do what is necessary to avoid useless tensions.

18. A. If it makes the other person happy, I might let them maintain their views.

   B. I will let the other person have some of their positions if they let me have some of mine.

19. A. I try to get all concerns and issues immediately out in the open.

   B. I try to postpone the issue until I have had some time to think it over.

20. A. I attempt to immediately work through our differences.

   B. I try to find a fair combination of gains and losses for

both of us.

21. A. In approaching negotiations, I try to be considerate of the other person's feelings.

B. I always lean toward a direct discussion of the problem.

22. A. I try to find a position that is intermediate between mine and another person's.

B. I assert my wishes.

23. A. I am often concerned with satisfying all my wishes.

B. There are times when I let others take responsibility for solving problems.

24. A. If the other's position seems important to them, I would try to meet their wishes.

B. I try to get the other person to settle for a compromise.

25. A. I try to show the other person the logic and benefits of my position.

B. In approaching negotiations, I try to be considerate of the other person's wishes.

26. A. I propose a middle ground.

B. I am nearly always concerned with satisfying all my wishes.

27. A. I sometimes avoid taking positions that would create controversy.

B. If it makes the other person happy, I might let them maintain their views.

28. A. I am usually firm in pursuing my goals.

B. I feel that differences are not always worth worrying about.

29. A. I propose middle ground.

B. I feel that differences are not always worth worrying about.

30. A. I try not to hurt the other person's feelings.

B. I always share the problem with the other person so that we can work it out.

Scoring the Thomas-Kilmann Conflict Mode Questionnaire:

	Competing (Forcing)	Collaborating (Problem Solving)	Compromising (Sharing)	Avoiding (Withdrawal)	Accommodating (Smoothing)
1.				A	B
2.		B	A		
3.	A			B	
4.			A		B
5.				B	A
6.	B			A	
7.			B	A	
8.	A	B			
9.	B			A	
10.	A		B		
11.		A			B
12.			B	A	
13.	B	A			
14.	B	A			
15.				B	A
16.	B				A
17.	A			B	
18.			B		A

	Competing	Collaborating	Compromising	Avoiding	Withdrawing
19.		A		B	
20.		A	B		
21.		B			A
22.	B		A		
23.		A		B	
24.			B		A
25.	A				B
26.		B	A		
27.				A	B
28.	A	B			
29.			A	B	
30.		B			A

Total the number of letters circled in each column.

	Competing	Collaborating	Compromising	Avoiding	Withdrawing
	(Forcing)	(Problem Solving)	(Sharing)	(Withdrawal)	(Smoothing)

LEARNING STYLE ASSESSMENT

LEARNING STYLE QUESTIONNAIRE

To complete this learning style questionnaire, read each sentence carefully and consider if it applies to you. On the line in front of each statement, indicate how often the sentence applies to you, according to the chart below. Please respond to all questions.

1	2	3
Never applies to me.	Sometimes applies to me.	Often applies to me.

Section One:

___I enjoy doodling and even my notes have lots of pictures and arrows in them.

___I remember something better if I write it down.

___I get lost or am late if someone tells me how to get to a new place, and I do not write down the directions.

___When trying to remember someone's telephone number, or something new like that, it helps me to get a picture of it in my mind.

___If I am taking a test, I can "see" the textbook page and where the answer is located.

___It helps me to look at the person while listening; it keeps me focused.

___Using flashcards helps me to retain material for tests.

___It is hard for me to understand what a person is saying when there are people talking or music playing.

___It is hard for me to understand a joke when someone tells me.

___It is better for me to get work done in a quiet place.

Total_____

Section Two:

___My written work does not look neat to me. My papers have crossed-out words and erasures.

___It helps to use my finger as a pointer when reading to keep my place.

___Papers with very small print, blotchy dittos, or poor copies are tough on me.

___I understand how to do something if someone tells me, rather than having to read the same thing to myself.

___I remember things that I hear, rather than things that I see or read.

___Writing is tiring. I press down too hard with my pen or pencil.

___My eyes get tired fast, even though the eye doctor says that my eyes are ok.

___When I read, I mix up words that look alike, such as "them" and "then," "bad" and "dad."

___It is hard for me to read other people's handwriting.

___If I had the choice to learn new information through a lecture or textbook, I would choose to hear it rather than read it.

Total_____

Section Three:

___I do not like to read directions; I would rather just start doing.

___I learn best when I am shown how to do something, and I have the opportunity to do it.

___Studying at a desk is not for me.

___I tend to solve problems through a more trial-and-error approach, rather than from a step-by-step method.

___Before I follow directions, it helps me to see someone else do it first.

___I find myself needing frequent breaks while studying.

___I am not skilled in giving verbal explanations or directions.

___I do not become easily lost, even in strange surroundings.

___I think better when I have the freedom to move around.

___When I cannot think of a specific word, I will use my hands a lot and call something a "what-cha-ma-call-it" or a "thing-a-ma-jig."

Total_____

Scoring:

Now, add up the scores for each of the three sections and record below. The maximum score in any section is 30 and the minimum score is 10. Note the preference next to each section.

Section One score: ____(Visual)
Section Two score: ____(Auditory)
Section Three score: ____(Kinesthetic)

EVALUATING THE LEARNING STYLE QUESTIONNAIRE

The modality type with the highest score indicates your preferred learning channel. The higher the score, the stronger the preference. If you have relatively high scores in two or more sections, you probably have more than one strength. If the scores in the sections are roughly equal, you probably do not have a preferred learning channel; you are a multi-sensory learner.

The following table summarizes the observable characteristic indicative of the three learning styles. It provides an informal means of assessing your preferred approach to learning.

MODALITY	VISUAL	AUDISTORY	KINESTHETIC
PREFERRED LEARNING STYLE	Learns by seeing or watching demonstrations.	Learns through verbal instructions from self or others.	Learns by doing and direct involvement.
SPELLING	Recognizes words by sight; relies on configurations of words.	Uses a phonics approach; has auditory word attack skills.	Poor speller; writes words to determine if they "feel" right.
READING	Likes description; sometimes stops reading to stare into space and imagine scene; intense concentration.	Enjoys dialogue and plays; avoids lengthy descriptions; unaware of illustrations; moves lips or sub-vocalizes.	Prefers stories where action occurs early; fidgets while reading; not an avid reader.

HANDWRITING	Tends to be good, particularly when young; spacing and size are good; appearance is important.	Has more difficulty learning in initial stages; tends to write lightly.	Good initially, but deteriorates when space becomes smaller; pushes harder on writing instrument.
MEMORY	Remember faces, but forgets names; writes things down; takes notes.	Remembers names, but forgets faces; remembers by auditory repetition.	Remembers best what was done, but not what was seen or talked about.
IMAGERY	Vivid imagination; thinks in pictures; visualizes in detail.	Sub-vocalizes; imagines things in sounds; details are less important.	Imagery not important; images accompanied by movement.
DISTRACTABILITY	Unaware of sounds; distracted by movement.	Easily distracted by sounds.	Not attentive to visual or auditory presentation so may seem distracted.
PROBLEM SOLVING	Deliberate; plans in advance; organizes thoughts by writing them; lists problems.	Talks problems out; tries solutions verbally or sub-vocally; talks self through problems.	Attacks problem physically; impulsive; selects option with greatest activity.
RESPONSE TO PERIODS OF INACTIVITY	Stares or doodles; finds something.	Hums, talks to self, or talks to others.	Fidgets or finds reasons to move.
RESPONSE TO NEW SITUATIONS	Looks around or examines structure.	Talks about situation; discusses pros and cons of what to do.	Tries things out; touches, feels, or manipulates.

GRIT SCALE

For each sentence, provide a number that best describes you at the present time:

Not at all like me	Not much like me	Somewhat like me	Mostly like me	Very much like me
5	4	3	2	1

1. New ideas and projects sometimes distract me from previous ones____

2. Setbacks do not discourage me. I do not give up easily_____

3. I often set a goal but later choose to pursue a different one_____

4. I am a hard worker_____

5. I have difficulty maintaining my focus on projects that take more than a few months to complete_____

6. I finish whatever I begin____

7. My interests change from year to year_____

8. I am diligent. I never give up_____

9. I have been obsessed with a certain idea or project for a short time but later lost interest_____

10. I have overcome setbacks to conquer an important challenge_____

To calculate your total grit score, add up all the points and divide by 10. The maximum score on this scale is 5 (extremely gritty), and the lowest possible score is 1 (not at all gritty). You can use the chart below to see how your scores compare to a large sample of American adults.

Percentile	Grit Score
10%	2.5
20%	3.0
30%	3.3
40%	3.5
50%	3.8
60%	3.9
70%	4.1
80%	4.3
90%	4.5
95%	4.7
99%	4.9

Keep in mind that your score is a reflection of how you see yourself right now. How gritty you are at this point in your life might be different from how gritty you were when you were younger. And if you take the Grit Scale again later, you might get a different score. Grit has two components: passion and perseverance.

Personality Assessments

The theory of psychological type says that people with different preferences naturally have different interests and views, behave differently, and are motivated by different things. Awareness of differences between types can help people understand and value other people who think and act quite differently. There are many valid tests for determining personality. Listed below are a few personality tests that can determine personality types.

BIG FIVE INVENTORY (BFI)

Description of Measure:
Forty-four item inventory that measures an individual on the Big Five Factors (dimensions) of personality:

Big Five Dimensions	Facet (and correlated trait adjective)
Extraversion vs. introversion	Gregariousness (sociable) Assertiveness (forceful) Activity (energetic) Excitement-seeking (adventurous) Positive emotions (enthusiastic) Warmth (outgoing)
Agreeableness vs. antagonism	Trust (forgiving) Straightforwardness (not demanding) Altruism (warm) Compliance (not stubborn) Modesty (not show-off) Tender-mindedness (sympathetic)

Conscientiousness vs. lack of direction	Competence (efficient) Order (organized) Dutifulness (not careless) Achievement striving (thorough) Self-discipline (not lazy) Deliberation (not impulsive)
Neuroticism vs. emotional stability	Anxiety (tense) Angry hostility (irritable) Depression (not contented) Self-consciousness (shy) Impulsiveness (moody) Vulnerability (not self-confident)
Open vs. closed to experience	Ideas (curious) Fantasy (imaginative) Aesthetics (artistic) Actions (wide interests) Feelings (excitable) Values (unconventional)

THE BIG FIVE INVENTORY (BFI) TEST

Here are a number of characteristics that may or may not apply to you. Please write a number next to each statement to indicate the extent to which you agree or disagree with that statement.

Disagree strongly	Disagree a little	Neither disagree nor agree	Agree a little	Agree strongly
1	2	3	4	5

I see Myself as Someone Who...

___1. Is talkative

___2. Tends to find fault with others

___3. Does a thorough job

___4. Is depressed, blue

___5. Is original, with new ideas

___6. Is reserved

___23. Tends to be lazy

___24. Is emotionally stable, not easily upset

___25. Is inventive

___26. Has an assertive personality

___27. Can be cold and aloof

___28. Perseveres until task is finished

___7. Is helpful and unselfish

___8. Can be somewhat careless

___9. Is relaxed, handles stress well

___10. Is curious about many things

___11. Is full of energy

___12. Starts quarrels with others

___13. Is a reliable worker

___14. Can be tense

___15. Is ingenious, a deep thinker

___16. Generates a lot of enthusiasm

___17. Has a forgiving nature

___18. Tends to be disorganized

___19. Worries a lot

___20. Has an active imagination

___21. Tends to be quiet

___22. Is generally trusting

___29. Can be moody with others

___30. Values artistic, aesthetic experiences

___31. Is sometimes shy, inhibited

___32. Is considerate and kind to most

___33. Does things efficiently

___34. Remains calm in tense situations

___35. Prefers work that is routine

___36. Is outgoing, sociable

___37. Is sometimes rude to others

___38. Makes plans and follows through

___39. Gets nervous easily

___40. Likes to reflect, play with ideas

___41. Has few artistic interests

___42. Likes to cooperate with others

___43. Is easily distracted

___44. Is sophisticated in the arts

Scoring:

BFI scale scoring ("R" denotes reverse-scored items):
Extraversion: 1, 6R, 11, 16, 21R, 26, 31R, 36
Agreeableness: 2R, 7, 12R, 17, 22, 27R, 32, 37R, 42
Conscientiousness: 3, 8R, 13, 18R, 23R, 28, 33, 38, 43R
Neuroticism: 4, 9R, 14, 19, 24R, 29, 34R, 39
Openness: 5, 10, 15, 20, 25, 30, 35R, 40, 41R, 44

⸻ INTROVERT/EXTROVERT QUESTIONNAIRE ⸻

Introversion is a personality trait characterized by a focus on internal feelings rather than on external sources of stimulation. Introverts draw energy from their internal world of ideas, emotions, and impressions. Introverts and extroverts are often viewed in terms of two extreme opposites, but the truth is that most people lie somewhere in the middle. An introverted personality would include the following characteristics: 1. Being around lots of people drains your energy; 2. You enjoy solitude; 3. You have a small group of close friends; 4. People often describe you as quiet and may find it difficult to get to know you; 5. Too much stimulation leaves you feeling distracted and unfocused; 6. You are very self-aware; 7. You like to learn by watching; 8. You are drawn to jobs that involve independence.

Extroversion is a personality trait characterized by a focus on external sources of stimulation rather than on internal feelings. Extroverts are energized by activities, people, places, and things. Some of the general characteristics associated with extroversion include: 1. Numerous, broad interests; 2. Likes to communicate by talking; 3. Enjoys being at the center of attention; 4. Tends to act first before thinking; 5. Enjoys group work; 6. Feels isolated by too much time spent alone; 7. Looks to others and outside sources for ideas and inspiration; 8. Likes to talk about thoughts and feelings.

Introverts make up an estimated 25 to 40 percent of the population. You need to know the differences between introverts and extroverts in resolving conflicts effectively. One personality type is no better than the other type. They are just different.

The short quiz below can help determine whether you are an introvert or an extrovert. Answer "Yes" or "No" to each preference.

INTROVERT/EXTROVERT QUIZ

Preferences A

_____Like to be in the thick of things.

_____Relish variety; bored with sameness.

_____Know many people, consider them friends.

_____Enjoy chitchatting, even with strangers.

_____Feel stoked after activity, eager for more.

_____Speak or act without needing to think first.

_____Are generally peppy.

_____Tend to talk more than listen.

Preferences B

_____Prefer to relax alone or with a few close friends.

_____Consider only deep relationships as friends.

_____Need to rest after outside activities, even ones you enjoy.

_____Often listen but talk a lot about topics of importance to you.

_____Appear calm, self-contained, and like to observe.

_____Tend to think before you speak or act.

_____Experience mind going blank in groups or under pressure.

_____Do not like feeling rushed.

If you have stated "Yes" to most of the preferences in list A, you are an extrovert. If you have stated "Yes" to most of the preferences in list B, you are an introvert.

—— INTROVERT/EXTROVERT ASSESSMENT TEST ——

A longer test to determine your personality type is provided below. Consider each statement in terms of what is generally true or false for you. Answer the following statements "True" or "False." Then add up your "True" answers to determine where you are on the introvert/extrovert continuum.

___When I need to rest, I prefer to spend time alone or with one or two close people rather than with a group.

___When I work on projects, I like to have larger uninterrupted time periods rather than smaller chunks.

___I sometimes rehearse things before speaking, occasionally writing notes for myself.

___In general, I like to listen more than I like to talk.

___People sometimes think I'm quiet, mysterious, aloof, or calm.

___I like to share special occasions with just one person or a few close friends, rather than having big celebrations.

___I usually need to think before I respond or speak.

___I tend to notice details many people don't see.

___If two people have just had a fight, I feel the tension in the air.

___If I say I will do something, I almost always do it.

___I feel anxious if I have a deadline or pressure to finish a project.

___I can "zone out" if too much is going on.

___I like to watch an activity for a while before I decide to join in.

___I form lasting relationships.

___I don't like to interrupt others; I don't like to be interrupted.

___When I take in a lot of information, it takes me a while to sort it all out.

___I don't like overstimulating environments. I can't imagine why people want to go to horror movies or go on roller coasters.

___I sometimes have strong reactions to smell, tastes, foods, weather, noises, etc.

___I am creative and/or imaginative.

___I feel drained after social situations, even when I enjoy myself.

___I prefer to be introduced rather than introduce others.

___I can become grouchy if I'm around people or activities too long.

___I often feel uncomfortable in new surroundings.

___I like people to come to my home, but I don't like them to stay too long.

___I often dread returning phone calls.

___I find my mind sometimes goes blank when I meet people or when I am asked to speak unexpectedly.

___I talk slowly or have gaps in my words, especially if I am tired or if I am trying to speak and think at once.

___I don't think of casual acquaintances as friends.

___I feel as if I can't show other people my work or ideas until they are fully formulated.

___Other people may surprise me by thinking I am smarter than I think I am.

Add up the number of Trues, and then read the following to see where you fall on the scale.

20-29 True: Introverted.
10-19 True: Somewhere in the middle.
1-9 True: Extroverted.

It is important to understand your personality type and the personality type of the person you are in conflict with, since introverts and extroverts process information differently and communicate differently.

Introverts tend to:

- Keep energy, enthusiasm, and excitement to themselves and share only with those they know very well.
- Hesitate before sharing personal information with others.
- Need time to think before responding.
- Need time to reflect before reacting to outside events.
- Prefer communicating one-to-one.
- Need to be drawn out or invited to speak and may prefer written to verbal communication.
- May occasionally think they told you something they did not (always going over things in their head).

Extroverts tend to:

- Share their energy, excitement, and enthusiasm with almost everyone in the vicinity.
- Respond quickly to questions and outside events.
- Share personal information easily.
- Communicate one to one or in groups with equal ease and enjoyment.
- Think out loud, interacting with others, and in the process, reach their conclusions.
- They often do not give others a chance to speak and do not always attach tremendous meaning to what they say.
- Prefer face-to face oral communication over written communication.

DARK TRIAD TEST – SHORT FORM

Rate each item on a 7-point scale from 1 being the lowest and 7 being the highest to determine where the person fits on the scale as you think it applies to this person. You can also rate yourself on these qualities to see how you measure up:

___1. I tend to manipulate others to get my way.

___2. I tend to lack remorse.

___3. I tend to want others to admire me.

___4. I tend to be unconcerned with the morality of my actions.

___5. I have used deceit or lied to get my way.

___6. I tend to be callous or insensitive.

___7. I have used flattery to get my way.

___8. I tend to seek prestige or status.

___9. I tend to be cynical.

___10. I tend to exploit others toward my own end.

___11. I tend to expect special favors from others.

___12. I want others to pay attention to me.

The total score can range from 12 to 84, but you can also break down the scales into the three traits as follows: Machiavellianism = 1, 5, 7, 10; Psychopathy = 2, 4, 6, 9; Narcissism = 3, 8, 11, 12.

PARANOIA TEST—SHORT FORM

Symptoms of paranoid personality disorder

- believing that others have hidden motives or are out to harm them.
- doubting the loyalty of others.
- being hypersensitive to criticism.
- having trouble working with others.
- being quick to become angry and hostile.
- becoming detached or socially isolated.

Instructions: Below is a list of questions that relate to life experiences. Please read each question carefully, and indicate how often you have experienced the same or similar challenges in the past few months.

1. Are you ever suspicious of other people or question their motives?

    ☐ Never
    ☐ Rarely
    ☐ Sometimes
    ☐ Often
    ☐ Very Often

2. Do you believe people are trying to harm or trick you, even if there's no evidence?

    ☐ Never
    ☐ Rarely
    ☐ Sometimes
    ☐ Often
    ☐ Very Often

3. Do you feel suspicious of people who have acted loyally towards you?

    ☐ Never
    ☐ Rarely
    ☐ Sometimes
    ☐ Often
    ☐ Very Often

4. Do you hesitate to confide in others?

    ☐ Never
    ☐ Rarely
    ☐ Sometimes
    ☐ Often
    ☐ Very Often

5. Do you perceive nonthreatening remarks as insults or as personal attacks?

- ☐ Never
- ☐ Rarely
- ☐ Sometimes
- ☐ Often
- ☐ Very Often

6. Do you respond with hostility or anger when you feel insulted?

- ☐ Never
- ☐ Rarely
- ☐ Sometimes
- ☐ Often
- ☐ Very Often

7. Do you hold grudges?

- ☐ Never
- ☐ Rarely
- ☐ Sometimes
- ☐ Often
- ☐ Very Often

8. Do you suspect that your romantic partner is unfaithful?

- ☐ Never
- ☐ Rarely
- ☐ Sometimes
- ☐ Often
- ☐ Very Often

9. Do you suspect that others are exploiting, harming, or deceiving you?

- ☐ Never
- ☐ Rarely

- ☐ Sometimes
- ☐ Often
- ☐ Very Often

10. Do you read hidden, insulting, or threatening meanings into remarks or events?

- ☐ Never
- ☐ Rarely
- ☐ Sometimes
- ☐ Often
- ☐ Very Often

Score 1 for Never; 2 for Rarely; 3 for Sometimes; 4 for Often; 5 for Very Often.

If you scored...	Paranoid Personality is...
40 & up	Very Likely
30 – 39	Possible
20-29	Unlikely
0 – 10	Very Unlikely

EMOTIONAL INTELLIGENCE

There are hundreds of emotions, together with variations, blends, and nuances. While there is no consensus as to which emotions may be considered primary, Professor Paul Ekman of the University of California at San Francisco has identified specific facial expressions for four of them: (1) fear; (2) anger; (3) sadness; (4) enjoyment. These four facial expressions are recognized by people in cultures all over the world.

The primary emotions would include:

Anger: annoyed; cross; peeved; cranky; crabby; critical; cold; displeased; mad; offended; arrogant; affronted; incensed; fury; outrage; resentment; wrath; exasperation; indignation; vexation; acrimony; animosity; annoyance; irritability; hostility; hatred; livid; seething; vicious.

Disgust: contempt; disdain; scorn; abhorrence; aversion; distaste; revulsion.

Fear: anxiety; apprehension; nervousness; concern; consternation; misgiving; wariness; qualm; edginess; dread; fright; terror; panic.

Happiness: upbeat; peaceful; calm; open; friendly; hopeful; inspired; jovial; glad; optimistic; cheerful; rejuvenated; pleased; excited; gleeful; merry; playful; elated; enthralled; jubilant; ecstatic; overjoyed; encouraged; joy; relief; contentment; bliss; delight; amusement; pride; thrill; rapture; gratification; satisfaction; euphoria; whimsy; mania.

Jealousy and Envy: suspicious; insecure; distrustful; protective; jealous; envious; threatened; greedy; possessive; resentful; avaricious; gluttonous; green with envy.

Love: acceptance; friendliness; trust; kindness; affinity; devotion; adoration; infatuation.

Sadness: regret; disappointment; mournful; grief; sorrow; gloom; melancholy; self-pity; loneliness; dejection; despair; depression; discouraged; bleak; despondent; anguished; hopeless; inconsolable; heartbroken; morose; bereaved.

Shame: guilt; embarrassment; chagrin; remorse; humiliation; regret; mortification; contrition; self-conscious; flushed; speechless; discomfited; awkward; humble; reticent; abashed; flustered; withdrawn; ashamed; intimidated; penitent; culpable; rueful; guilt-ridden; guilt-stricken; disgraced; stigmatized; demeaned; degraded; shamefaced; belittled; ostracized; self-condemning.

Surprise: shock; astonishment; amazement; wonder.

— EMOTIONAL INTELLIGENCE ASSESSMENT TEST —

Answer Each Statement using the following scale:

Not at all	Rarely	Sometimes	Often	Very Often
1	2	3	4	5

_____1. I can recognize my emotions as I experience them.

_____2. I lose my temper when I feel frustrated.

_____3. People have told me that I am a good listener.

_____4. I know how to calm myself down when I feel anxious or upset.

_____5. I enjoy organizing groups.

_____6. I find it hard to focus on something over the long term.

_____7. I find it difficult to move on when I feel frustrated or unhappy.

_____8. I know my strengths and weaknesses.

_____9. I avoid conflict and negotiations.

_____10. I do not enjoy my work.

_____**11.** I ask people for feedback on what I do well, and how I can improve.
_____**12.** I set long-term goals, and review my progress regularly.
_____**13.** I find it difficult to read other people's emotions.
_____**14.** I struggle to build rapport with others.
_____**15.** I use active listening skills when people speak to me.

Now add up your score:_____

Score Comments

15-34 You need to work on your emotional intelligence. You may find that you feel overwhelmed by your emotions, especially in stressful situations; or, you may avoid conflict because you think that you will find it distressing. It is likely, too, that you find it hard to calm down after you have felt upset, and you may struggle to build strong working relationships.

35-55 Your emotional intelligence level is okay. You probably have good relationships with some of your colleagues, but others may be more difficult to work with.

56-75 You are an emotionally intelligent person. You have great relationships, and you probably find that people approach you for advice. However, when so many people admire your people skills, it is easy to lose sight of your own needs.

Characteristics of Emotional Intelligence

Psychologist Daniel Goleman, in his book, "Emotional Intelligence: Why it can Matter More Than IQ" identified five elements that make up emotional intelligence:

1. **Self-awareness** (Questions 1, 8, 11) (The ability to recognize and understand personal moods and emotions and drives, as well as their effect on others. Hallmarks of self-awareness include self-confidence, realistic self-assess-

ment, and a self-deprecating sense of humor. Self-awareness depends on one's ability to monitor one's own emotion state and to correctly identify and name one's emotions).

2. **Self-regulation** (Questions 2, 4, 7) (The ability to control or redirect disruptive impulses and moods, and the propensity to suspend judgment and to think before acting. Hallmarks include trustworthiness and integrity; comfort with ambiguity; and openness to change).

3. **Motivation** (Questions 6, 10, 12) (A passion to work for internal reasons that go beyond money and status, which are external rewards, - such as an inner vision of what is important in life, a joy in doing something, curiosity in learning, a flow that comes with being immersed in an activity. A propensity to pursue goals with energy and persistence. Hallmarks include a strong drive to achieve, optimism even in the face of failure, and organizational commitment).

4. **Empathy** (Questions 3, 13, 15) (The ability to understand the emotional makeup of other people. A skill in treating people according to their emotional reactions. Hallmarks include expertise in building and retaining talent, cross-cultural sensitivity, and service to clients and customers).

5. **Social skills** (Questions 5, 9, 14) (Proficiency in managing relationships and building networks, and an ability to find common ground and build rapport. Hallmarks of social skills include effectiveness in leading change, persuasiveness, and expertise building and leading teams).

Acknowledgments

There are so many people to thank for their contributions to my knowledge of conflict resolution that it is not possible to name them all.

I had the privilege of working with educators at a number of different schools. Northeastern University provided me the first opportunity to teach labor and employment law, organizational behavior, and conflict resolution. Thanks to my colleagues at Northeastern, particularly A. Howard Myers, Albert Ross, and John Martin; at Harvard Law School, Charles Ogletree, Elizabeth Bartholet, Alan Dershowitz, Arthur R. Miller, Mary A. Glendon, Archibald Cox, Charles Fried, Derek Bok, Donald T. Trautman, Roscoe Pound, and Peter Murray; at New York University Law School, Maurice Trotta, Thomas G. S. Christensen, Jack Kroner, Steve Vladeck, and Sam Kaynard; at Suffolk University Law School, John Fenton, Jack Nolan, Paul Sugarman, Alfred Maleson, Samuel B. Horowitz, and Frank Sargent; at Emory University School of Law, Molly O'Brien; at the Massachusetts School of Law, Lawrence Velvel, Michael Coyne, Louise Rose, Anthony Copani, Tim Cagle, Paula Kaldis, Diane Sullivan, Paula Colby-Clements, Joseph Devlin, Peter Malaguti, Thomas Martin, Kurt Olsen, Shane Rodriguez, Phillip Copploa, Connie Rudnick, Andy Starkis, Daniel Harayda, Jeff Kitaeff, Shukla Biswas, Jean Landers, and Laura Lussier; and all the others.

Thanks to the students I have taught and from whom I have learned.

Thanks to the Community Dispute Settlement Center (CDSC), a private, not-for-profit mediation and training center dedicated to providing an alternative and affordable forum for resolving conflicts. Thanks to Gail Packer, Jim Grumbach, Vivian Hsu, Freddie Kay,

Jack Wofford, Amy Cashore Mariani, Esther Lin, John Maiona, Patricia Bernstein, Mark Bamford, Harry Manasewich, Miriam Mandell, Melissa Brodrick, Jeanne Cleary, Thomas Marton, Mindy Milberg, Amy Nee, Shippen Page, Lydia Edwards, Jane Hoffmann, Richard Reilly, Cathleen Finn, Jeffrey Fink, Molly Froelich, Deborah Heller, Robert Smith, Maria Joseph, Roberta Kosberg, Cynthia Runge, Ruth Freedman, Steven Seeche, Steve Lilly-Weber, John Cratsley, Danae Kristiansen, Soraya Tramontozzi, and Mimi Grosser for their dedication to the peaceful resolution of conflicts and disputes.

Thanks to the people at the Program on Negotiation (PON) at Harvard Law School, a university consortium dedicated to developing the theory and practice of negotiation and dispute resolution. Founded in 1983 as a special research project at Harvard Law School, PON includes faculty, students, and staff from Harvard University, Massachusetts Institute of Technology, and Tufts University. Roger Fisher, William Ury, David Hoffman, Frank Sander, Deborah Kolb, Bruce Patton, and Douglas Stone were valuable resources for understanding and dealing with conflicts constructively.

Thanks to the people who worked with me in these programs to resolve conflicts: the Association of Conflict Resolution; the Conflict Intervention Team: Massachusetts Attorney General; the United States Federal District Court Mediation Program; the Massachusetts Association of Mediation Programs, and Practitioners; the Labor and Employment Panels for the American Arbitration Association; the Massachusetts Board of Conciliation and Arbitration; the Mediation and Arbitration panel for New Hampshire; the Mediation and Arbitration panel for Rhode Island; the Middlesex Multi-Door Courthouse; the Essex County Superior Court, Conciliation Program; the Middlesex Mediation Program; and the Essex County Dispute Resolution Services.

Thanks to the people who entrusted me with their disputes and conflicts.

Thanks to Ian Hughes for reviewing my manuscript and making valuable suggestions to improve the design and format of the book. Professor Hughes is a Senior Research Fellow at MaREI Centre for Energy, Climate and Marine at University College, Cork, Ireland, and author of *Disordered Minds: How Dangerous Personalities Are Destroying Democracy*. Professor Hughes' website, www.disorderedworld.com, provides a stark warning for our future. A small proportion of people who suffer from psychologically abnormal personalities have, throughout history, had an immeasurable detrimental impact on our societies, our politics, and our world. Professor Hughes wants us to prevent these psychologically impaired people from obtaining positions of power and influence.

Thanks to Mihaly Csikszentmihalyi for reviewing my manuscript and for his valuable insights and suggestions. Professor Csikszentmihalyi is the Claremont Graduate University Distinguished Professor of Psychology and Management, and is the founder and co-director of the Quality of Life Research Center (QLRC). The QLRC is a nonprofit research institute that studies positive psychology, the study of human strengths such as optimism, creativity, intrinsic motivation, and responsibility. Professor Csikszentmihalyi is known for his research on the experience of flow, a psychological concept introduced in his best-selling book *Flow: The Psychology of Optimal Experience*.

Thanks to John D. Mayer for his valuable input. Professor Mayer is one of the founders of emotional intelligence theory and continues his vital work as the Director of the Personality Laboratory at the University of New Hampshire, focusing on people-centered intelligences, including primarily personal intelligence and emotional intelligence, and how mental abilities are best conceptualized, measured, and their relationships to life outcomes.

Thanks to Peter David Orr for reading my manuscript, providing valuable input, encouragement, and wise counsel.

Thanks to Debbie Carvalko who provided suggestions, which improved the format of the book.

Thanks to the people at Luminare Press, Kim Harper-Kennedy, who did an amazing job managing this book project; Melissa Thomas, who created a great cover; Nina Leis, who designed the interior of the book; Jamie Passaro, for her edits; and Patricia Marshall, who guided me from the beginning.

Thanks to my children Rachel, her spouse Michael Kesselman; David, his spouse Shera; Naomi, her spouse Joseph Spak; and to my beautiful grandchildren, Jared Kesselman and Noah Kesselman; Pauline Golder and Alexandra Golder; Hannah Spak and Emma Spak. They provided the inspiration for this book. Resolve conflicts constructively, not through confrontation, but through cooperation.

None of this would be possible without the love of my life, Caron. Not only for putting up with me, but for her incredible editing skills.

Bibliography

Arbinger Institute. *The Anatomy of Peace, 2nd Ed.* (Berrett-Koehler Publishers, 2015).

Arendt, Hannah. *The Origins of Totalitarianism* (Harvest-Harcourt, 1951).

Ariely, Dan. *The (Honest) Truth about Dishonesty* (Harper-Collins Publishers, 2012).

Ayer, Alfred Jules. *Language, Truth & Logic* (Dover Publications, Inc., 1952).

Bondurant, Joan V. *Conquest of Violence* (University of California Press, 1967).

Cialdini, Robert B., Ph.D. *Influence: The Psychology of Persuasion* (HarperCollins Publishers, 1984).

Coleman, Peter T.; Ferguson, Robert. *Making Conflict Work* (Houghton Mifflin Harcourt, 2014).

Csikszentmihalyi, Mihaly. *The Evolving Self* (Harper Perennial, 1993).

Dawkins, Richard. *The Blind Watchmaker* (W.W. Norton Company, Inc., 1986).

Dawkins, Richard. *The Selfish Gene* (Oxford University Press, 2006).

Darwin, Charles. *On the Origin of Species* (John Murray, 1859).

Darwin, Charles. *The Descent of Man and Selection in Relation to Sex* (John Murray, 1871).

Dershowitz, Alan M. *The Abuse Excuse* (Little Brown & Co., 1994).

Dershowitz, Alan M. *The Genesis of Justice* (Warner Books, 2000).

Dershowitz, Alan M. *Rights from Wrongs* (Basic Books, 2005).

Elgin, Suzette Haden. *The Gentle Art of Verbal Self-Defense* (Dorset Press, 1980).

Fisher, Roger; Ury, William L.; Patton, Bruce. *Getting to Yes: Negotiating Agreement without Giving In* (Penguin Books; 3rd edition, 2011).

Frankl, Victor E. *Man's Search for Meaning* (Beacon Press, 2006).

Gardner, Howard. *Frames of Mind* (Basic Books, 1983).

Goldberg, Bernard. *Arrogance* (Warner Books, 2003).

Golder, Frederick T. *Uncivil Rights: A Guide to Workers' Rights* (Beachfront Press, 2009).

Goleman, Daniel. *Emotional Intelligence: Why It Can Matter More Than IQ* (Bantam Books, 2005).

Harari, Yuval Noah. *Sapiens: A Brief History of Humankind* (Penguin Random House, 2014).

Harari, Yuval Noah. *21 Lessons for the 21st Century* (Penguin Random House, 2018).

Hill, Anita. *Speaking Truth to Power* (Random House, 1998).

Hoffer, Eric. *The True Believer* (Harper & Row, Publishers, Inc., 1951).

Huff, Darrell. *How to Lie with Statistics* (W.W. Norton & Company, Inc., 1954).

Hughes, Ian. *Disordered Minds: How Dangerous Personalities Are Destroying Democracy* (Zero Books, 2018).

Keating, Daniel P. and Hertzman, Clyde, Eds. *Development Health and the Wealth of Nations* (The Guilford Press, 1999).

Jensen, Arthur R. *The g Factor* (Praeger Publishers, 1998).

Laney, Marti Olsen, Psy.D. *The Introvert Advantage: How Quiet People can Thrive in an Extrovert World* (Thomas Allen & Son Limited, 2002).

Lujala, Paivi and Sirleaf, Ellen Johnson. *High-Value Natural Resources and Post-Conflict Peacebuilding* (Taylor and Francis Group, 2012).

Lynn, Richard and Vanhanen, Tatu. *IQ and the Wealth of Nations* (Praeger Publications, 2002).

MacDonald, Heather. *The Diversity Delusion* (St. Martin's Press, 2018).

Maslow, Abraham H. *Motivation and Personality, 2nd Ed.* (Harper & Row, 1970).

Mayer, John D. *Personal Intelligence: The Power of Personality and How It Shapes Our Lives* (Scientific American/Farrar, Straus and Giroux, 2014).

Mayer-Schonberger and Cukier, Keneth. *Big Data* (Houghton, Mifflin, Harcourt, 2013).

Max-Neef, Manfred A. *Human Scale Development* (Apex Press, 1991).

Murray, Charles. *In Pursuit of Happiness and Good Government* (Simon & Schuster, 1988).

Newberg, Andrew B., M.D. and Mark Robert Waldman. *Words Can Change Your Brain* (Penguin Group, 2013).

Nunnally, Jum C. *Psychometric Theory, 2nd Ed.* (McGraw-Hill, 1978).

Pinker, Steven. *The Blank Slate: The Modern Denial of Human Nature* (Penguin Books, 2003).

Pinker, Steven. *The Language Instinct* (HarperCollins Publishers, 2007).

Pinker, Steven. *The Better Angels of Our Nature: Why Violence Has Declined* (Penguin Books, 2012).

Pinker, Steven. *Enlightenment Now* (Penguin Books, 2018).

Rosenberg, Marshall B., Phd. *Speak Peace in a World of Conflict* (PuddleDancer Press, 2005).

Rosenberg, Marshall B., Phd. *Nonviolent Communication: A Language of Life* (PuddleDancer Press; 3rd edition, 2015).

Seelye, H. Ned. *Teaching Culture, Strategies for Intercultural Communication, 3rd Ed.* (National Textbook Company, 1993).

Stone, Douglas, Patton, Bruce, and Heen, Sheila. *Difficult Conversations: How to Discuss What Matters Most* (Penguin Group, 2010).

Satir, Virginia. *Conjoint Family Therapy, 3rd Ed.* (Science and Behavior Books, 1983).

Stephens-Davidowitz, Seth. *Eveybody Lies* (HarperCollins Publishers, 2017).

Tannen, Deborah. *You Just Don't Understand: Women and Men in Conversation* (HarperCollins Publishers, Inc., 1990).

Tannen, Deborah. *The Argument Culture: Stopping America's War of Words* (Ballantine Books, 1999).

Tatter, Ian; Desalle, Rob. *The Accidental Homo Sapiens* (Pegasus Books, 2019).

Wade, Nicholas. *Before the Dawn* (Penguin Group, 2006).

Endnotes

1   Pinker, Steven. *Enlightenment Now*, p. 51 (Penguin Random House LLC, 2018).

2   Cialdini, Robert B., Ph.D. *Influence: The Psychology of Persuasion* (HarperCollins Publishers, 1984).

3   Frankl, Victor E. *Man's Search for Meaning*, p. 66 (Beacon Press, 2006).

4   Frankl, Victor E. *Man's Search for Meaning*, p. 131 (Beacon Press, 2006).

5   Richard Dawkins, who created the word, defines a *meme* as the cultural equivalent of a gene. Anything that could be the basis for an evolutionary process is a meme, simply by becoming more frequent in the population, in the meme pool, in the same way the gene becomes more frequent in the gene pool.

6   Csikszentmihalyi, Mihaly. *The Evolving Self*, p. 22 (Harper Perennial, 1993).

7   There are no black or white skinned humans. Humans come in many shades. People with dark skin are sometimes referred to as "black." People with light skin are sometimes referred to as "white." Skin color has nothing to do with intelligence, morality, or any other human quality or trait.

8   Abraham H. Maslow was an American psychologist who was best known for creating Maslow's hierarchy of needs. Lawrence Kohlberg was an American psychologist best known for his theory of stages of moral development.

9   This may soon change due to scientific advances in gene editing.

10 Seelye, H. Ned. *Teaching Culture, Strategies for Intercultural Communication, 3rd Ed.* (National Textbook Company, 1993). The book contains an excellent bibliography on cultural issues.

11 There is recent evidence to suggest that modern humans may have started migrating out of Africa about 200,000 years ago and continued to migrate ever since.

12 Nunnally, Jum C. *Psychometric Theory, 2nd Ed.* (McGraw-Hill, 1978).

13 Gardner, Howard. *Frames of Mind* (Basic Books, 1983).

14 Neuroticism: tendency toward anxiety, depression, self-doubt, and other negative feelings.

    Openness: receptivity to new ideas and new experiences.

    Agreeableness: cooperative, polite, altruistic, empathetic, kind, and friendly.

    Extraversion: outgoing, self-confident, sociable, and need for external stimulation.

    Conscientiousness: responsible, reliable, organized, and hard-working. Some psychologists identify a sixth personality trait that does not overlap with the others—character. They call it the "H Factor," for honesty-humility. Humility reflects the degree to which a person promotes or does not promote their own interests above those of others. The H factor underlies people's approach to money, power, and sex; their inclination to commit crimes; and their choice of friends and spouse.

15 Lynn, Richard and Vanhanen, Tatu. *IQ and the Wealth of Nations* (Praeger Publications, 2002).

16 Keating, Daniel P. and Hertzman, Clyde, Eds. *Development Health and the Wealth of Nations* (The Guilford Press, 1999).

17 Dawkins, Richard. *The Selfish Gene* (Oxford University Press, 2006).

18 See https://www.richarddawkins.net

19 See https://centerforinquiry.org

20 Murray, Charles. *In pursuit of Happiness and Good Government* (Simon & Schuster, 1988).

21 From the preamble of the Democratic Party Platform. See https://democrats.org.

22 From the preamble of the Republican Party Platform. See https://www.gop.com.

23 From the Libertarian Party's Platform. See https://www.lp.org.

24 See https://policy.greenparty.org.uk/core-values.html.

25 See https://www.constitutionparty.com.

26 For further information see www.moreincommon.com.

27 Golder, Frederick T. *Uncivil Rights: A Guide to Workers' Rights* (Beachfront Press, 2009).

28 The total *land* surface *area of Earth* is about 57,308,738 square miles, of which about 33% is desert and about 24% is mountainous. Subtracting this uninhabitable 57% from the total *land area* leaves 24,642,757 square miles or 15.77 billion acres of habitable *land*.

29 See https://www.nafcm.org

30 See https://arbinger.com.

31 Mayer-Schonberger and Cukier, Keneth. *Big Data*, p. 176 (Houghton Mifflin Harcourt, 2013).

32 For more information about this system of conflict resolution, go to smartsettle.com.

33 Huff, Darrell. *How to Lie with Statistics* (W.W. Norton & Company, Inc., 1954).

34 The Mayer-Salovey-Caruso Emotional Intelligence Test (MSCEIT™) evaluates Emotional Intelligence (EI) through a series of objective and impersonal questions. It tests the person's ability to perceive, use, understand, and regulate emotions. Based on scenarios typical of everyday life, the MSCEIT measures how well people perform tasks and solve emotional problems, rather than having them provide their own subjective assessment of their emotional skills.

The MSCEIT considers Four Branches of Emotional Intelligence:

Perceiving Emotions: The ability to perceive emotions in oneself and others as well as in objects, art, stories, music, and other stimuli.

Facilitating Thought: The ability to generate, use, and feel emotion as necessary to communicate feelings or employ them in other cognitive processes.

Understanding Emotions: The ability to understand emotional information, to understand how emotions combine and progress through relationship transitions, and to appreciate such emotional meanings.

Managing Emotions: The ability to be open to feelings, and to modulate them in oneself and others so as to promote personal understanding and growth.

35 Rosenberg, Marshall B., Phd. *Nonviolent Communication: A Language of Life* (PuddleDancer Press; 3rd edition, 2015).

36 Newberg, Andrew B., M.D. and Mark Robert Waldman. *Words Can Change Your Brain* (Penguin Group, 2013).

37 (c) 2005 by Center for Nonviolent CommunicationWebsite: www. cnvc.org; Email: cnvc@cnvc.org Phone: +1.505-244-4041

38 Satir, Virginia. *Conjoint Family Therapy, 3rd Ed.* (Science and Behavior Books, 1983).

39 Max-Neef, Manfred A. *Human Scale Development* (Apex Press, 1991).

40 See https://kilmanndiagnostics.com

41 For a more complete list, see Brown, Donald E. *Human Universals* (McGraw-Hill, 1991).

42 Paulhus, D. L., and Williams, K. M. (2002). The Dark Triad of personality: Narcissism, Machiavellianism, and Psychopathy. *Journal of Research in Personality, 36,* pgs. 556–563.

43 Hughes, Ian. *Disordered Minds: How Dangerous Personalities Are Destroying Democracy* (Zero Books, 2018).

Index

Made in the USA
Middletown, DE
09 December 2021